DATE DUE

A FINE WILL BE CHARGED FOR EACH OVERDUE MATERIAL.

The Immigrant
Experience in North
American Literature

Recent Titles in
Contributions to the Study of American Literature

The Short Fiction of Kurt Vonnegut
Peter J. Reed

Enchanted Places: The Use of Setting in F. Scott Fitzgerald's Fiction
Aiping Zhang

Solitude and Society in the Works of Herman Melville and Edith Wharton
Linda Costanzo Cahir

The Immigrant Experience in North American Literature

Carving Out a Niche

Edited by
Katherine B. Payant
and Toby Rose

Contributions to the Study of American Literature, Number 4

GREENWOOD PRESS
Westport, Connecticut • London

Library of Congress Cataloging-in-Publication Data

The immigrant experience in North American literature : carving out a
   niche / edited by Katherine B. Payant and Toby Rose.
         p.   cm.—(Contributions to the study of American literature,
   ISSN 1092–6356 ; no. 4)
      Includes bibliographical references and index.
      ISBN 0–313–30891–8 (alk. paper)
      1. American literature—Minority authors—History and criticism.
   2. Canadian literature—Minority authors—History and criticism.
   3. Immigrants' writings, American—History and criticism.
   4. Immigrants' writings, Canadian—History and criticism.
   5. Emigration and immigration in literature.   6. Ethnic groups in
   literature.   7. Immigrants in literature.   8. Minorities in
   literature.   9. Ethnicity in literature.   I. Payant, Katherine B.
   II. Rose, Toby.   III. Series.
   PS153.M56I56   1999
   810.9′920691—dc21   98–46823

British Library Cataloguing in Publication Data is available.

Library of Congress Catalog Card Number: 98–46823
ISBN: 0–313–30891–8
ISSN: 1092–6356

First published in 1999

Greenwood Press, 88 Post Road West, Westport, CT 06881
An imprint of Greenwood Publishing Group, Inc.
www.greenwood.com

Printed in the United States of America

The paper used in this book complies with the
Permanent Paper Standard issued by the National
Information Standards Organization (Z39.48–1984).

10 9 8 7 6 5 4 3 2

Copyright Acknowledgments

The editors and publisher gratefully acknowledge permission for use of the following material:

A similar version of chapter 3, "Fighting the Trolls on the Dakota Plains: The Ecstasy and the Agony of Norwegian Immigrants' Lives in O. E. Rolvaag's *Giants in the Earth*" originally appeared as "Almost Like a Fairy Tale: The Ecstasy and the Agony of Norwegian Immigrants' Lives as Seen in *Giants in the Earth* by O. E. Rolvaag" in *North Dakota Quarterly* (Fall 1998). Reprinted by permission of Raychel Haugrud Reiff and *North Dakota Quarterly*.

A similar version of chapter 4, "*Jasmine* or the Americanization of an Asian: Negotiating between 'Cultural Arrest' and Moral Decay in Immigrant Fictions" appeared in *Journal of American Studies of Turkey* 2 (Fall 1995). Reprinted by permission of Gönül Pultar and *Journal of American Studies of Turkey*.

Excerpts reprinted by permission of Riverhead Books, a division of The Putnam Publishing Group from *Native Speaker* by Chang-rae Lee. Copyright © 1995 by Chang-rae Lee.

This book is dedicated to our parents,
who taught us of our heritage and the struggles of our immigrant ancestors,
and to our children, who will continue that heritage.

Contents

Preface

Toby Rose

Once upon a time I had two grandmothers, immigrants from Russia, whose identities were as different as if they had come from Venus and Mars. One grandmother chose to remain old world and unwashed in the ways of refined middle-class ladies. She spoke in broken English punctuated by Yiddish, stuck close to her family, and was relatively uninterested in the ways of gentile neighbors. The other grandmother polished both her English and her image, becoming a leader in charitable organizations and aspiring to be an American through and through, though one who never forgot her traditions. These variations on the theme of the immigrant experience in North America will, perhaps, give the reader an insight into the approach we as editors and our contributing essayists have taken in deciding on the tone for this study. We are scholars and critics of our literary heritage, but we are equally family members or descendants of immigrants whose choices in the way they would approach life in their adopted homeland influenced the culture and identities we inherited, along with the diversity, richness, and conflictedness of vision in contemporary North America. Therefore, we write with both objectivity and personal insight about our own experiences and those of our forebears.

One of the controversial issues among scholars and critics that we had to address in editing this volume was whether or not to hyphenate the terms used to refer to ethnic groups in North America. Some writers resist being referred to in hyphenated terms because of the political and social connotations such usage implies for them. Others do not have a problem with this issue. We have decided to let our contributing scholars decide whether to hyphenate or not, and Katherine Payant and I have similarly made individual choices.

We would like to thank all of the people who assisted in our research and in the production of this manuscript.

Acknowledgments

The authors would like to thank Northern Michigan University's College of Arts and Sciences Advisory Council and the Department of English for financial support on this project. Also we thank Mary Letts, Secretary, Department of English, for assistance; and Karen Wallingford for preparing the manuscript.

Introduction: Stories of the Uprooted

Katherine Payant

More than forty years ago, in his now-classic study *The Uprooted,* the historian Oscar Handlin declared that when he set out to write a history of immigration in the United States, he discovered that the "immigrants were American history" (3). Today in the field of literary criticism it is commonplace to say that "ethnic literature" (of which immigrant literature is a part), in the past seen as a tributary or branch of the mainstream of American literature, *is* American literature. In fact, it is frequently argued that terms such as "ethnic," "immigrant," or the currently fashionable "multicultural" tend to ghettoize this literature and therefore devalue it (Ferraro 1; Sollors, *Beyond Ethnicity* 8). As early as 1940, Caroline Ware in *The Cultural Approach to History* stated that the culture of immigrants "*is* American culture, not merely a contributor to American culture" (87).

Despite such positive support, the fact is that literature about immigration has had a long struggle to be accepted as worthy of scholarly study, and it is still seldom taught as an integral part of the canon of American literature. As Thomas Ferraro points out in his 1993 study of ethnic narratives, the first critical studies of Jewish immigrant fiction done by scholars such as Leslie Fielder and Irving Howe tended to dismiss this writing as "regional," narrowly parochial, and defensive, being overly concerned with prejudice and thus suffering aesthetically (2). In 1964 Daniel Aaron suggested that an immigrant writer could come into his own only by "dehyphenating" himself through coming out from "behind the minority barricade," and becoming a writer in a "universal republic" of letters (215). Such an artist did not have to give up ethnic subject matters, but somehow he had to universalize his material. In all of this criticism, there was the tacit assumption that ethnic subjects could not be universal, of interest to audiences outside the ethnic groups, or part of the main body of American literature.

In the 1970s, with the birth of the "new ethnicity" influenced by the civil rights movement of the 1960s, ethnicity suddenly became acceptable, in some circles even fashionable. Sociological studies such as Michael Novak's *The Rise of the Unmeltable Ethnics* (1972) and Nathan Glazer and Daniel Moynihan's *Beyond the Melting Pot* (1970) pointed out the "myth of the melting pot," that, in fact, the stew of America had not assimilated differences between groups, and that ethnicity persisted. Novak called for a celebration of diversity: "by each of us becoming more profoundly what we are, we will find greater unity in those depths in which unity irradiates diversity . . . " (71). Glazer and Moynihan stated that "the ethnic pattern was American, more American than the assimilationist," and the ethnic pattern offers hope of a diverse but common society (xxii–xxiv).

Just as sociologists began to study and celebrate ethnic differences in the 1970s, literary critics began to take an interest in ethnic literature, including the literature of immigration. As more young writers, including those of the "new" immigrant groups, began writing of their experiences and those of their predecessors, critics began studying their work. For example, the 1970s saw the publication of Maxine Hong Kingston's *The Woman Warrior* (1976), and Rudolfo Anaya's *Bless Me, Ultima* (1972), as well as the founding of *MELUS*, the Journal of the Society for the Multi-Ethnic Literature of the United States (1973). On college campuses, anthologies of ethnic writers began to appear as well as a few representations in "mainstream" textbooks such as the Norton Anthology.

Equally concerned with prejudice, especially that faced by ethnic, nonwhite writers, literary criticism of the new ethnic fiction often expressed anger at how these writers had been excluded from the canon. Perhaps the most well-known example is *Aiiieeeee!: An Anthology of Asian-American Writers* edited by Jeffrey Paul Chan, Frank Chin, Lawson Fusao Inada, and Shawn Hsu Wong (1974). The editors criticize the lack of attention to Asian American literature by reviewers and scholars, and also fault some of the literature of the past and present for being inauthentic and ingratiating to the dominant white culture.

In the 1980s, new studies of ethnicity by Werner Sollors, *Beyond Ethnicity* and *The Invention of Ethnicity* (1986; 1989), took a seemingly radical new direction by suggesting that rather than being an "essentialist" condition acquired by biological and cultural "descent" from one's foreparents, ethnicity is an invented condition, one of "consent," discovered by various groups *after* they immigrated to the United States. In this viewpoint, ethnicity is part of fiction making whereby a group continually reinvents itself as it negotiates and renegotiates its identity vis à vis the larger society. In an example given by many sociologists, Italians of the late nineteenth century (the various provinces of the Italian peninsula were united into a nation only in the 1860s) had little sense of being Italian but rather thought of themselves as Sicilians or Calabrians (Hechter xiv–xv; Portes and Rumbaut 104). When they discovered that others thought of them as "Italian" and often were prejudiced against them, they began to acquire an ethnic identity.

According to Sollors, the formation of an ethnic identity, which began in eighteenth-and nineteenth-century Europe of growing, competing nation-states, involves the creation of national or ethnic symbols as obvious as a St. Patrick's Day parade or a Chinese New Year's Day parade, or as complex as a group's literature and folklore. This is not to suggest that there is no such thing as "Irish" or the "Chicanos," only that ethnic groups should not be imagined as "natural, real, eternal, stable, and static units" (*The Invention of Ethnicity* xiii–xiv). Rather, they are constantly reinventing and reinterpreting themselves in each generation and by each individual, and it is this reinterpretation that is the project of the literature of these groups. Similarly, another critic, William Boelhower, in 1987 argued in *Through a Glass Darkly* that in the United States ethnicity is not a definable cultural essence but is constantly in flux (31–32).

Sollors and Boelhower's work turns literature by immigrant groups outward, arguing that it has much more in common with the mainstream of American culture than its creators would acknowledge. By examining a number of examples from America's literary and popular culture throughout history, Sollors demonstrates their debt to broader cultural symbols such as the myth of Pochahontas, or the West. As such, since his purpose is to show the commonality of this literature with mainstream American culture, his work does not consider in detail how writers interpreted the experience of immigration or adaptation to an unfamiliar culture.

In addition to hundreds of essays on individual writers and works, there have been many books and anthologies in the last twenty years dealing with ethnic literature, such as *Reading the Literatures of Asian America* (1992), edited by Shirley Geok-lin Lim and Amy Ling; and *Criticism in the Borderlands: Studies in Chicano Literature, Culture, and Ideology*, edited by Hector Calderon and José D. Saldivar (1991). However, few have concentrated specifically on the experience of immigration, and instead are concerned with larger issues of cultural conflict and theoretical issues of interest to scholars. *New Immigrant Literatures in the United States* (1996) edited by Alpana Sharma Knippling provides surveys of the literatures of nearly every major ethnic group, but much of this material does not speak directly to the experience of immigration. Thomas Ferraro's *Ethnic Passages: Literary Immigrants in Twentieth-Century America* (1993) concentrates on narratives of immigration, but the scope of the works he studies is fairly limited, dealing mostly with works about earlier European immigrant groups and only one work by the newer non-European immigrants. In his Introduction, Ferraro explains that he is interested specifically in immigration and social mobility, how ethnics become writers, their cultural distancing, and the ways in which they encompass national and rhetorical traditions in constructing their narrations of "up from the ghetto" stories. Another anthology, *How We Found America* (1995) by Magdalena J. Zaborowska, focuses on gender themes in East European immigrant narratives, but discusses only one author born since 1900.

Our focus in this volume of essays on immigrant literature attempts to fill a gap—to present essays about literature that deal in very direct ways with the experience of immigrating to a new culture. Unlike Ferraro, we are not especially concerned with artistic formation, but rather with commentaries on how immigrant authors have portrayed their experiences coming to America or in the cases of second- or third- generation writers, those of their parents and grandparents. We are also particularly interested in presenting the experiences of non-European groups, especially those immigrants who have come to America since 1965, most of whom are non-European and nonwhite, and to assess how their writing may be different from the earlier groups of immigrants. We are not alleging that these works are necessarily "authentic" in the sense of being an accurate historical record of immigration, but rather that they are artistic visions of the writers' views of their own experiences or of their ethnic groups' experiences.

One question we had when we began compiling these essays was whether the literature would reflect the assimilatory pattern that is part of the mythology of immigration in America—the idea that people come here as aliens, as uprooted strangers in a strange land, are thrown into the stew pot of America, pick up the ways of the native-born, and eventually, perhaps not until the second generation, join the throng of assimilated Americans. We suspected that this theme would be found in the earlier literature by writers of European roots, but that a new paradigm would be found in the literature of more recent non-European immigrants. As will be seen, our suspicions were correct concerning the newer writers, but we found that the assimilatory pattern was problematic, even in the older writing.

Another theme that emerged as we began to collect essays was gender and the immigrant experience. We found many essays by women critics about women authors writing about women protagonists. In all these essays and works, the gender of the author and characters were important factors in the types of experiences recounted in the literature. Earlier history, sociology, and literary criticism had tended to focus on the male immigrant, his experience as being the norm (Oscar Handlin almost always gave male examples to illustrate his themes), but there was obviously a body of literature written in earlier times and being written today that concentrates on the experiences of women immigrants and their descendants. In fact, today it appears that of the immigrant writers currently being studied, women authors outnumber the men.

When studying the literature of immigration—to understand its composition, why some groups are underrepresented, for example, and to read its themes perceptively—it is helpful to know something about the history of immigration, as well as cultural attitudes toward immigrants, and cultural mythology about the formation of the so-called national character. There have been three great waves of immigration to the United States. During the first wave, which lasted from about 1830 to 1860, immigrants came from northwestern Europe, specifically the British Isles, including Ireland, Germany, and Scandinavia. Often English speaking, these people sometimes were fleeing revolutions or religious persecution—famine in the case of the Irish—and many were searching for economic opportunity. They were fairly similar to those native-born Americans descended from the earliest settlers. It is these people who formed what has sometimes been called the "old stock" of Americans, and from their ranks have come many of the mainstream writers still composing the canon of American literature. Few of these writers have written extensively of the immigrant experience.

During the first half of the nineteenth century, cultural attitudes toward immigration were very positive, one could say welcoming (Handlin 264). Even when the flow of immigrants in the 1840s and 1850s became heavy, immigrants faced little opposition because it was believed that all these new people would contribute to the melting pot. Differences, which were not very great anyway, would disappear as immigrants became Americans. European travelers to the United States such as de Tocqueville remarked that America was creating a "new man" from the mixture of European nationalities composing it.[1] This "new Adam in a new Eden" was someone different, a new breed of human, more freedom loving and independent, more practical, more hardworking, and less likely to bow to arbitrary authority than the Europeans who were his ancestors. Crèvecoeur, another Frenchman who immigrated to America prior to the Revolution, asked:

What then is the American, this new man? He is either an European, or the descendent of an European, hence that strange mixture of blood, which you will find in no other country. . . . He is an American, who, leaving behind him all his ancient prejudices and manners, receives new ones from the new mode of life he has embraced, the new government he obeys, and the new rank he holds. (qtd. in Sollors, 1986, 75)

Although the east coast of America had been first settled in the seventeenth century by the English, according to early nineteenth-century mythology (the effects of which still reverberate in the popular culture today) this new American being created in the "great melting pot" of the new nation was decidedly not English (Handlin 265). In 1920, nearly two centuries after Crèvecoeur, the historian Frederick Jackson Turner expressed this mythology in his famous study of the effects of the frontier on American society: "In the crucible of the frontier the immigrants were Americanized, liberated, and fused into a mixed race, English in neither nationality nor characteristics" (23). The greatness of America, seen to be the hope of the human race, was derived from this stew of humanity, each nationality contributing important parts of the national character. Instead of taking on any particular prescribed traits, this newcomer to America would contribute what he brought with him to the new land.

These attitudes began to change with the arrival of new immigrants in the later part of the nineteenth century, a change that produced the first extensive literature of immigration. Lasting from the 1880s to the 1920s, this wave of immigration was composed of people from southern and eastern Europe, peasants or uneducated urban people from Italy, Greece, the Slavic countries, and another somewhat different group, Jews from the *shtetls* of Eastern Europe. These non-English-speaking people dressed differently, and they had different religions from the Protestant majority composing most of the native born. Roman Catholic, Orthodox, and Jewish, these "huddled masses" of Emma Lazarus's famous poem crowded into ghettos in the urban centers of the United States. In the minds of the native born, they created unsanitary conditions and taxed public resources. Up until this time, other than the Catholic Irish, who came after the famine, and the Chinese, who came during the mid-nineteenth century to work in mining and on the railroads, immigrants had faced little overt prejudice. However, that began to change with the continual flow from Europe.

Assimilation began to mean something different in the national mythology. Rather than all groups stewing together, each contributing something to the national character, creating a new creature, "an American," scholars and social scientists began searching for a predetermined definition of national character, a type to which immigrants would have to aspire if they wished to be accepted. Unfortunately, in developing their thinking, they were influenced by European writers on racial differences, men such as Houston Stewart Chamberlain and Arthur Gobineau, who were saying that northern Europeans were racially superior to people of other national or ethnic groups such as southern European, Jewish, or Asian. And it seemed to sociologists who studied the social pathologies of immigrant groups that these theories were borne out in the disease, alcoholism, crime, and poverty sometimes prevalent in the tenements.

American intellectuals influenced by these racist theories (later used by Hitler in developing his ideas) began to suggest that the national character was northern European—rooted in the culture and traditions of pre-Norman England, or perhaps the Teutonic tribes of Germany. This, of course, made it difficult for Irish, Slavs, or Jews ever to achieve this status, except by consciously adopting the culture, behavior, and customs of the native-born groups. Because it was now expected that an immigrant would have to assimilate to these predetermined standards, the effect these developments had on the immigrant experience was profound. In examining the work of the fiction writers from these groups, such as the Jewish writers featured in our collection, the reader can see these ideals and sometimes a willingness, even eagerness, to conform to them.

Prejudice toward immigrants grew during the latter part of the nineteenth century and first decades of the twentieth. As Oscar Handlin recounts, the media, intellectuals, and politicians began to call for restriction of these "inferior" groups. Amid these commonly accepted, we would now say racist, theories, the first major restriction of immigration, the Chinese Exclusion Act, was passed by Congress in 1882, in response to the growing nativist alarm in California about the Chinese who had immigrated to work in mining and in railroad construction. After this, the doors remained open to Europeans for over forty more years, allowing in a growing flood of immigrants. But because of nativist fears of these newcomers, concern over jobs and the effects of these different cultural groups on American culture, and buttressed by the pseudo-scientific studies mentioned above, Congress finally passed the National Origins Act in 1924.

This set up a system of quotas based on percentages of national groups already in the United States, thereby giving precedence to nations in northern Europe. Though many people had immigrated from southern and eastern Europe, the American stock was still heavily weighed toward northern Europeans. Thus, as Handlin said, "Now the moving men [came] to rest" (293). From the founding of the republic in 1797 until 1924, more than 35 million had flowed into the United States, 23.5 million of them during the years of 1880–1920 (Handlin 35; Knippling xv). From this point on, literature of immigration, at least that written by first-generation immigrants, diminished greatly in prominence, not to resume until the changes of the 1960s.

With a few exceptions, such as the Jews, many of these earlier ethnic groups produced little literature of note. Even the Irish, from whose ranks later came great American writers such as Eugene O'Neill, produced little notable literature during the nineteenth century, the peak years of their immigration. According to Daniel J. Casey and Robert E. Rhodes in their survey of Irish American literature, the immigrants of the famine were mostly illiterate peasants who poured into the urban slums and struggled at menial labor jobs to survive amid prejudice and almost intolerable living conditions. The works that came out of this period served to confirm stereotypes of the Irish as shiftless, ignorant, and a burden on society. Irish immigrants were urged to emulate the Yankee work ethic and disavow their Irish roots (265–269).

Other groups such as Italian and Polish who came in large numbers in the late nineteenth and early twentieth century were composed mostly of peasants who came mainly from oral cultures with little literary tradition. These groups did not produce much literature about their immigration experiences. In the case of Italians, the little that was published was influenced by this oral style (Gardaphe 282). According to Yiorgos D. Kalogeras, another group who came in large numbers during these years, Greek Americans, have written relatively little of their immigration experiences. Says Kalogeras, "The immigration story has always had little appeal to the Greeks, and this fact has determined . . . their exclusion from company of canonized immigrant writers such as Abraham Cahan and Anzia Yezierska [two Jewish writers]" (254). In *The Rise of the Unmeltable Ethnics* (1972) Michael Novak laments this lack of literary documentation of the experiences of white ethnics. He says, "Concerning the urban experience of immigration, it is as though our grandfathers did not live" (169). Novak goes on to say that to some extent the Jewish writers have spoken for these relatively silent groups, though there are important differences between the Jews and other white ethnics. Though Novak underestimates the amount of literature produced by these immigrant groups, it is true that in comparison to Jewish writers and the outpouring from the newer writers, which are the main subject of these essays, non-Jewish white ethnic groups have produced little.

For the next forty years, immigration was very sparse compared with the years from 1880 to 1924. During the 1930s, few had the means to immigrate because of the worldwide Depression, and during World War II they could not (Glazer, *New Immigration*, 2–3). During the late 1940s and 1950s, considerable numbers of refugees came from Europe fleeing the devastation of the war, and some from China (Chinese restrictions had been lifted since it was embarrassing to disallow immigration from a World War II ally). However, in comparison with the numbers who would have wished to come, immigration was limited in the postwar years. During this period, attitudes toward immigrants were less hostile, perhaps because fewer were coming, and the assimilatory mythology held firm in the national consciousness. And, certainly there were exceptions such as Paule Marshall, whose Afro-Caribbean parents immigrated from Barbados in the 1930s, to find not only racial prejudice from whites, but resentment from Southern-born blacks.

As in many areas of national life, great changes came in the 1960s with the advent of the black civil rights movement, which spilled over and affected other disadvantaged or excluded groups in American life. Long-silent groups such as Mexican Americans and Asian Americans began speaking out angrily against discrimination and formed their own movements for civil rights, similar to those of the African Americans. Part of this awakened awareness resulted in the creation of new literature by these groups. Whereas many of the first generation of immigrants had clung to the old world ways, and many of the second generation had embraced all things American and urged their children to become Americans, their children, the third generation, were less anxious about their ethnicity and more interested in exploring their roots. In addition, a different, more tolerant attitude toward difference and an appreciation for diversity created an audience for such literature.

This literature is also the result of a new immigration policy. It had long been obvious that the national quotas set up in 1924 were racist, and many had spoken out against them during the years following their enactment. In 1965, reflecting the new attitudes toward civil rights and racism, Congress abolished the system of quotas set up under the National Origins Act and allowed many more immigrants to come each year. This momentous event set up the third great wave of immigration in American history, a stream of immigrants from around the world that has increased each year and has greatly affected American life, including its literature. Though this stream of immigrants has never reached the record levels of 1900–1920 (in 1990, 7.9 percent of the population was foreign-born, compared with 14.7 percent in 1910), it has caused upheavals in many areas of the national consciousness (Portes and Rumbaut 6). It is the literature of this group immigrating since 1965 that is primarily the subject of the essays in this book.

How does the new immigration differ from the older immigration, and how does its literature differ? Though there are many similarities between these two groups of immigrants—two major examples being that the vast majority have settled in urban areas and many are willing to do jobs rejected by the native-born—differences between the groups are most often noted (Portes and Rumbaut 7). These new immigrants are overwhelmingly from what we would call undeveloped nations. In 1994 the top five nations sending immigrants to the United States were Mexico, China, the Philippines, the Dominican Republic, and Vietnam, and the next five were India, Poland, Ukraine, El Salvador, and Ireland. If one goes back just a couple of decades, we can see that into the 1980s many immigrants came from Korea as well as the Caribbean area.

Thus, because they are non-European (though some come from areas colonized by European nations), these new immigrants bring different cultural baggage with them: different religions (non-Judeo-Christian totally or in part), unusual, "exotic" languages, and different customs. Perhaps the greatest difference is that the newer groups are mostly nonwhite, or at least darker-skinned people whom white Americans perceive as "colored." For example, Mexican Americans are usually *mestizos*, mixtures of Spanish and Indian stock. Racial prejudice is certainly nothing new to American immigration (discussions were actually held in the 1880s about whether an Italian was white), but these new immigrants face a degree of racial prejudice unprecedented in earlier waves of immigration. This theme of racial prejudice is certainly important in the literature of these groups. It could be argued that the previously mentioned "reaction formation," a term used to describe an ethnic group's awareness of discrimination and resultant militancy on the part of the educated, English-speaking second and third generations, has produced much of this immigrant group's outpouring of literature in the last thirty years.

Another distinguishing characteristic of this new group setting them apart from earlier waves of immigrants is that they tend to maintain close ties with their former countries for several generations. Rather than severing ties and not looking back as many earlier immigrants were forced to do,[2] modern communications and travel have made it possible to communicate with those "back home" frequently, to send children to be with grandparents during the summer, and to travel home frequently for visits. This new "transnationalism" (and sometimes dual citizenship), plus the acceptance of multicultural lifestyles in the United States, has slowed the process of assimilation greatly. Many of these people live in ethnic enclaves and continue with the customs of their native lands; though considering themselves American, they consciously choose not to assimilate to certain aspects of the American lifestyle they consider undesirable for themselves and their children. These closer ties with the homeland and admiration for their national cultures certainly can be seen in the literature, where writers often find fault with certain aspects of American life, and where characters often return home for visits, or reflect on the strengths of their cultural heritage.

Another important difference that has contributed to the greater production of literature about the immigration experiences of these groups is that many of their members, especially in the second and third generations, are not only literate, but well educated. Contrary to popular stereotypes of most immigrants being peasants or laborers in big cities, a good number of immigrants are high school or college educated—in the case of some groups, more educated than the native born.[3] This situation was partly aided by statutes passed in the 1980s allowing special status to professionals such as engineers and doctors.

After the initial liberalizing legislation of the 1960s, the numbers of immigrants allowed in during a given period were consistently raised, leading to the point where nearly one million are coming legally each year, not including the thousands of illegals. This flood, perceived as destructive to mainstream culture by some conservative intellectuals and threatening to job security by some blue-collar workers, has led to largely ineffective measures to curb immigration. For example, the infamous Proposition 187 abolished welfare benefits in California for illegal immigrants, and on the national scene, in 1996 Congress withdrew some welfare benefits to legal immigrants, although the hardship to the elderly and children caused the benefits to be reinstated.

The growing nativist agitation against the newcomers bears a strong resemblance to the old prejudices against the earlier immigrants. In 1998 California voted to abolish bilingual programs in its schools, a measure that can partly be traced to anti-immigrant sentiment among the native-born. Much of the writing of this movement, such as Peter Brimelow in *Alien Nation* (1995), sounds eerily like that of the earlier period. Readers are warned that this influx of alien cultures will change the American character and will jeopardize the culture of the older, native-born stock. One could argue that in academe the canon wars of the 1990s between multiculturalists and traditionalists are an intellectual aspect of these arguments. One of the points we hope this volume will make is that rather than corrupting the culture of America, the outpouring of literature by these ethnic groups, greater in volume than that produced by earlier immigrant groups, is greatly enriching our culture and adding to the vibrancy of American literature.

The essays in this volume represent a good sampling of both the immigrant literature from the past and present, and the writers and nationalities current scholars are studying. For example, concerning the older immigrant groups, we found many essays and proposals on Jewish American literature, and relatively few on literature produced by non-Jewish white ethnics. The majority of the proposals and essays concerned second- and third-generation writers from the third group of immigrants described above—authors whose heritage lies in the nations of Asia, the Caribbean, and Spanish-speaking nations. This reflects the fact that first-generation, non-English speakers of any nationality seldom produce much literature, the exception being the Jews who did produce some well-known first-generation writers, though most of these immigrated as children or teenagers and were educated in the United States. Other first-generation immigrant writers such as Jamaica Kincaid, Paule Marshall, and Bharati Mukherjee are from English-speaking nations, former British colonies. Though certain national groups are not represented—for example, Filipino, Vietnamese, and Central and South American—we believe the essays represent a wide variety of American writers from immigrant backgrounds.

It will be noticed that of the eleven essays dealing with one work (one essay discusses a theoretical issue in immigrant writing), only two concern male authors. As stated earlier in the chapter, this reflects the fact that at present it appears that more female than male writers are writing on the immigrant experience. Apparently, in the field of ethnic literature and the literature of immigration, gender issues and writing by women immigrants is very popular now. We will speculate in our concluding chapter as to why this is so. Suffice it to say for now that many of the writers represented here, including the older ones, are grappling with conflicts between the patriarchal cultures of their heritage and the supposed greater autonomy and opportunity offered women by American culture. Donna Gabaccia points out in her study of gender in immigration that many immigrants saw American women as symbols of individualism, but at the same time feared a loss of community support and kinship (74, 111).

The first two essays in our collection represent early Jewish American women's immigrant writing. Though written at least half a century before the works discussed later, this early immigrant writing sets many of the themes for the contemporary literature to follow: issues of identity formation, cultural and generational conflict, assimilation and guilt, and alienation, sometimes from the old world traditions and sometimes from American culture. Unlike other immigrant groups, even though English was not their first language, Jewish people, perhaps because they are the "people of the word," and have long valued literacy and scholarship, produced a considerable body of first-generation immigrant writing. Though these women deal with some of the same issues as male immigrant writers such as Abraham Cahan and Henry Roth, issues of assimilation and cultural conflict, they do so from the vantage point of their gender. Mary Antin, Elizabeth Stern, and Anzia Yezierska are all traditionally read as assimilationist writers who strongly reject their cultures in favor of American values and lifestyles. Wendy Zierler in her essay "In(ter)dependent Selves: Mary Antin, Elizabeth Stern and Jewish Immigrant Women's Autobiography," though agreeing that these writers are seemingly assimilationist, finds that the assimilationist theme is problematic. In "Justifying Individualism: Anzia Yezierska's *Bread Givers*" (1925), Martin Japtok states that in her autobiographical novel, Yezierska shows her struggle with the patriarchal traditions of her orthodox scholar father. Like Antin and Stern's, Sara Smolinsky's drive for assimilation is fraught with conflict.

The next essay deals with immigrant pioneers on the frontier, a type of experience that looms large in the national mythology although it was experienced by only a small percentage of immigrants. Perhaps the best-known work of this type is Ole Edvart Rolvaag's *Giants in the Earth* (1927), a very popular saga of Norwegian pioneer life on the Dakota prairies. A first-generation Norwegian immigrant himself, Rolvaag tells their story as a series of gender contrasts between the man's experience, a fairy-tale-like adventure similar to the tales of Norwegian folklore, and the woman's, a grim struggle with loneliness and alienation. In a landmark essay in 1928 called "Human Migration and the Marginal Man," sociologist Robert Park described the "inner turmoil" and alienation experienced by the individual torn from his roots and placed in an unfamiliar new culture (893), and certainly some of the characters in *Giants in the Earth*, especially Beret, the wife, experienced this alienation. Not overtly concerned with assimilationist issues, but rather survival against the natural elements, the lonely life of the barren prairies separated the pioneers from all the culture they knew. It is this aspect of the pioneer immigrant experience that Raychel Haugrud Reiff documents in her essay "Fighting the Trolls on the Dakota Plains."

One salient difference between older and more recent immigrant writing is the tendency of newer writers to critique American culture and find it wanting. Though acknowledging the lure of American freedom and affluence, newer immigrant writers see a loss of their cultural roots, the racism and violence of American city life, and the materialism and hypocrisy of middle-class American mainstream culture. We begin our survey of later immigrant writing with two essays that cast a critical eye on the American society into which protagonists seek entry. The first essay on Bharati Mukherjee's *Jasmine*, represents an immigrant group, Indians,

who are exceptionally well educated, many of them relatively affluent professionals (Portes and Rumbaut 59). Gönül Pultar in *"Jasmine* or the Americanization of
an Asian" gives Mukherjee's novel quite a different reading than it is usually given.
Often seen as an upbeat tale of the protagonist's assimilation by adopting of successive identities, Pultar reads *Jasmine* as a negative critique of American violence
and materialism.

The next work discussed also takes a negative view of much of American culture. Jamaica Kincaid, who immigrated, like her protagonist Lucy, as a teenager
from the formerly British island of Antigua, often creates characters who face
gender conflicts as well as identity issues in a world that presents many obstacles
to self-realization. The adolescent protagonist of *Lucy* rejects much of the American culture she encounters as a nanny in an upper-middle-class home, but at the
same time she rejects the British-influenced culture of postcolonial Antigua, which
she associates with the domination of her mother. Jacqueline Doyle in her essay
"Developing Negatives: Jamaica Kincaid's *Lucy*" concentrates on the metaphor of
photography in the novel, which Lucy uses to create a new version of herself that
she hopes is free of the negative influences of both her new and older homes.

One of the most important efforts of both older and recent immigrants has been
to learn English as soon as possible. America tends to be very intolerant of non-
English speakers, and English acquisition becomes a primary step toward acculturation. At the same time, since language is so much a part of identity and culture,
acquisition of a new language can involve guilt and anxiety about giving up one's
cultural roots. June Dwyer's essay on Chang-rae Lee's *Native Speaker,* "Speaking
and Listening: The Immigrant as Spy Who Comes in from the Cold," deals with
the issue of language and speech as part of the acculturative process as the young
second-generation Korean American protagonist struggles to find his niche in
American society.

The rest of the essays, though concerning many different racial and ethnic groups,
all deal with what is probably the most prominent theme of recent immigrant literature: hybridity, which can mean a number of things from cultural syncretism or
blending, to the coexistence of two or more cultural/national identities in the same
individual.

Qun Wang's essay on recent Asian American literature deals with the issue of
essentialism, or an emphasis on cultural retention or purity versus a looser adaptation of cultural traditions to meet the needs of people living in contemporary American society. Several recent Chinese American writers such as Maxine Hong Kingston
and Amy Tan have freely altered Chinese myth and folklore in their works, a practice harshly criticized by another Chinese American novelist Frank Chin, who
calls such writing by Americanized, Christianized writers of Asian ancestry "fake"
(93). Wang's essay, "Repositioning the Stars: Twentieth-Century Narratives of Asian
American Immigration," explains such practices as realizing a new postcolonial
view of culture, which would reject all attempts at cultural hegemony, whether by
dominant Westernized groups or the formerly colonized groups.

Gender issues are prominent in recent literature by women writers of immigrant backgrounds as protagonists often find themselves in a new society with seemingly different attitudes and values than their cultures of birth. For example, Katherine Payant's essay, "Borderland Themes in Sandra Cisneros's *Woman Hollering Creek,*" argues that Chicana feminist Cisneros's female characters are searching for a hybridity that would leave them comfortable on the borders of several cultures: Mexican, Indian, and Anglo. This search often pits them against cultural traditions seen as restricting to their development.

Like Cisneros, many authors from a Caribbean background reveal similar conflicts in their fiction. Toby Rose's essay "Crossroads Are Our Roads" concerns such issues in Paule Marshall's novels. The work of a second-generation Barbadian, Marshall's fiction, says Rose, moves from young protagonists facing basic questions of racism, identity, and gender to a global vision of women of color united in their dedication to create humane societies of class and gender justice. The later characters' quests often involve a "return" both literally and figuratively to their ancestral roots, roots that they have lost; at the same time they often come up against current postcolonial rulers and figures of power in both their island societies and in the United States. Though they usually develop comfortable hybrid identities, such struggles are fraught with conflict.

Carmen Faymonville's essay on Judith Ortiz Cofer's *The Line of the Sun* "Motherland Versus Daughterland" deals with similar assimilationist and boundary issues. Cofer contrasts a young American-born woman, Marisol, who attempts to assimilate thoroughly to American culture, with her mother, Ramona, who attempts to maintain her Puerto Rican identity by living in "El Building," a high-rise ghetto in New York City. Explicitly in her statements and implicitly in her fiction, Cofer deals with issues of "transnationalism" (see conclusion), whereby individuals can be truly binational, that is, members of two different nations or cultures simultaneously.

Japanese Canadian writer Joy Kogawa's *Obasan* explores the key historical experience for Japanese Americans and Canadians, the internment and relocation of World War II, a theme often treated by Japanese American writers. According to Matthew Beedham in "*Obasan* and Hybridity: Necessary Cultural Strategies," Kogawa not only movingly tells the story of this traumatic experience and its effect on her characters, but also uses the story to explore profound questions of national identity relating to issues of hybridity. Kogawa asks a very basic question: "What does it mean to be Canadian?"

The final essay in our volume, Zhou Xiaojing's "Becoming Americans: Gish Jen's *Typical American,*" argues that unlike Kingston and Tan, the work of Gish Jen, a third-generation Chinese American writer, suggests a possible new direction for fiction by writers from immigrant backgrounds. Jen, says Zhou, is less concerned with issues such as racism and identity and more with the inner life of her characters.

Our concluding chapter explores the themes of these essays more deeply and ties them into some broad conclusions about the subjects and themes of immigrant literature. In particular we examine some of the differences between the older and newer immigrant literature.

We will end this introduction by referring to a question raised at the beginning of this discussion. Does discussing "immigrant literature" categorize it as a subgenre, worthy only of sociological and historical interest? First, our approach is thematic and we see no problem with discussing immigration as a theme in American literature, any more than we would with examining "the theme of the West" in American literature. Second, we would argue that much of the literature discussed in these essays is of high aesthetic quality, fit to stand alongside writing by "mainstream" American writers. Finally, until this literature find its way into the canon and is thus well represented in literary histories and college courses, it needs to be treated separately so that it receives the attention it deserves. We can only hope that in the future, writing that deals with immigration, a central experience of our culture—one could argue *the* central experience—will be recognized as an important, integral part of American literature.

NOTES

1. We use the male pronoun here since all the writing and expressions of the mythology of the time seemed to assume that the immigrant was a male.

2. Actually, a fairly large percentage, 25–33 percent (Novak 80; Sontag and Dugger 13) of earlier immigrants in fact, returned to their homelands after many years in the United States. However, the contemporary phenomenon of binationalism was not possible in earlier decades.

3. For example, from 1980 to 1990, eight nations, most of them Asian, sent immigrants whose level of education was well above the U.S. average (Portes and Rumbaut 59).

WORKS CITED

Aaron, Daniel. "The Hyphenate Writer and American Letters." *Smith Alumae Quarterly.* (July 1964): 215.

Boelhower, William. *Through a Glass Darkly: Ethnic Semiosis in American Literature.* New York: Oxford UP, 1987.

Casey, Daniel J., and Robert E. Rhodes. "Irish-American Literature." *New Immigrant Literatures: A Sourcebook to Our Multicultural Literary Heritage.* Ed. Alpana Sharma Knippling. Westport: Greenwood, 1996.

Chan, Jeffrey Paul, Frank Chin, Lawson Fusao Inada, and Shawn H. Wong, eds. *AIIIEEEEE!: An Anthology of Asian-American Writers.* Washington: Howard UP, 1974.

Ferraro, Thomas J. *Ethnic Passages: Literary Immigrants in Twentieth-Century America.* Chicago: U of Chicago P, 1993.

Gabaccia, Donna. *From the Other Side: Women, Gender and Immigrant Life in the U.S., 1820–1990.* Bloomington: Indiana UP, 1994.

Gardaphe, Fred. "Italian/American Literature." *New Immigrant Literatures in the United States: A Source to Our Multicultural Literary Heritage.* Ed. Alpana Sharma Knippling. Westport: Greenwood, 1996.

Glazer, Nathan. *The New Immigration: A Challenge to American Society.* San Diego: San Diego State University P, 1988.

Glazer, Nathan, and Daniel Moynihan. *Beyond the Melting Pot: The Negroes, Puerto Ricans, Jews, Italians, and Irish of New York City.* 2nd ed. Cambridge: MIT P, 1970.

Handlin, Oscar. *The Uprooted: The Epic Story of the Great Migrations that Made the American People.* Boston: Little, 1951.

Hechter, Michael. *Internal Colonialism: The Celtic Fringe in British National Development, 1536–1966.* Berkeley: U of California P, 1977.

Kalogeras, Yiorgos D. "Greek-American Literature." *New Immigrant Literatures in the United States: A Sourcebook to Our Multicultural Literary Heritage.* Ed. Alpana Sharma Knippling. Westport: Greenwood, 1996.

Knippling, Alpana Sharma, ed. *New Immigrant Literatures in the United States: A Sourcebook to Our Multicultural Literary Heritage.* Westport: Greenwood, 1996.

Novak, Michael. *The Rise of the Unmeltable Ethnics: Politics and Culture in the Seventies.* New York: Macmillan, 1972.

Portes, Alejandro, and Ruben G. Rumbaut. *Immigrant America: A Portrait.* 2nd ed. Berkeley: U of California P, 1996.

Sollors, Werner. *Beyond Ethnicity: Consent and Descent in American Culture.* New York: Oxford UP, 1986.

———, ed. *The Invention of Ethnicity.* New York: Oxford UP, 1989.

Sontag, Deborah, and Celia W. Dugger. "The New Immigrant Tide: A Shuttle Between Worlds." *New York Times* 19 July 1998, sec. 1: 1+.

Ware, Caroline F. *The Cultural Approach to History.* New York: Columbia UP, 1940.

1

In(ter)dependent Selves: Mary Antin, Elizabeth Stern, and Jewish Immigrant Women's Autobiography

Wendy Zierler

The waves of Eastern European immigration to America at the end of the nineteenth and beginning of the twentieth centuries gave rise to a new genre of Jewish literature: Jewish women's autobiography. In a 1927 introduction to the published memoirs of American Jewish women's activist Rebekah Kohut, Henrietta Szold chronicles the emergence of this new genre, outlining several factors leading to the rise during this period of Jewish autobiography, in general, and Jewish women's autobiography in particular. Like the well-known theorist of autobiography Georges Gusdorf, who argues in his seminal 1956 essay "Conditions and Limits of Autobiography" that "autobiography is not possible in a cultural landscape where consciousness of self does not, properly speaking, exist" (Gusdorf 29–30), Szold contends that for Jews to begin writing autobiography, they needed first to discover the self, that is, to begin to consider their personal experience a fit subject for writing. For this, they needed to individuate and oppose themselves to others, to shrug off the strictly communal perspective that had characterized Jewish writing for generations as a result of centuries of collective persecution.

According to Szold, the emancipation of the Jews in Europe in the eighteenth and nineteenth centuries, with its possibilities for self-transformation and improvement, encouraged this process of Jewish literary self-revelation; the waves of Jewish immigration to America provided an even greater impetus. Crossing over to the American "Promised Land" of democracy and individual rights, of opportunity and upward mobility, the Jew invented a new self, and this story of self-discovery and transformation was the subject of a great many immigrant autobiographies. And for virtually the first time in history—scholars know of less than a handful of autobiographies by Jewish women that antedate this period, most notably, the *Memoirs of Gluckel of Hameln* and Pauline Wengeroff's Haskalah autobiography, *Memoiren Einer Grossmutter: Bilder aus der Kultugeschichte der Juden Russlands im 19 Jahrhundert*—Jewish women began to write autobiography, to tell the story of their own border-crossings and metamorphoses. As Szold writes, "who in his progress has more obstacles to overcome than the immigrant...? And if the immigrant is a woman to boot, then the tale thrills with the threefold interest and victory over hindrances barring the path of the Jew, the immigrant and the woman" (Szold ix–xi).

What happens when Jewish women begin to write in a generic form in which there have been virtually no Jewish women's contributions in the past? What happens when this form is autobiography, a genre the definitions of which have been predominantly drawn from the ways in which remarkable men—St. Augustine, Jean Jacques Rousseau, Montaigne, Benjamin Franklin, and Henry Adams—wrote their lives? How does the Jewish woman immigrant autobiographer, a figure whose *shtetl* background often discouraged the development of an individualistic, autobiographical subjectivity, establish what feminist theorist Sidonie Smith has called "the discursive authority to interpret herself publicly in a patriarchal culture and an androcentric genre" (Smith 45)? What "anxieties" of autobiographical "authorship" (to adapt a term from feminist critics Sandra Gilbert and Susan Gubar) attend the writing of her autobiography, and what strategies does she develop to cope with these anxieties?

In this essay, I will address these questions by looking at the autobiographies and autobiographical fiction of two Jewish immigrant women, Mary Antin (1881–1949) and Elizabeth Gertrude Levin Stern (1889–1954). Both Antin and Stern immigrated to America from Poland, Antin from Polotzk when she was thirteen years old, and Stern from Skedel when she was a young child; both inaugurated their literary careers through the writing of immigrant autobiography and associate their coming to America with their coming into writing; and both recycle this autobiographical story in various other forms in their fiction writing. The version of self presented in these fictional rerenderings, however, is often very different from that presented in the autobiography. The flip-side of their sense of exhilarating "firstness" as Jewish women autobiographers is a sense of discomfort over the repudiations of the old world that accompany their new versions of self. And so, although Mary Antin claims in the introduction to *The Promised Land* that in writing her autobiography, she is taking her cue from The Ancient Mariner, "who told his tale in order to be rid of it"—I will write a bold "Finis" at the end, and shut the book with a bang!"—a reading of her stories reveals just how anxious she is about closing the book of her past. Similarly, although Elizabeth Stern ends her first autobiography, *My Mother and I*, with a resignation to the reality that she has become forever estranged from Judaism and can never restore her relationship with her old world mother to its former condition, in two later works, a fictional autobiography entitled *I am a Woman and a Jew*, and a novel entitled *A Marriage Was Made*, this ending is largely, if not entirely reversed.

In my framing the issues to be addressed in this essay, I have intentionally cited the work of Georges Gusdorf along with certain feminist critics, because I see my observations on Antin and Stern as an effort to mediate between Gusdorf's theory and the feminist critique thereof. According to Gusdorf, a precondition for autobiography is a "conscious awareness of the singularity of each individual life" (29); autobiographical writing cannot take place in a society where "lives are so thoroughly entangled that each of them has its center everywhere and its circumference nowhere" (31). The late emergence of Jewish autobiography in general, and Jewish women's autobiography in particular, seems to support Gusdorf's linkage between autobiography and the development of individualistic cultures. In the past decade and a half, however, there has been a virtual outpouring of feminist theoretical and critical interest in women's autobiography, much of which challenges the relevance of Gusdorf's individualistic concept of the autobiographical self. The critical approaches of Sidonie Smith in *A Poetics of Women's Autobiography* (1987) and Susan Stanford Friedman in her well-known essay "Women's Autobiographical Selves: Theory and Practice" (1988) are two cases in point. Both of these critics assert the "fundamental inapplicability" of Gusdorf's individualistic models of self to the autobiographical writings of women (Friedman 34), resting their arguments on feminist theoretical writings, such as Nancy Chodorow's feminist reinterpretation of feminine and masculine development, which posits that males develop through individuation and separation from their mothers, whereas females develop through continued relation.

According to Susan Stanford Friedman, "[i]solate individualism is an illusion. It is also a privilege of power. A white man has the luxury of forgetting skin color and sex and can think of himself as an individual. Women and minorities . . . have no such luxury" (Friedman 39). Where do Jewish women immigrant autobiographers fit into this theoretical debate? It is my contention in this essay that the version of immigrant American selfhood presented in the writings of Antin and Stern represents a middle ground between Gusdorf and the feminists, between individuation and relation. In their autobiographies, both Antin and Stern often assume the privileged stance of the isolate American individual—in fact, their individualism represents a paradoxical admixture of individualism and collectivism, in its reliance on mainstream, assimilationist, and therefore collectivist notions of American-ness. At the same time, they remain preoccupied with the impact of this authorial individuation upon what George Gusdorf would refer to as their "interdependent existence (Gusdorf 29)—their Jewish religious past and their relationship with their immigrant mothers and sisters. And, in their fictional rerenderings of the autobiographies, the pressures of this interdependent existence challenge, even overtake the versions of self delivered in the autobiographies.

I've chosen to begin my discussion with Mary Antin, specifically because so many critics read *The Promised Land* (1912), Antin's autobiographical account of life in the Russian Pale of Settlement and subsequent immigration with her family to Boston, as an unequivocal celebration of both the individual ego and the Americanization process. In comparison with the more sober versions of the immigrant experience presented by such writers as Abraham Cahan (*The Rise of David Levinsky*, 1917), Ludwig Lewissohn (*Up Stream*, 1922), Anzia Yezierska (*Hungry Hearts*, 1920), and Rose Cohen (*Out of the Shadows*, 1918), Antin's shiningly positive depiction of her immigrant entry into American life and letters "is seen by most critics as a naive, unrealistic portrayal of the difficulties of immigration and acculturation, the story of a woman who too eagerly surrendered her past, her culture, and her religion for the promise of America" (Rubin 289). Alvin Rosenfeld characterizes Antin's account of her past life in Polotzk and her subsequent immigration to America as a kind of personal exorcism of the past (Rosenfeld 133–156). Sarah Blacher Cohen goes even further and calls Antin's account of her Americanization as a "religio-cultural striptease" which "may have made her more appealing to her Gentile friends, but it certainly prevented her from becoming a profound writer of Jewish-American literature, or for that matter, any kind of literature" (Blacher Cohen 32). More recently, however, critics such as Steven J. Rubin (1986), Gert Buelens (1994), and Betty Bergland (1994) have begun to look beneath the surface of Antin's narrative of assimilation to detect the various anxieties pertaining to her construction of an individualistic American identity and the surrendering of her past. This essay contributes to this ongoing reevaluation of Antin's work, through close attention to the autobiography as well as to those other writings by Antin that seem to be in dialogue therewith.

To be sure, the most readily apparent version of self presented in *The Promised Land* is autonomous and oppositional. Antin's parents may have initially directed her education, she writes, but "I soon chose my own books, and built me a world of my own. In these discriminations, *I* emerged, a new being, something that had not been before (Antin, 1912 xix–xx). "Since I have stood on my feet," she proclaims with Emersonian conviction, "I have never met my master. I can think of no cataclysm that could have the force to make me move from my path" (59). In keeping with Gusdorf's male-centered paradigm, Mary's individualistic assertions are often associated with images of maleness or male figures, in opposition to the interdependence of the women of her family. In one episode in the first half of the autobiography which deals with life in Polotzk, Mary tests the boundaries of her religious faith by stepping outside her gate on the Sabbath with a handkerchief in her pocket, thereby violating the laws that prohibit the Jew from carrying anything outside the house on the Sabbath. When the thunders of Jehovah fail to strike, she goes back into her house and gazes with a new curiosity at her mother and grandmother dozing in their chairs. "When they awoke," Antin writes, "and stretched themselves and adjusted wig and cap, they looked *very* strange" (125). The strangeness that Mary observes arises from her having ventured outside the company of her pious mothers, both literally and figuratively. Indeed, while her female relatives remain steadfast in their observance of the Day of Rest (they are asleep during this episode, and when they wake up, their first action is to adjust their ritual hair-covering, a symbol of their faithful adherence to the laws of female modesty), Mary daringly violates God's with seeming impunity. Soon after this episode, Mary's transgressiveness takes on an explicitly patrilineal form, when she witnesses her father turn off a light on the Sabbath, thus discovering that she is not the only "doubter in Polotzk" (128).

In this alliance with the transgressive behavior of her father, Mary begins to carve out what will become her (masculine) immigrant self. Indeed, from the very beginning of her immigrant voyage, Antin's autobiographical narrator imagines herself emulating men not women, and not just any man, but the prototype of the self-sufficient, middle-class, modern man—Robinson Crusoe. Antin first discovers secular literature during a stay at her uncle's house in Vitebsk (156); significantly, of all the secular books and stories she reads while she is away from home, Defoe's story of a lone man's sojourn on a desert island is the only one she remembers by name. Later, while standing on the deck of the ship bound for the new world, Mary imagines herself "all alone on the ocean, and Robinson Crusoe was very real to me" (179). Like Robinson Crusoe, indeed, Mary has embarked on a sea voyage to discover a new world and has ventured to write a "history" of her discoveries. And like Crusoe, who is left alone and shipwrecked on a faraway island, Mary's metaphorical voyage into the world of American letters carries her away from her old world origins and from her family circle.

Later on in the narrative, when Mary is firmly ensconced in American life, she supplements the Crusoe model of solitary male individualism and enterprise with the quintessential American model of male heroism, George Washington. In a chapter entitled "My Country," which chronicles Antin's public school experiences, Antin describes in religious terms her newfound reverence for the first president of the United States, elevating Washington even above God. "As I read about the noble boy who would not tell a lie to save himself from punishment," Antin writes, "I was for the first time truly repentant of my sins" (223).

As Mary Dearborn has observed, it is her discovery of the gospel of George Washington that launches Mary Antin's career as a public author (Dearborn 71–72). On the occasion of Washington's birthday, Antin composes a poem in honor of her newfound hero, recites it at school in front of her classmates, and dazzles them with the pathos and sophisticated vocabulary of her poetic praise. Encouraged by the reception of her poem, Antin enacts a kind of mini-immigrant voyage into the world of published writing. Boldly she crosses the Mystic River into downtown Boston, and hits "Newspaper Row," where she submits the poem for publication in the *Boston Transcript*.

Significantly, when Mary discovers George Washington and crosses over into the world of writing, we also read of Mary's steady alienation from her older sister Frieda. In Poland, Mary and Frieda attended school together and shared similar aspirations. Upon their arrival in America, however, Frieda is singled out for a very different fate than that of her academically talented younger sister. Unlike Mary and the younger Antin children who are enrolled in school, Frieda is sent to work as a milliner, participating in the grammar school experience only insofar as she sews Mary's calico school frock. Lacking the opportunity for schooling, Frieda makes an immediate transition into womanhood, a state Mary associates with the drudgery of housework, marriage, and motherhood. Antin's description of her school years as a "dance at the May festival of untroubled childhood" (199–200), with its associations with maidenhood, courtship, and fertility, is particularly curious, given that in *The Promised Land* she completely avoids addressing issues of female sexuality or sexual maturity. Mary's life history begins with her birth and ends with her high school years; nowhere is there anything more than an oblique mention of her marriage to Lutheran geologist William Amadeus Grabau, nor of the birth of their daughter, Josephine Esther. The American educational "May festival" enjoyed by Mary, then, is a de-gendered intellectual experience, in contrast to the conventionally feminine nature of Frieda's domestic work.

Mary further differentiates herself from her sister's old-world feminine role by repeatedly declaring that although she had a number of good female friends, her "favorite playmates were boys." Mary prefers the world of boys—its slapdash adventure, its opportunities to dodge trains, peer into saloons, and laugh at drunken men—not only in real-life but also in writing. Although Mary expresses her fondness early in the autobiography for Louisa May Alcott and her tales of little American women, she admits a particular fondness for boys' books and their adventurous heroes. "In the boys' books I was fond of reading," she writes,

I came across all sorts of heroes and I sympathized with them all. The boy who ran away to sea; the boy who delighted in the society of ranchmen and cowboys; the stage-struck boy, whose ambition was to drive a pasteboard chariot in a circus; the boy who gave up his holidays in order to earn money for books; the bad boy who played tricks on people; the clever boy who invented amusing toys for his blind little sister—all these boys I admired. I could put myself in the place of any one of these heroes, and delight in their delights. (322)

To "put herself in the place of any one of these heroes"—to construct a narrative of immigrant self-transformation and growth that measures up to the stories of notable American male—is, in large measure, the project of *The Promised Land*. In the absence of appealing models of old world Jewish femininity and the Jewish female written life, Antin chooses a version of self that is more male than female, more wild than tame, more sinful than pious, more individualistic than relational. Repeatedly, Antin repudiates the kind of feminine piety that she identifies with her mother (who continues to attend synagogue long after the Antin family immigrates to America even though the rest of the family has desisted from religious observance) and feminine self-sacrifice that she identifies with her "poor" sister Frieda, who was married off within two years of her arrival in America and led a life of domestic drudgery.

At the same time, Mary's (masculine) individualism repeatedly cracks under the pressure of her prior "interdependent existence," and it is at these points in Antin's narrative when the feminist critique of Gusdorf's autobiographical paradigm becomes especially relevant. Every so often, during her accounts of her academic and literary triumphs, Mary casts a regretful glance backward at what and whom she has left behind, as if to reject the privilege of isolate individualism. Immediately following her account of her repudiation of the Jewish faith and her embrace of the Constitution, for example, Mary admits a few misgivings: "My grandchildren, for all I know, may have a graver task than I have set them. Perhaps they may have to testify that the faith of Israel is a heritage that no heir in direct line has the power to alienate from his successors" (249). Even more pronounced than these parenthetical admissions is her sense of regret over the breakdown of the structure of her family as a result of the immigrant experience. In the absence of firsthand knowledge of "good American form," Antin recalls that her parents were forced to take their cues from their children. "The result," she writes, "was a laxity of domestic organization, that inversion of normal relations which makes for friction, and sometimes ends in breaking up a family that was formerly united and happy" (270).

Most of all, Antin repines the discrepant lot of her sister Frieda. Persistently in the narrative, Antin punctuates her exultant descriptions of her education and transformation with doleful references to her sister's sacrifices and missed opportunities. In the middle of her joyous account of her first day at school in America, Antin shifts focus to Frieda, who gave up her own hopes of education for the sake of the family. "I was so blind," Antin writes, "that I did not see that the glory lay on her, and not on me" (202). Although it is Mr. Antin, the father of the house, who ordains that Frieda must go to work rather than school, and who arranged Frieda's swift marriage, Mary exonerates her father and heaps the guilt for Frieda's fate upon herself: "I remember that I accepted the arrangements made for my sister and me without reflection," she writes, "and everything that was planned for my advantage I took as a matter of course. I was no heartless monster, but a decidedly self-centered child" (201).

In this passage, Antin attempts to apologize for the self-centeredness of her youth and her authorial pursuits, and for her part in contributing to Frieda's fate. It is in her fiction, rather than her autobiographical writing, however, that Antin provides a kind of imaginative restitution for her wronged sister. Throughout *The Promised Land*, Antin refers to her propensity to lie, that is to embellish the truth for the sake of constructing a good story. In her 1913 story "The Lie," Antin puts this talent for "lying" to good use and creates a fiction that smooths over the inequities and harsh realities of Frieda's immigrant experience. Significantly, in this reinvention of Frieda's life, Antin transforms Frieda into a male character, an imaginative move that reinforces Antin's association in *The Promised Land* of strong versions of self with male rather than female experience, and suggests, perhaps, that if Frieda had been a firstborn son rather than daughter to the Antin family, hers might have been a very different fate. [1]

In the figure of David Rudinsky, the protagonist of "The Lie," Frieda and Mary Antin effectively merge into one. Like Frieda Antin, David is the eldest child in his family, the one who would be expected to go off to work to help support the family. And like Mary Antin, David Rudinsky writes compositions about vacations spent in the public library and adulates George Washington. As in Antin's own story, David's zealous pursuit of knowledge earns him extra attention from his teacher Miss Ralston, a figure reminiscent of Mary's beloved teacher Miss Dillingham. Similarly reminiscent of *The Promised Land* is the figure of David's poor immigrant father, who, like Israel Antin, conducts his children to school for their first day with a kind of religious pride. "If I didn't have to make a living," Mr. Rudinsky declares in the story, "I'd like to stay here all day and see my son David get educated" (Antin, 1965, 580). Unlike Mr. Antin, however, who sends his daughter off to work to be a milliner, Mr. Rudinsky takes concrete steps to prevent David's premature entry into the workforce. When Mr. Rudinsky learns of the American system of compulsory education, he deliberately falsifies David's age on his school certificate, making him ten instead of twelve, thus ensuring David four full years of American schooling. Compulsory education, he decides, "will be the policeman that will keep me from robbing my David if I fail in business" (591).

It is Mr. Rudinsky's lie on the school certificate that furnishes this story with its title and its central plot conflict. Troubles begin two years after David's entry into public school, when David, enchanted with the story of George Washington's inability to tell a lie, is selected to play the role of Washington in a school play. When Miss Ralston asks David his age in order to ascertain the proper size for his George Washington costume, David replies that he is twelve years old, reiterating his father's original lie. After telling this lie, David becomes literally sick with regret. Echoing Mary Antin's awestruck declaration in *The Promised Land* that "this George Washington was as inimitable as he was irreproachable. Even if I have never told a lie, I could not compare myself to George Washington," (224) David becomes convinced that his lie not only disqualifies him from playing the part of Washington in the play, but taints his aspirations to be a good, proper citizen of America. Confined to his bed, he sends a cryptic note to his beloved teacher Miss Ralston, refusing to play the part of Washington in the play.

When Miss Ralston receives this note, she goes to visit David and his parents at their tenement home, hoping to uncover the root of David's concerns. During a conversation with Mr. Rudinsky, she refers incidentally to David as being twelve years old; it is then that she learns David's true age, and by extension, the meaning of his message. Quickly she goes to David's bedroom to speak to him about "the lie" and assuage his crippling guilt. Antin does not give her readers the direct content of this conversation between Miss Ralston and David. Instead, she provides an indirect account, in terms that resonate with both erotic and religious meanings. "Miss Ralston never forgot the next hour," Antin writes,

and David never forgot. The woman always remembered how the boy's eyes burned through the dusk of the shadowed corner where he lay. The boy remembered how his teacher's voice palpitated in his heart, how her cool hands rested on his, how the lamplight made a halo of her hair. To each of them the dim room with its scant furnishings became a spiritual rendezvous. (595)

The polemical point of this grandiloquent ending is patently, perhaps too simplistically clear: through her revision of the George Washington myth, Antin demonstrates how the immigrant newcomer renews and revivifies the founding principles of America. On a more personal level, the story imagines away those details from Antin's autobiography that undercut or refute the promise of the Promised Land. In the person of David Rudinsky, Frieda Antin, who was sent to work and married off at a young age and was thus unable to share in Mary's patriotic revelations, is born again not only as a boy, but also as the genuine spiritual offspring of George Washington. Unlike the Founding Father, this boy does tell a lie, but it is a noble one, for the sake of the best of America. In the person of Mr. Rudinsky, Israel Antin is similarly reborn as an immigrant saint, one who sacrifices potential extra income in order to secure his child's continuing education. Through these imaginative rewritings, Antin rehabilitates the hopes of her sister Frieda, seemingly writing away the anxieties surrounding her self-centered pursuit of the American Dream.

In yet another story called "Malinke's Atonement," Antin enacts an even more imaginative fictionalization of the plot of *The Promised Land*. Published in September 1911 in *The Atlantic*, the same year that magazine began serializing the first chapters of *The Promised Land*, "Malinke's Atonement" extends the American promise of education even back to the old world of Polotzk. Like David Rudinsky, Malinke boasts an interesting combination of both Mary and Frieda Antin's character traits. Recalling Frieda, Malinke is a diligent little housewife, long entrusted by her mother, Breine Henne, with a large measure of housekeeping responsibilities. Recalling Mary, as well, she demonstrates intellectual curiosity, outspokenness, and a penchant for mischief. Malinke (a name not all that different from Mashke, Mary's old-country name) audaciously ridicules the traditional explanation of the origins of God; like Mary in *The Promised Land,* she questions the role divisions of men in women in Polotzk as evidenced in the discrepancy between her education and that granted her brother. In fact, the central conflict of this story concerns Malinke's refusal to strictly conform to her proper feminine role. Malinke's rebellious tendencies come to the fore when a piece of chicken wire is discovered in the bowels of a lean hen that her mother has slaughtered in honor of the Sabbath, and that Malinke has been so hungry to eat. Malinke is sent with the chicken to the home of Reb Nossen, who determines that the wire has rendered the chicken unkosher. Malinke, however, refuses to accept his pronouncement. Daringly she decides to report to her family that Reb Nossen has pronounced the chicken kosher after all. To protect the innocence of her family members, however, she makes a deal with God that if the chicken is indeed unkosher, she alone should be punished.

And so, when during dinner Malinke nearly chokes to death on the bone of this same chicken, she immediately recognizes and confesses her sin. Word soon gets around Polotzk, and Malinke becomes a pariah in the community. Longing to atone for her sin, she sacrifices her two most beloved possessions—her Sabbath dress and shoes, ironically symbolic of the feminine role she has stubbornly opposed, and in contrition ought to embrace rather than cast out—and throws them in the river. Reb Nossen soon hears of Malinke's sacrifice and takes her under his pedagogical wing. During this meeting, Reb Nossen, an old-world version of Miss Dillingham in *The Promised Land* and Miss Ralston in "The Lie," expresses his regret for not having made a more sensitive and thoughtful ruling on the status of the chicken and takes it upon himself to provide for Malinke's education.

Ironically, then, it is independence not interdependence, impiety not compliance, that allows Malinke to receive the education for which she has long envied her brother Yossele. ("Oh will you teach me everything? . . . the same as a boy— the same as Yossele?" she asks. "I'd like to read *everything*. Yossele says a girl can't understand but I don't think that's true, do you?" Antin, 1990, 55.) As William Proefriedt observes, Malinke gets it all: "the education denied to her as a girl, the independence of a free thinker, and absolute acceptance, even adulation within the Jewish community" (Proefriedt 87). Unlike Mary in *The Promised Land*, Malinke's yearning for a "male" education does not led her to suppress her religion. Both of these concerns are brought together in a harmonious union. In the person of Malinke, Antin wishfully—and quite implausibly—reinvents the old world which she so shuns in her autobiography and envisions the possibility of feminine fulfillment within the traditional Jewish fold. In this sense, "Malinke's Atonement" becomes "Mary's Atonement," a fantastic rediscovery of her past.

Elizabeth Stern's *My Mother and I* (1917) does not present the same boldly independent and stubbornly individualistic version of self that Antin so often delivers in *The Promised Land*. Whereas Antin's anxieties of immigrant female autobiographical authorship need to be teased out from in between the lines of her ebullient narrative of self, they are readily confessed in Stern's autobiographical story of her relationship with, and eventual estrangement from, her old world immigrant mother. Stern received much praise from reviewers for her frank account of her adoration of her mother and of the Americanization process, which eventually leads her away from her mother's kitchen for good. As one contemporary reviewer writes, "the note struck in Mrs. Stern's book appears to be more sincere than that sounded by Miss Antin, because though the narrative is a personal one, the reader is not oppressed by the ego of the writer," (*New York Call* 1917)—a critical response that reflects a measure of incredulity and intolerance in the face of female expressions of individualism. Antin's autobiography sets her up as a propagandist for the melting pot, but it also articulates an iconoclastic form of female independence, which, while the product of privilege, also demonstrates the ability of girls and women to make their own way. Stern's autobiography, in contrast, conforms more readily to Susan Stanford Friedman's description of women's autobiographical identity as merging "the shared with the unique" (40). Indeed, as the title itself suggests, this is the story not only of the development of Elizabeth's independent "I" or self, her "coming to America" and to writing, but also of her relationship with her mother. Stern's account of one of her first writing assignments in America is emblematic of the combination of independent and interdependent selves in Stern's narrative. Recognized for her writing talents at a very young age, Elizabeth is commissioned by the illiterate immigrants of her neighborhood to write letters on their behalf to their relatives in the old country, a task that Stern insists most strenuously that she would not have been able to accomplish if not for the help of her beloved mother. "Many of the letters," Stern writes,

could not have been written at all had not mother been at hand to help me. Despite a most fluent use of speech during every moment of their lives, the mere sight of my pen transferring their words indelibly upon paper seemed to give them an extraordinary affection of tongue and throat. . . . I could never have written one letter for him had my mother not translated [his] grunts and embarrassed blushes, and extracted by sympathetic questions and tactful suggestions the information he wished to send to his father and to his sweetheart in Europe. "I tell you it takes a scholar's daughter to look paper in the face," [Perez the huckster] would declare to mother. And mother, yielding the compliment to me, would say,

"I am proud to have a scholar for a husband." (Stern, 1917, 32–33)

This passage is particularly suggestive in that it deals both literally and figuratively with a girl's entry into the world of male "letters." It also introduces two conflicting notions of literary inheritance. Perez the huckster attributes Elizabeth's literary talents to her identity as a male scholar's daughter. Elizabeth's mother endorses this patrilineal view and dismisses her own part in Elizabeth's accomplishments by announcing her pride in having "a scholar as a husband." In contrast to this patriarchal view, Elizabeth insists upon a literary matrilineage, sharing credit for her literary accomplishments with her mother. As a lone female, Elizabeth does not feel she has the literary authority to author letters for the immigrant men. Grouped with her mother, however, a female co-author, Elizabeth is indeed able to take her place in the male world of writing.

Unlike Mary Antin, then, who develops an identity very much apart from the female members of the family, Elizabeth Stern develops her authorial and autobiographical "self" alongside her mother. However, in the same way that further education widens the gap between Mary and Frieda Antin, Elizabeth's high school experience draws her away from her mother's kitchen. Slowly but surely, Elizabeth replaces her mother's friendship with her new high school girlfriends, sharing with them her love of books and reading (105). More and more, Elizabeth becomes enchanted with the home-life of her American-born classmates, "whose ancestors had fought in the Revolutionary and Civil Wars, girls whose very life was bound into the life of our country" (107). When Elizabeth attends a party at the home of one of her classmates, she is astonished to meet her friend's beautifully ebullient, educated mother. "A woman in *white!*" she writes, "Why, mothers dressed in brown and black, I always knew. And this mother sang to us. She romped through the two steps with us" (110). From there on in, Elizabeth becomes allied with a new model of middle-class feminine identity, entirely other than that represented by her mother. "To my eyes," Stern writes, "my mother's life appeared all at once as something to be pitied—to be questioned" (Stern 110). After graduating high school, Elizabeth goes to college herself and marries, and the cultural chasm between her and her mother widens even further. "There is little to say of mother and myself during these college years," writes Stern, "because she had so little part in them" (133). It is in this second half of the narrative, then, that Stern separates herself from her prior interdependence, fashioning a multifold version of self that combines (Gusdorfian) individualism, middle-class femininity, and melting pot assimilationism.

But like Antin, who writes the story of her past "to be rid of it" only to repeat it again and again in her short stories, Stern's fiction provides a similar opportunity to revisit her initial autobiographical plot. The first rewriting occurs in a fictional autobiography entitled *I am a Woman and a Jew,* which Stern published in 1926 under the pseudonym Leah Morton. This pseudonym, composed of a biblical first name, and a gentile/American family name, highlights Stern's desire to reinvent her autobiographical self and heightens the conflict of the original plot. Like Elizabeth in *My Mother and I*, Leah Morton, the protagonist of *I am a Woman and a*

Jew, experiences conflict with her father over her desire to pursue a secular education; also like Elizabeth, Leah enjoys a close relationship with her mother but finds herself drifting away from her as her schooling progresses. Again, like Elizabeth, Leah meets an American-born man in New York, whom she comes to marry. But whereas Stern does not specify the religious background of Elizabeth's husband in *My Mother and I*, in *I am a Woman and a Jew*, Leah's American-born spouse is specifically designated as a Gentile. Leah's marriage thus takes on an added significance, symbolizing an even more radical rejection of her Jewish immigrant origins.

Ironically, this same act of marrying out of the faith and repudiating her Jewishness leads Leah to re-embrace her Jewish self. "I had thought that, by marrying a Christian," Leah confesses, "I who was in my heart no longer a Jew, would be free. I was to find out not only on that day of my father's death, but twice again, how mistaken I had been" (Morton 2). The role of Leah's father's death in precipitating Leah's search for a Jewish self is significant in that it suggests a desire to stake a claim to her patriarchal heritage. In contrast to *My Mother and I*, then, where Elizabeth's Jewish past is metonymically represented by her mother's kitchen, Leah search for the meaning of her Jewish-ness becomes associated with an effort on the part of a woman writer to find her place in a male literary and intellectual tradition.

What Leah discovers (or attempts to argue) in *I am a Woman and a Jew*, is that merely by writing, she is able to forge a link with her Jewish past. In contrast to both Mary Antin in *The Promised Land* and Elizabeth in *My Mother and I*, who write themselves away from Judaism, Leah's writing metaphorically returns her to the bosom of her people. This idea is first articulated by Leah's brother Robert, one of the few members of Leah's family who maintains contact with her after her intermarriage. "The children of your brain," Robert says, "are more Jewish than those of your body, Leah!" (123) Toward the end of the book, she generalizes this observation and contends that Jewish-ness is expressed in every kind of work that Jews do in this world. "Now I knew," she writes toward the end of *I am a Woman and a Jew*, that

what every Jew is and does, is something which must, indeed, belong to his people; that no other people living have our peculiar quality, which is not individual but racial, and which gives to each of us who accomplishes with genius, the ability to express through himself only the accumulated genius of his race, so that every Jewish writer, statesman, actor, is not only himself, but the mirror of his people, the voice of his people. (358)

One can certainly quarrel with the facile, self-serving, jingoistic message of this passage, which allows Leah/Elizabeth to have her assimilationism and her Judaism, too. What, after all, is the "peculiar quality" of the Jewish people, "which is not individual but racial"? Leah's definition of Jewish-ness stretches so far and so thinly across the whole range of Jewish contributions to politics and culture that it becomes virtually meaningless. What is clear from Leah Morton's insistence on the essential Jewish-ness of her writing project, however, is her unwillingness to accept the notion of the isolate writing self, existing in its own center, without a deep awareness and connection to community and tradition.

In her 1928 novel, *A Marriage Was Made*, Stern once again revisits these same themes, reinventing the characters and rewriting the ending of her first two autobiographies. In contrast to her earlier autobiographical works, *A Marriage Was Made* is not an explicitly Jewish novel; although some Jewish characters are featured in the book, the mother and daughter characters in the novel are neither Jewish nor European immigrants. In this novel, Stern sustains the mother-daughter theme, but universalizes its application, transforming the "up-from-the ghetto" plot of the earlier autobiographical works into a story of the metaphorical emigration of a mother (Mrs. Dreiser) and a daughter (Millie Dreiser) from a poor and dreary life in small-town Pennsylvania to a life of culture, art, affluence, and high society in New York City. Like Elizabeth and Leah, whose academic and literary talents provide a way out of the ghetto, Millie Dreiser possesses a remarkable talent as a concert pianist that serves as her ticket out of rural Pennsylvania. Unlike Elizabeth and Leah, however, Millie has no strong desire to leave her native Derrick City. It is her mother who dreams of leaving her marriage and dreary small-town life; it is for her mother that Millie pursues a concert career; and when the social and professional responsibilities of a concert career begin to threaten her filial bond, Millie consistently chooses Mother over music. When Millie is offered a chance to travel to Vienna to study with a European master and give a few concerts, she refuses to go unless assured that Mama can come along too. Millie's teacher warns her that her attachment to her mother is compromising her artistic individuality and hindering the development of her talents. "You play nice, pretty," he says. "But no passion, no feeling, no courage, Millie" (Stern, 1928 174). As the novel progresses, however, it becomes clear that more than music, Millie's relationship with her mother is her art, and her filial love the medium through which she crafts her life's best work. "Mama lived in me," Millie says to herself, "as some musicians live in their work. She put her courage, her fearlessness into making my life. Making something of my life" (210).

In contrast to Elizabeth, then, who carves out her own career and emotional life apart from her closest kin, Millie consistently defines her self in strict correspondence with her mother's wishes. The only time she dares to act independently occurs when at age sixteen, she falls in love with her country bumpkin, slightly dull-witted cousin Allan and accepts his proposal of marriage, only to back down when her mother expresses her disapproval of the match. Years later, when the handsome, wealthy, and distinguished Judge Fairlie, widowed of his first wife, asks Millie for her hand in marriage, Millie accepts his proposal and discontinues her concert career, even though she does not love him, because she knows it will make her mother happy to see this "marriage made," hence the title of the novel. *A Marriage Was Made* thus represents the absolute reverse of the story of individuation that is told in *My Mother and I*. Read in conjunction with the autobiographies, Millie's story might be interpreted as an effort to rewrite to correct the filial estrangement that attends Stern's more individualistic articulations of the written self.

At the same time, Stern's novel teaches a lesson on the necessity of individuation. Millie not only listens to her mother, she is utterly eclipsed by her. As one contemporary reviewer writes, in comparison with the colorful, strong-willed Mrs. Dreiser, Millie is "a shadowy, colorless, rather tiresome creature who never seems more than half awake, and in whose one emotional potentialities one never believes (*New York Times*, 1928), Clearly, the story of Millie Dresier's life would not make an interesting autobiography; drained of its singularity, taken over in its interdependence, her life becomes a mere backdrop for the far more interesting and devious machinations of her mother. A text steeped in images of interdependence, connection, and permeable ego boundaries, *A Marriage Was Made* sounds something of an alarm for a feminist theory, which, in an effort to embrace alternative female forms, too readily devalues the individual self as a masculine notion.

Isolate individualism may be a privilege of power, as Susan Stanford Friedman argues, but for precisely this reason it was a stance that many immigrant women autobiographers strove to assume. In their attempts to clear a space for themselves in Jewish and American literary tradition, which previously had known no female autobiographical contributions, immigrant autobiographers such as Antin and Stern were eager to stake a claim to a powerful authorial self. As members of an ethnic, religious, and gender group that knew more than its fair share of collective persecution, however, they carried with them an interdependent identity as well. In the case of Elizabeth Stern, this interdependent identity exerted an even greater force; at the same time, it is in her writing (particularly *A Marriage Was Made*) that the dangers of retreating too far into essentialist definitions of female identity, grounded entirely in relation and connection, are most readily apparent.

NOTES

1. It came to my attention after the completion of this essay, that in the original manuscript version of *The Promised Land*, Antin reveals the autobiographical origins of the plot of "The Lie"; in actuality, Isral Antin, recognizing Mary's academic talents, falsified Mary's age on her school certificate, making her eleven instead of thirteen to ensure her two more years of compulsory education. An awareness of this autobiographical information necessarily adds an additional dimension to one's interpretation of "The Lie." While Antin ultimately chose to delete this story from her autobiography, lest she cast doubt upon the moral rectitude of her father and the Jewish immigrant community as a whole, she chose to confess the truth in the safer form of "The Lie." Nevertheless, I believe my interpretation of the story can still stand. In confessing this "truth," Antin made some significant changes to the original autobiographical plot, transforming her protagonist into the eldest child in the family (conforming to Frieda Antin's position) and a boy, thus creating a kind of factional distance between so-called "fiction" and fact. From this fictional distance, Antin was able to confess and justify a lie from her own past, as well as to offer imaginative restitution for the older sibling who did not benefit from her father's (and her own) lies. For more information on this manuscript variant, see Werner Sollors' introduction to the recently published Penguin edition of *The Promised Land* (1997), xxvii–xxviii.

BIBLIOGRAPHY

Antin, Mary. *The Promised Land*. Boston: Houghton, 1912.

———. "The Lie." *The Atlantic Monthly*. 3 (January 1913) 31–41. Reprinted in *The Jewish Caravan*. Ed. Leo Schwarz. New York: Rinehart, 1965. 578–595.

———. "Malinke's Atonement." *America and I: Short Stories by American Women Writers*. Ed. Joyce Antler. Boston: Beacon, 1990.

Bergland, Betty. "Photographs and Narratives in Ethnic Autobiography: Memory and Subjectivity in Mary Antin's *The Promised Land*." *Memory, Narrative and Identity: New Essays in Ethnic American Literatures*. Ed. Amritjit Singh, Joseph T. Skerett, and Robert E. Hogan. Boston: Northeastern UP, 1994. 45–88.

Blacher Cohen, Sarah. "Mary Antin's *The Promised Land*: A Breach of Promise." *Studies in American Jewish Literature* 3.2 (1977–78): 28–35.

Buelens, Gert. "The New Man and the Mediator: (Non-) Remembrance in Jewish American Immigrant Narrative." *Memory, Narrative and Identity: New Essays in Ethnic American Literatures*. Ed. Amritjit Singh, Joseph T. Skerett, and Robert E. Hogan. Boston: Northeastern UP, 1994. 89–113.

Chodorow, Nancy. *The Reproduction of Mothering: Psychoanalysis and the Sociology of Gender*. Berkeley: U of California P, 1978.

Dearborn, Mary. *Pocahontas's Daughters: Gender and Ethnicity in American Culture*. New York: Oxford UP, 1986.

Friedman, Susan Stanford. "Women's Autobiographical Selves: Theory and Practice." *The Private Self: Theory and Practice of Women's Autobiographical Writings*. Ed. Shari Benstock. Chapel Hill: U of North Carolina P, 1988. 34–62.

Gilbert, Sandra M., and Susan Gubar. *The Madwoman in The Attic*. New Haven: Yale UP, 1977.

Gluckel of Hameln. *The Memoirs of Gluckel of Hameln*. Trans. Marvin Lowenthal. New York: Schocken, 1977.

Gusdorf, Georges. "Conditions and Limits of Autobiography." Trans. James Olney. *Autobiography: Essays Theoretical and Critical*. Ed. James Olney. Princeton: Princeton UP, 1980.

Ludwig Lewissohn. *Up Stream*. New York: Boni & Liveright, 1922.

Morton, Leah. *I am A Woman and a Jew*. New York: J.H. Sears, 1926. 1986 ed. Ed. Ellen Umansky. New York: Marcus Wiener, 1986.

Proefriedt, William A. "The Education of Mary Antin." *The Journal of Ethnic Studies* 17. 4 (Winter 1990).

Rev. of *My Mother and I*. NY Call. 9 Sept. 1917: 15.

Rev. of *A Marriage Was Made*. The New York Times Book Review. 19 Feb. 1928: 18.

Ravage, Marcus. *An American in the Making*. New York: Harper and Brothers, 1917.

Rosenfeld, Alvin. "Inventing the Jew: Notes on Jewish Autobiography." *The American Autobiography: A Collection of Critical Essays*. Englewood Cliffs: Prentice Hall, 1981. 133–156.

Rubin, Steven J. "American Jewish Autobiography." *Handbook of American Jewish Literature*. Ed. Lewis Fried. Westport: Greenwood, 1988. 287–313.

———. "Style and Meaning in Mary Antin's *The Promised Land*: A Re-evaluation," *Studies in American Jewish Literature* 5 (1986): 35–43.

Smith, Sidonie. *A Poetics of Women's Autobiography: Marginality and the Fictions of Self-Representation*. Bloomington: Indiana UP, 1987.

Sollors, Werner. *Beyond Ethnicity: Consent and Descent in American Culture*. New York: Oxford UP, 1986. v–xiv.

Stern, Elizabeth. *My Mother and I*. New York: Macmillan, 1917.

———. *A Marriage Was Made*. New York: J. H. Sears, 1928.

Szold, Henrietta. Introduction. *My Portion*. By Rebekah Kohut. New York: Albert & Charles Boni, 1927.

Wengeroff, Pauline Epstein. *Memoiren Einer Grossmutter: Bilder aus der Kultugeschichte der Juden Russlands im 19 Jahrhundert*.

2

Justifying Individualism: Anzia Yezierska's *Bread Givers*

Martin Japtok

Anzia Yezierska's *Bread Givers* (1925) describes a time span of about twenty years, presumably from the 1890s to some time before the 1910s, which roughly parallels Yezierska's own life history (Kessler Harris vii–ix). Her novel does not supply any obvious temporal markers, however. It is about a Jewish immigrant world that has its specific historical location but is isolated to an extent from the outside world, though it is subject to its dynamics. This isolation reflects the immigrant status of the community depicted in *Bread Givers*. Ethnic customs abound and create a world different from the "mainstream." This difference is primarily marked by language. Direct speech is often rendered in the distinctive vernacular (Yiddish—rendered in English, though) of the Eastern European (Russian-Polish Jewish) immigrant community in juxtaposition to the narration, which is in American English. The duality of language used in the novel reflects "the general idea of the interdependence of language and identity—you are the way you speak" (Ashcroft 54)—and in this context, it is significant that the protagonist does not speak with the inflection of her community in the latter part of the novel. Nonetheless, the use of dialect highlights cultural specificity. At the same time, the text "employ[s] vernacular as a linguistic variant to signify the insertion of the outsider into the discourse" (Ashcroft 57). The very rendering of the vernacular in written English gives it equal status to "mainstream" English and linguistically symbolizes the act of immigration. This culturally specific community serves as the background for the coming of age of a protagonist born into a family recently immigrated to the United States.

Like many coming-of-age novels, *Bread Givers* is autobiographical in nature. Alice Kessler Harris says in her foreword to the novel: "all of the six books Anzia Yezierska published between 1920 and 1932 are in some sense autobiographical, but none more so than *Bread Givers*. . . . Anzia Yezierska and Sara Smolinsky, the novel's narrator, are emotionally interchangeable" (v, xvii). At the same time, the novel seems to fit the traditional *Bildungsroman* mold in its insistence on individualism and its protagonist's rebellion against her community. But almost as if to forestall the conclusion that individualism rules, the novel devotes considerable time to delineating other characters' lives, particularly that of the dominant father figure who comes to represent the ethnic community. In this, and in many other respects, the novel can be understood as a constant battle between individualism and communalism.

This is so because Yezierska also depicts her protagonist as experiencing the ethnic community as oppressive or confining at times. What Carole Boyce Davies has said about autobiographical writings by black women holds true for *Bread Givers*: "The mystified notions of home and family are removed from their romantic, idealized moorings, to speak of pain, movement, difficulty, learning and love in complex ways. Thus, the complicated notion of home mirrors the problematizing of community/nation that one finds in Black women's writing from a variety of communities" (21). The traits of the Jewish immigrant community that the protagonist dislikes are clearly shown to be a response to socioeconomic conditions, though, not essential characteristics of the ethnic group. The protagonist resents the materialism of her father, for example—but comes to understand it as a defense mechanism against oppression and poverty. Because the novel, for the most part, does not see ethnicity in essentialist terms, the protagonist is not forced to decide between individualism and ethnicity, between "Americanization" and conformity to ethnic group norms—though those choices do present themselves in the plot, and even in those terms. The narrative does not portray Sara as a betrayer of ethnicity for leaning toward individualism, even though the novel shows an awareness of the possibility of seeing individualism as betrayal of the ethnic community. The constructionist bent in the novel—seeing ethnicity as social construct rather than as essence—can thus be interpreted as both the result of the protagonist's strong individualist leanings and as a way of making those leanings possible in the first place while not showing them as an expression of unmitigated selfishness.

As Carole Boyce Davies's remark already implies, the struggle the protagonist has to go through to arrive at a hybrid form of individualism and communalism is expressive of the narrative's struggle with ethnic nationalism. Nationalism, whether ethnic, cultural, or nation-state based, demands group cohesion and solidarity. Jewish American nationalism, of course, can be seen as a response to the virulent American nativism—partly in response to Jewish immigration—of the turn of the century and is thus protective in nature, as becomes evident in Emma Lazarus's complaint about a supposed Jewish lack of solidarity: "I do not hesitate to say that our national defect is that we are not 'tribal' enough. . . . We have not sufficient solidarity to perceive that when the life and property of a Jew in the uttermost provinces of the Caucasus are attacked, the dignity of a free Jew in America is humiliated" (qtd. in Urofsky 44). Carol B. Schoen, commenting on the gender implications of ethnic solidarity, sees *Bread Givers* "most of all [as an exploration of] the unresolvable tensions between the ancient Jewish mores that assumed male domination and the American ideal of individual freedom" (61), tensions that the novel—as I will argue—does resolve, however uneasily. Accordingly, Sam Girgus has noted the similarity between the ideology Yezierska's narratives seem to embrace and Supreme Court Justice Louis Brandeis's Zionism, which proposed the compatibility of Zionist aspirations and American citizenship (109). But far from simply subscribing to Zionism, the novel is locked in a dialectical struggle with the notion of ethnic solidarity. It is thus characterized by dualities: its protagonist rebels against a communally prescribed ethnic identity and yet comes to a kind of reconciliation with her community; it both harshly criticizes and at the same time celebrates the ethnic community. The result for the protagonist is a reluctant but inescapable hybridity.

Bread Givers tells the story of a young girl with immigrant parents growing up in a section of New York inhabited primarily by Eastern European Jews. The protagonist's life is lived partly in response to what she sees as the model of ethnicity that her father, Reb Smolinsky, embodies for her. He dominates the household through determining economic matters, even against the resistance of his wife, and by attempting to mold his children's lives. The novel depicts him at times as ruthless and cruel. Resistance against him apparently is futile—but also becomes a mark of the protagonist's growth and character. In her attempts at resisting her father's influence, in her fears of being or becoming like him, and in her ability to reach a kind of peace with him, Sara Smolinsky establishes her individuality and her relationship to Jewish-ness.

Bread Givers reverberates with ambiguities. Carol Schoen has described the various forces pulling at Sara: assimilation versus tradition, feminist self-realization versus marriage and children, the wish for wealth and comfort versus scholarly success and the life of the mind (62). As a result of such ambiguities, the novel recognizes the necessity of ethnic solidarity, associated with the "old world," *and* affirms individuality, associated with the "new," as equally important, making the protagonist paradigmatic of a new and uneasy ethnicity. In Werner Sollors's words, "In the complicated American landscape of regional, religious, and ethnic affiliation, it could be very difficult to construct the self as autonomous individual and as fated group member" ("Ethnicity" 173).

One strategy through which the novel accomplishes the affirmation of the equal importance of individualism and communalism is by establishing its heroine as a highly idiosyncratic character. Even though, as a child, Sara fully immerses herself in her family and community, she also feels or is depicted as somehow precocious. This narrative strategy bases itself on the assumption that ethnicity is something constructed, something negotiated by members of the ethnic group. The novel allows individuals to differ from one another without calling into question their "ethnic-ness" and without attaching any obvious judgment to "intra-ethnic difference." If anything, when the protagonist's differences first appear, and they do so in the opening pages of the novel, they are seen as positive, quite in accordance with the *Bildungsroman* model of the youthful and rebellious hero/ine. Not until later in the plot do these differences become problematic and connected to the question of "betrayal" of ethnicity.

Sara shows strength of character early on and appears old beyond her years. She is described as small for her age and thin, yet full of energy and determination, as indicated by her nickname, "Blut-und-Eisen" [Blood-and-Iron] (20). She is a precocious child, often taking on the responsibilities of an adult. Sara is old beyond her years because of the pressures of poverty, the fear of being evicted into the street for all to see. Although all her sisters share poverty with her, she is more enterprising than they are, insisting on peddling to make some money for her family. In this enterprise, her strong sense of her own individuality is revealed. Indeed, her personhood becomes defined by her ability to do business like an adult. When a friendly neighbor offers simply to give her some fish for starting her peddling business, she replies vehemently that rather than begging, she "want[s] to go into business like a person" (21). She is able to prove wrong her mother's doubt about her ability to earn money and finally triumphs in her success. Resenting having been treated condescendingly, she establishes her personhood by accomplishing adult feats. Through this act the novel establishes her as a dynamic character; just as she, not her sisters, shows initiative in an emergency situation, only she will break the pattern of poverty and/or dependence on a man, whereas her sisters end up in marriages not unlike that of their parents. Girgus notes that the "ideology of the individual self at the core of Yezierska's writings represents basic American attitudes towards freedom, success, and culture" (111), and the above episode exhibits Sara's individualism at a young age. To underline Sara's individualism, the novel has both of Sara's parents register her difference from her sisters through nicknaming her "Blood-and-Iron," her mother explaining the significance of that name: once Sara has set her sights on a goal, "there is no rest . . . till she gets it" (20).

Sara's independence is linked to her attitude toward values that come to be connected with her ethnic group, specifically through her father. Because the novel depicts her as independent and strong willed, it appears consistent—particularly in terms of the *Bildungsroman* genre—that she would rebel at some point against what is outlined as the "norm," and in this case as the "ethnic norm." Sara's rebellion takes religion as one of its focal points. Since her father devotes his life to studying the Torah, her rejection of the ethnic life she sees around her is strongly linked to the issue of religion. Yezierska responds here to the image of the "pious scholar" as it had "emerge[d] in American Jewish fiction by the turn of the century. . . . The figure of the reflective, otherworldly scholar struggling to survive in the harsh grind of the sweatshop and bemoaning his children's apostasy, serves as a metaphor for the tensions inherent in new conditions" (Baum 189). Although this metaphor serves the same function in *Bread Givers*, Yezierska revises it substantially by making the scholar not only a victim of changed conditions but also an oppressor in his own small world. The focus thus shifts from the plight of the scholar, which the novel nonetheless depicts, if most unsympathetically, to those suffering under the tyranny of that scholar. In turn, this shift in focus emphasizes less—at least at times—the oppressive circumstances caused by economic conditions in the United States than the domestic oppression occurring within that larger framework. Not until the protagonist experiences the "outside world" does her resentment vanish and her view of the ethnic world start appearing in a different light.

Before that, however, Sara resents her sisters' and mother's subjection to her father, a custom she connects with her ethnicity, while linking greater freedom to a "nonethnic" state. Thinking of the men who court her sisters, she resolves that she does not want a suitor from the Lower East Side but an American who would have to be self-employed and grant her autonomy. And, she adds, "no fathers, and no mothers, and no sweatshops, and no herring!" (66). Her rejection of these "icons" of ethnicity points to—among other things—her wish to escape poverty. But poverty, in *Bread Givers*, appears in part to be caused by religion, at least for Sara's family. Her father's resolve not to work, his exploitation of his daughters, his inept selection of husbands for his daughters, and his failure in business are all the result of his inexperience in the world of business, which he despises. As S. M. Dubnow has said of rabbinic education in nineteenth-century Russia, "The scholastic education resulted in producing men entirely unfit for the battle of life, so that in many families energetic women took charge of the business and became the wage earners, while their husbands were losing themselves in the mazes of speculation" (qtd. in Baum 55). This quote adequately represents not only the role of the protagonist's father but also the narrator's attitude toward that role. Sara thinks and says, and the author has other characters say, that her father should contribute to earning a living for the family. In fact, though, having the women of the family earn its income on their own if the father was a scholar was not unusual in Eastern European Jewish communities (Baum 67). Such scholars were respected in the old world *shtetl*, and supported by it (Rose). With this in mind, one might say that the extent of Sara's resentment of this arrangement illustrates the extent of her Americanization.

Sara's dislike of poverty, a poverty which she, as narrator, attributes in part to her father, then also leads to a rejection of religion: after revealing how much both she and her sisters dislike her father's preaching, she confesses she wakes up at night crying, "'I hate my father. And I hate God most of all for bringing me into such a terrible house'" (65/66). One can see how "father" and "God" are paralleled here in a conflation of her feelings of anger toward her father (the man of God), and God. Her anger also determines her feelings toward the religious injunction to honor and obey one's parents. Her feelings of difference and her independence thus come to be defined in reaction to Judaism, which, in turn, is a sign of ethnicity. That the novel constructs religion as such a sign becomes clear when Sara's father counters her assertion, after she has left the family, that she is an American with the exclamation, "You blasphemer! . . . Denier of God!" (138). He, too, sees no difference between a denial of religion and a denial of ethnicity. Thus, Sara, in establishing her independence, refuses to embrace one of the core values that defines her ethnic community.

The core value rejected—religion—turns out to be very closely related to pov-

erty-driven acquisitiveness in the way the novel constructs both religion and acquisitiveness. *Bread Givers* interweaves religious and materialist elements until
both seem inextricably connected. Reb Smolinsky, Sara's father, repeatedly preaches
the value of poverty and the richness of a life devoted to religion. However, when
it comes to his daughters, he exhibits ruthless materialism. He wants to be paid for
his oldest daughter Bessie by her potential groom and expects to be set up in
business by him, which turns the custom of offering a bride price on its head.
Thomas Ferraro comments: "In the Russia-Poland of Mrs. Smolinsky's memory,
fathers exercise nearly complete authority over their daughters' marriages, but they
are obligated to provide as opulent a dowry as possible. While deriving his authority to intervene from tradition, Smolinsky reinterprets the obligation to provide a
dowry as an opportunity to secure economic peace" (68). Reb Smolinsky despises
the suitor of one of his daughters for his poverty, making clear that his concern is
not the welfare of his daughter but his own well-being. Accordingly, once he has
married off two of his daughters successfully, he expects to be served better. Reb
Smolinsky derives his authority for these marital transactions from traditional religion—indeed, one might say that he practices a religion with materialist overtones.

And it is exactly the materialism in his religion as he interprets it that alienates
Sara from her father. She points out his double standard concerning his view of
poverty when he ignores the poet Lipkin as his daughter Fania's suitor when she
reminds him that he himself had said the previous day that "'poverty is an orna-
ment on a good Jew'" (70). In the course of the conflict over Fania's suitor, she
asserts the value of love by implying that Fania should have been allowed to marry
for love. The basic value of dualistic materialism versus idealism is an important
factor in the estrangement between Sara and her father. Before deciding to leave
the family after a clash with her father over a small sum of money, she thinks of the
various acts of her father that have caused unhappiness in the family, such as spoil-
ing his oldest daughter's chances at happiness because of bargaining too hard with
her suitor and "his bargaining away Fania to a gambler and Masha to a diamond-
faker"; she concludes that those combined "tyrannies crashed over me" (135).
Because the novel associates the ethnic community as exemplified by Sara's father
with materialism in a number of passages, it can be read as a critique of what
William Boelhower has identified as a basic plot for most immigrant novels: "With
construction as the master topic, goals are still relatively uncomplicated, cultural
motives are few, simple, public in character, and usually agreed upon by all. The
ethnic project inspires consensus, and consensus inspires the building of an ethnic
community" (101–102). Sara does not subscribe to that consensus and demands
room outside the parameters it prescribes. *Bread Givers* explores the potential of
coercion behind the notion of ethnic solidarity (which also takes a patriarchal guise).

Ironically, the novel's critique brings it closer to the ideology of individualism,
a feature of an "Americanism" or mainstream nationalist self-definition, from which
the ethnic community finds itself excluded. But is the novel therefore unmitigat-
edly assimilationist? The answer is no, because rather than accept the definition of

ethnicity represented by the domineering father figure or reject ethnicity as a whole, it creates new ethnic boundaries, illuminating, as Werner Sollors has said in a discussion of Mark Twain's *Connecticut Yankee*, "Frederick Barth's thesis that ethnicity rests on the boundary, not the 'cultural stuff it encloses'" ("Ethnicity" 299). This shifting of boundaries, however, while creating distance from the parents' version of ethnicity, does not result in an uncritical embrace of individualism.

Bread Givers' protagonist attempts to establish her independence from her father, who is symbolic of the coercive aspect of the ethnic community, through a refusal to conform to one of the main tenets of her ethnic community, namely adherence to traditional religious doctrine—which Sara breaks by opposing her father. However, this refusal is not equivalent to a renouncement of ethnicity. The novel provides characters located between absolute ethnic solidarity and unmitigated individualism, and it depicts these characters in positive or sympathetic terms (of that later). This strategy becomes necessary because the protagonist still has to deal with the ethnic consensus described above and establish some kind of truce, since ethnicity, as the novel makes clear, goes into the making of her personality.

The awareness that ethnicity cannot be simply discarded undergirds *Bread Givers*. Yezierska, in "We Can Change Our Moses but not Our Noses," a story she never published, invented a protagonist who changed her name so she could get a job. She finds that she is unable to "pass": "But I couldn't get away with it . . . the day I gave up my Jewish name, I ceased to be myself. I ceased to exist. A person who cuts himself off from his people cuts himself off at the roots of his being, he becomes a shell, a cipher, a spiritual suicide" (qtd. in Schoen 7). Here she expresses unequivocally that the cultural ties to one's ethnicity are an integral part of an individual's personality, and are beyond choice, since one, as the metaphors strongly suggest, leaves the realm of the living when one deserts one's ethnicity. Looking at *Bread Givers* through the lens of this unpublished story, one can see that the overall constructionism of ethnicity at work in the novel has its limits. One may choose not to follow one's ethnic group's mores and traditions to the full extent, as the short story's title suggests, but one cannot and should not give up one's cultural heritage—so Yezierska's message.

Sara does have role models located between the conflicting demands of (novelistically constructed) ethnicity and individualism: her mother, who does not adhere to the ruthless materialism of her father, supports Sara in her "escape" by giving her the family's savings, and occasionally contradicts her husband. For the most part, however, she accepts her subordinate role, and her posture when Sara leaves is indicative of her position: before leaving the house, Sara sees her mother "clutching at her heart in helplessness, her sorrowful eyes gazing at me" (136). In the conflict between father and daughter, her mother is an onlooker; although she is able to secretly slip Sara some money, she does not have a voice to take her side, only a silent look expressive of her suffering. To that extent, Sara's breakaway from her family, although prepared by years of resentment, appears almost as a solitary act.

Though Sara's mother and Mummenkeh, a neighbor woman, to some extent provide alternative role models to Sara's father's ruthless patriarchy by their un-conditional acts of giving, these are not the modes of behavior after which Sara patterns her own life, even if they do defy the notion of an overall ethnic essential-ism. As both of the characters exhibiting complete selflessness are women, how-ever, the question of gender essentialism arises, since their altruism might be "noth-ing more" than an acting out of culturally ascribed gender roles, reintroducing a gender-informed ethnic essentialism along with it. In this scenario, Sara would have to go up against a combined ethnic/gender cultural essentialism to completely invent a new role for herself. However, this is not fully the case: not only her iron-willed father but also her sister Masha, whose stubbornness the protagonist/narra-tor often comments on in negative terms, live out before her eyes how to go up against the combined wills of the rest of the family and accomplish one's goals. In addition, Sara's individualist escape from a confining family life may not have been as unusual as the novel suggests: according to a study cited in *The Jewish Woman in America*, "about 40 percent of the women attending evening schools in New York were Jewish. . . . If most first-generation immigrant women seemed to be living within the confines of the Old World traditions, Van Kleeck's study indi-cates many were breaking with the customs of the past, and indeed some of them were in open rebellion" (Baum 129).

The character who most confirms Sara's course, however—Hugo Seelig— ap-pears only belatedly when she has already finished her college education. His appearance is important, though, because it, together with Sara's history, maps out the course of a certain section of the second generation of Jewish immigrants. Sara's story takes on a paradigmatic character in that respect: she is a "breakaway" who assimilates to a certain extent to the "mainstream" while retaining a strong awareness of her ethnicity. Girgus has outlined this ideology in Yezierska's fiction and remarked on its similarity to Louis Brandeis's brand of Zionism: although an immigrant may wish to both be American and ethnic at the same time, this wish appears to create a dilemma which, however, can be resolved through "The idea elaborated upon by Brandeis and others that with honesty about being Jewish one can be faithful to the principles of pluralism and diversity that ultimately bring all people together as Americans. . . . She must compromise enough to achieve so-called Americanization but not change so much as to lose her ethnic identity" (110).

Americanization, of course, is a motto written all over *Bread Givers*. Consider the following description of Seelig (whose name, meaning as much as "extremely happy" or describing a state of holiness, indicates the novel's approval of this character), whose features are described in glowing terms—and in contradistinc-tion to her father's: "A Jewish face, and yet none of the greedy eagerness of Hester Street any more. It was the face of a dreamer, set free in the new air of America. Not like Father with his eyes on the past, but a dreamer who had found his work among us of the East Side" (273).

Although the passage emphasizes Seelig's Jewish-ness, it also stresses the power of the environment to determine what particular face Jewish-ness will take on, while at the same time flirting with projecting traits perceived as negative on a particular past that is rooted in social circumstances and geography. Old world ethnicity becomes personified by her father, whereas Seelig appears as model for a new world ethnicity, so much so that the passage suggests that it takes "America" to bring out the full potential of Jewish-ness. As Laura Wexler has noted, "[a]lthough Hugo Seeling is a Jewish immigrant, as a school principal he has also integrated himself socially into the new life without undue self-laceration. This figurative new American berth sustains him. It is also what makes him desirable to Sara. It is opposed to the lack of place in America for Sara's infuriated father" (171). The novel constructs this "new ethnicity" as a hybrid between "America" and "Jewish-ness," embodied by characters such as Sara and Seelig. Although this ethnicity is a hybrid one, it still maintains a boundary between "Jewish" and "American," in the above quote, apparently established through Seelig's idealistic qualities. Sara subscribes to this model of ethnicity, but her way to it is paved with the fear that she might be more like her father than she likes—as Girgus notes, "they are most like each other as character types" (113)—having set him up as a negative role model in the first third of the novel, titled "Hester Street." Already the passage quoted above shows that "Hester Street" is the protagonist/narrator's label for what she does not like about her ethnic group. Thus, the reconciliation of Jewish-ness and American-ness does not come to Sara as easily as the Brandeisian formula seems to suggest.

Indications of her similarity to her father appear early on, as she stresses her strong will and her opposition to her father, which she verbalizes in direct confrontations. To that extent, she engages in a power struggle with her father and is involved in a dialectic of sorts that ultimately leads to a synthesis in which she combines the traits of her parents. Sara's resemblance to her father is first explicitly commented on by her sisters when they come for a visit after she has left the family and started going to college; they expect to take her home to a visit with their parents, but she refuses, claiming that her work takes precedence. Her sister Fania responds, "'You hard heart!'" She then proceeds to tell her sister Bessie that it would be best to leave Sara, since the latter, in her pursuit of education, had become "worse than Father with his Holy Torah'" (178). The phrase "hard heart" connects her to her sister Masha who, according to the narrator, has "no heart" (6) because she single-mindedly invests her money in clothes or personal hygiene while her family starves; as opposed to Masha, Sara invests in her personal education, but also to the neglect of her family. The more important comparison for the purposes of this discussion is that of Sara to her father, though. Similarly to her father, she gives development of her mind in study precedence over any other matters, and she cannot be moved by appeals to emotion or family feeling. Education becomes her "god," a secularized version of her father's Torah, an all-consuming concern that comes before any more worldly considerations.

But the novel creates ambiguity about this. Because Sara has broken away from her family on account of an egotistical father, the discovery of the same trait in herself requires some explanation. Thus, when her father charges her with selfishness after she rejects a well-to-do suitor, she flings back that she has inherited this trait from him. Having recognized the similarity, however, Sara needs further explanation for her behavior in terms of her own value system. Whereas her father justifies his selfishness with reference to his calling, she justifies hers with reference to hers in a peculiar moment of hybridization of the two value systems, asking God to give her "the hard heart of reason" (230). The ultimate justification for her selfishness/independence—the two have become indistinguishable at this point in the novel—comes from the dean of her college, who assures her that "all pioneers have to get hard to survive" (232). This strategy, notes Girgus, is similar to the one she used in "American and I," in which she compares Jews to Pilgrims, thus providing "a vehicle for entrance into American culture" (109). Thus, from here on, selfishness and independence have become entangled again, because she can perceive herself as blasting a way for others, possibly—in an implicitly feminist interpretation—for other women, and specifically for other Jewish women. The plight of her married sisters invites such an interpretation; there is one problem, however: she shows no concern for her sisters once she has left home.

Although the feminist implications of her individualism remain questionable, the implications of her chosen course for her relationship to ethnicity are somewhat clearer. It appears that she attempts to combine individualism and ethnicity. Her intent of combining her individualist approach with the notion of ethnic solidarity becomes evident through her return to the Jewish neighborhood after her individualist goal has been reached; she assumes a job as a teacher, teaching Jewish children to speak "correct" English—which may be seen as an attempt to make them less "old world ethnic." Finally, she visits her parents again, and her visits to her father, once he is sickly, are particularly of symbolic import.

What enables Sara to develop a bond of sympathy with her father is her recognition of her father's—and, by extension, the old world Jewish community's—fragility. What before seemed an overwhelming pressure to conform has now lost its threat, and what remains are bonds of feeling and kinship. Acquisitiveness is understood as a fight against poverty and against the exclusiveness and "coldness" of Anglo-Americans she has experienced at college (who are described as beautiful but "too cool"—211). When her father remarries after her mother's death, she does not see him for a while. Just before their fateful encounter on the streets—poverty has driven him to become a peddler—she contemplates the fate of other peddlers as she is walking through Hester Street. She is still elated after a meeting with Hugo Seelig, but when seeing "[l]ines upon lines of pushcart peddlars" out on the streets in miserable weather, her joy begins to "hurt like guilt. . . . They were like animals helpless against the cold, pitiless weather. Wasn't there some way that I could divide my joy with these shivering pushcart peddlars, grubbing for pennies in the rain?" (281). The symbolic (and naturalist) overtones of the passage are strong. Where before she saw greed, she can now perceive a desperate fight for survival in a hostile environment, a perception triggering feelings of solidarity and compassion. Her attempt to reach out for happiness now includes those around her, and she feels it her responsibility to include them in her "American

Dream," symbolized by the red roses she has just received from Seelig but which she now wants to share since they, in view of the poverty she has just witnessed, are "so heartlessly perfect, so shamelessly beautiful that it hurt to look at them." She concludes that she does not want them "if they were only for me" (282). The description of the roses recalls her perception of Anglo-American college students as beautiful but cold and implies a comparison of the East Siders' fight for survival with the empty but comfortable life of nonethnics at college who, for the most part, simply ignore her presence.

Though she appears to have imbibed the value-system observed at college to an extent, as her attitude toward clothing and appearance reveal, she is really able to feel ethnic solidarity only after her return from college. For her, a "we-feeling" is possible only once she has experienced "them" and gains an appreciation of why tight ethnic in-group bonds are maintained; however, Sara's experience of prejudice at college—mostly exhibited in the other students' distance and their laughter at her speech or "clumsiness"—does not have a shattering effect on her (though she does shatter a hurdle in gym class when she feels that the nonethnic students regard her as an odd spectacle). This may be because the anti-Semitism she encounters is not blatant and is barely perceived as such by her. Nonetheless, one notices that after college, her Jewish identification is rendered in more positive terms than before. Seelig's description, quoted above, is one case in point, and her decision to teach in the Lower East Side another.

However, her acceptance of ethnicity, even of old world ethnicity, can be observed most clearly in her relationship to her father. Although she seems to dread the thought of having him be her responsibility for the rest of her life, she also feels a sense of tenderness and, most of all, of inevitability. Seeing him sick, she regrets her former dislike and affirms their oneness: "Can a tree hate the roots from which it sprang? Deeper than love, deeper than pity, is that oneness of the flesh that's in him and me. . . . If I grow, . . . if I ever amount to something, is it not his spirit burning in me?" (286).

Since her father is, for her, the most powerful symbol of ethnicity in general and of old world ethnicity in particular, her own conceptualization of her ethnicity is reflected in this relationship, which is considerably more complex than the simplistic old world/new world dichotomy she advances several times. Rather than merely leaving behind one kind of ethnicity and adopting another, the two interact continuously, as also manifested by her suitor's request to her father to teach him Hebrew. Although Sara has achieved the goals set by her individualist strivings, duty and love are bonds that tie her irrevocably to family and community.

Ironically, "she alone effectively challenges her father's authoritarianism but also becomes the only daughter capable of internalizing and accepting responsibility for his model of authority" (Girgus 114). What remains is ambiguity: on the one hand, Sara fully experiences feelings of ethnic solidarity, but only to come to see her ethnicity as a burden. The novel finishes with her and Hugo's decision to have her father live with them. And although she will marry the representative of a Jewish American ethnicity, she sees her father's presence as a "shadow still there, over me. It wasn't just my father, but the generations who made my father whose weight was still upon me" (297). Acceptance and alienation thus go hand in hand, mirroring the struggle between individualism and the perceived demands of ethnicity that pervades the novel.

Sara comes to accept ethnicity as inevitable, but something new and different emerges, a kind of hybrid ethnicity that is the product of the old world ethnicity represented by her father and the influences of the new world environment. In Werner Sollors's model of ethnic representation, ethnicity may be configured as either a consent or as a descent relationship. In the first case, ethnicity, like family descent, is not a choice. In the second case, ethnicity, particularly because it is embodied by her father, appears as an inescapable descent relationship, while individualist strivings may represent the sway of the U.S. environment—this individualism, in turn, is accepted by consent. However, U.S. influences are rarely specified in the novel. The protagonist's life is lived mostly within an ethnic community, her contact with nonethnics is relatively limited, and the nonethnic world is at times perceived as lifeless and shallow, making an "American" derivation of individualism less compulsory. Nonetheless, the presence of that almost stereotypically American value as an American value cannot be ignored in a story, which tells of a second-generation protagonist moving away from "old world" definitions of ethnicity. The emergence of individualism can be explained in part by the relative easing of those extreme pressures of the old world, which made for the cohesiveness of the Jewish communities, pressures to which the novel alludes. The struggle against poverty and discrimination brings on an emphasis on material acquisition as a safeguard against both, but it allows for greater ethnic diversification than an outright hostile environment does. The protagonist of Edna Ferber's *Fanny Herself* at one point comes to a similar conclusion, which is worth quoting here (though the tenor of that novel affirms the higher importance of ethnic solidarity in a much more unambiguous way than *Bread Givers*): "'We're free to build as many synagogues as we like, and worship in them all day, if we want to. But we don't want to. The struggle isn't racial any more, but individual'" (294).

Though *Bread Givers* does not claim that individualism completely overrules ethnic communalism, the novel recognizes a struggle between those two world views. The hybrid ethnicity of Sara, arrived at against the resistance of her father, is in an ironic sense the outcome of her parent's decision to flee more oppressive circumstances to allow for a fuller development of (ethnic) life; that decision did not take into account that less oppression also might give his children expanded opportunities to decide what shape ethnic life is to take. And it is the resulting hybridity that makes necessary the simultaneous assertions of and uneasy reconciliation between communalist ethnicity and individualism.

Bread Givers thus records ethnic adjustments in the new world. Its protagonist figures as a pioneer who points the way for developments within the community that are implicitly inevitable. However, the development is not from ethnicity to nonethnicity or "American-ness" but to a new kind of ethnicity that recognizes the necessity of solidarity in an adverse environment but rejects the absoluteness to a communal claim to solidarity that is the hallmark of nationalism: if the individuals making up a "nation" do not declare allegiance to it, then there is no "nation." Because the novel supports individualist aspirations, it cannot construct ethnicity in an essentialist fashion as (ethnic) nationalism would; nationalism, though always recognizing that it can exist only as long as it has the consent of the people who make up the "nation," nonetheless often employs a rhetoric that tends to emphasize relations of "blood" and "family." If the novel were to take such a view of ethnicity, it would force the implausible claim that the individualist protagonist is simply not ethnic anymore—by severing those "ties of blood," by rejecting part of the old world definition of ethnicity—but American. This, in turn, would align the novel's sympathy with "American-ness," which cannot be the intent in a work that in great detail outlines an ethnic world with characters the reader is supposed to empathize with, and which points out that hardship and prejudice remain factors in the life of the ethnic group and individual. Finally, Yeziersak avoids such a dualistic view of ethnicity and "American-ness" through the movement of a plot in which the protagonist comes to embrace the major antagonist (Reb Smolinsky). This simultaneous assertion of ethnicity and individualism is accomplished through a constructionist rhetoric of ethnicity—or, in other words, a rhetoric that allows one to see ethnic solidarity as an original response to an old world environment that still has validity in the new world, though maybe not the same urgency.

At the same time, *Bread Givers* responds to the ideological pressure of cultural nationalism in that it recognizes that the course of individualism needs justification. This need to justify creates a tension alluded to before: certain features of the ethnic community must appear oppressive in order to legitimize the heroine's quest for individualism. However, overtly negative depictions of the ethnic community might mean playing into the hands of a potentially biased readership and would raise questions about the author; first and foremost, it would put the protagonist into an almost self-destructive bind, since, having ethnic ancestry, she would have to create herself out of nothing if she wanted to acquire a positive self-image while creating a negative one of her own community. The resulting tension is partially resolved by the depiction of ethnic individuals who are selfless and/or on good terms with the heroine, such as Mummenkeh and Bessie, and by the reconciliation between Reb Smolinsky as symbol of old world ethnicity and Sara. I say "partially resolved" because the protagonist experiences unease with the realization that ethnicity is inescapable for her. Until the very end, Sara perceives ethnicity as a "weight" and "shadow." She stands half-willingly in a tradition that holds ethnic solidarity as the highest duty. Although she partly strives to alter this tradition, she remains bound to it to the extent that her individualism requires constant justification.

WORKS CITED

Ashcroft, Bill, Gareth Griffiths, and Helen Tiffin. *The Empire Writes Back. Theory and Practice in Post-Colonial Literatures.* London: Routledge, 1989.

Baum, Charlotte, Paula Hyman, and Sonia Michel. *The Jewish Woman in America.* New

York: Dial, 1976.

Boelhower, William. *Through a Glass Darkly: Ethnic Semiosis in American Literature.* New York: Oxford UP, 1987.

Davies, Carole Boyce. *Black Women, Writing and Identity: Migrations of the Subject.* New York: Routledge, 1994.

Dearborn, Mary V. "Anzia Yezierska and the Making of an Ethnic American Self." *The Invention of Ethnicity.* Ed. Werner Sollors. New York: Oxford UP, 1989.

Ferber, Edna. *Fanny Herself.* New York: Gross & Dunlap, 1917.

Ferraro, Thomas J. *Ethnic Passages. Literary Immigrants in Twentieth-Century America.* Chicago: U of Chicago P, 1993.

Girgus, Sam B. *The New Covenant. Jewish Writers and the American Idea.* Chapel Hill: U of North Carolina P, 1984.

Kessler-Harris, Alice. Introduction. *Bread Givers.* Anzia Yezierska. New York: Persea, 1975. v–xviii.

Rose, Toby. Letter to the author. June 1998.

Schoen, Carol B. *Anzia Yezierska.* Boston: Twayne, 1982.

Sollors, Werner. *Beyond Ethnicity. Consent and Descent in American Culture.* New York: Oxford UP, 1986.

———. "Ethnicity." *Critical Terms for Literary Study.* Eds. Frank Lentricchia and Thomas McLaughlin. Chicago: U of Chicago P, 1990. 288–305.

Urofsky, Melvin I. *American Zionism from Herzl to Holocaust.* Garden City: Anchor, 1976.

Wexler, Laura. "Looking at Yezierska." *Women of the Word: Jewish Women and Jewish Writing.* Ed. Judith R. Baskin. Detroit: Wayne State UP, 1994.

Yezierska, Anzia. *Bread Givers.* New York: Persea, 1975.

3

Fighting the Trolls on the Dakota Plains: The Ecstasy and the Agony of Norwegian Immigrants' Lives in O. E. Rolvaag's *Giants in the Earth*

Raychel Haugrud Reiff

After the Homestead Act was passed in 1862, poverty-stricken Norwegians flocked to America to claim land, hoping to make prosperous, happy lives for themselves and their families. Traveling west, they loaded all their belongings in wagons topped with curved branches and overspread with blankets. Wives and children, and often cows, accompanied these men who turned their eyes westward and coaxed their oxen to pull their wagons where none had traveled before. On and on they traveled, finally putting down roots on the Midwest plains.

In *Giants in the Earth*, Ole Edvart Rolvaag tells what life was like for those impoverished pioneers who emigrated from Norway to America in the 1870s and moved west by covered wagon, setting down stakes and carving homes in an untamed, unpeopled Dakota wilderness. He knew from firsthand experience, since he himself had emigrated from Norway in 1896, the happiness and the unhappiness experienced by Norwegian emigrants, and he wanted to write about both sides. In *Giants in the Earth*, Rolvaag tells the true story of immigration, the joys and the sorrows resulting from it. Both of these he portrays through his two protagonists, Per Hansa and Beret. Per Hansa's story is told as a fairy tale experience. He is a typical fairy tale hero—a young man who possesses nothing, but through bravery, insight, and cleverness defeats all the evil trolls that try to thwart his happiness, and finally wins both the "princess" and the "kingdom" (Rolvaag, Letter to Colcord). Per Hansa transforms the fairy tale into reality as he sees and reaps the benefits of America, the many and rich possibilities that Rolvaag felt America had to offer the individual: he gains wealth; he obtains a practical grasp of things through intense work; he develops himself through encounters with new people, absorbing new thoughts and new ideas; he enjoys political and religious freedom ("Country and Fatherland" 110).

But Rolvaag also turns the fairy tale inside out and examines the cost of the hero's success. He sees the loneliness, the suffering, the heartsickness, and finally the mental collapse of the isolated pioneer, particularly the female. This aspect of immigration he shows primarily through Beret, Per Hansa's wife. She is homesick for Norway and terrified of the strange, alien land she is supposed to tame. But perhaps the most important reason for Beret's unhappiness is the fact that she is a woman who has no control over her life. As Stevens points out, "Because she was a woman her status in America was much different from Per's. Her status alone (shared with all other women) could account for some of her unhappiness" (135). It is the man who makes the decisions; the woman submissively follows. She is not free to decide when the family will move or where they will live; she is not free to travel from her home to outlying communities to relieve her boredom; she has few friends living close by. The life of the pioneer woman, unlike that of the man, is a restricted, lonely life.

These, then, are the two sides of immigration—the adventurous, exciting ecstasy of fighting the trolls and founding a kingdom, balanced against the lonely, frightening agony of isolation and separation. Since *Giants in the Earth* is concerned with both the joys and the sorrows resulting from immigration, it has two moods. Half of it is an adventure-romance in which Per Hansa finds excitement and fulfillment in America; the other half is a penetrating study in the psychology of the lonely pioneer woman. Both the ecstasy and agony of conquering a new land are vividly portrayed.

When *Giants in the Earth* was published in 1927, it was hailed immediately as a great novel, which critic after critic recommended because of its realistic portrayal of immigrant life. Whereas earlier writers talked only about the romantic conquest of the West, Rolvaag also shows the great price paid for it. Parrington states that Rolvaag's treatment is very admirable. He explains that many writers have glorified the westward movement as a romantic epic, "but the emotional side . . . we have too little considered—the men and women broken by the frontier. . . . The cost of it all in human happiness—the loneliness, the disappointments, the renunciations, the severing of old ties and quitting of familiar places . . . too often have been left out of the reckonings in our traditional romantic interpretation" (ix).

This dual treatment is probably the primary reason for the novel's immediate and great success. Hutchison, reviewing *Giants in the Earth,* feels this way. On May 29, 1927, he writes: "Perhaps the author does nothing better in his narrative than the way he conveys . . . the vast solitude which engulfed and blanketed the pioneers of America's civilization. In the knowledge of what the immigrant accomplished, his overcoming of hostile men and an equally hostile nature, while we have marveled at his victory over enemies without, we have not grasped the intensity and long duration of his struggle with the subtle enemy within" (5). He recommends that this book be read as "a human document of pioneer days in this country" (5).

Critics universally have commented about Rolvaag's skillful portrayal of the joys and the sorrows of immigrant life as seen through Per Hansa and Beret, essentially stating that the two protagonists have very different personalities that cause them to respond to pioneer life in different ways. In 1927, Nevins writes that Per Hansa has the joy of fulfilling his destiny, but Beret never recovers from losing her fatherland (896). Boynton, two years later, says that Per Hansa lives with primitive strength and Beret with primitive fear (539). Parrington, writing in 1929, states that Per Hansa is a "type of the natural pioneer who sees the golden light of promise flooding the windswept plains, and Beret [is a] child of an old folk civilization who hungers for the home ways and in whose heart the terror of loneliness gathers" (ix). In 1932, Larsen writes that Per Hansa's nature is bold, restless, and self-reliant and Beret's gentle and sensitive (7). The biographers comment on the "inherently different natures" of Per Hansa and Beret (Jorgenson and Solum 345). Through these two conflicting personalities, Rolvaag is able to show both the joys and costs of immigration.

This observation, that Rolvaag's greatness results from his ability to see not only the economic benefits but also the psychological hardships involved in pioneering, continued as the focus of critical writing for decades. See Commager 10 (1951); Stevens 90 (1955); Boewe 8 (1957); Steensma, "Rolvaag" 101–103 (1959); Steensma, "The Land" 34 (1968); and Reigstad 118 (1972).

For many years, *Giants in the Earth* was a popular book because of its realistic portrayal of immigrant life. In addition, it was well received because it portrayed values that were important to Americans from the 1920s to the early 1970s. Per Hansa was seen as a role model for white Americans—a man who works hard, overcomes obstacles, and becomes a great success. Therefore, the novel appealed to the general public and to educators who used it as a text in high schools and colleges.

In more recent years, the novel has not been as well read for several reasons. No longer are people as interested in reading about life on the frontier, because it seems like ancient history. No longer are people as optimistic that strenuous labor will bring great rewards. No longer are people very enthusiastic about studying the European conquest of the West. With the current multicultural focus, Americans are seeing that there is another side to the westward movement—the losses experienced by the Native Americans. Since this newer topic is of more concern to modern readers, the book has been abandoned by the general reading public in large measure.

However, literary critics continue to study the book for not only its historical value but also its literary worth. Thus, new topics are analyzed. They include Rolvaag's use of Norwegian myths (Hahn 1979), comparisons between Beret and Ibsen's *Brand* (Homola 1986), an analysis of the novel as a work of fiction (Sledge 1991), Rolvaag's use of folklore to describe the landscape (Schultz 1992), and Rolvaag's use of gothicism and naturalism (Gross 1993). The novel is seen by modern critics as an excellent work of art and an accurate portrayal of immigrant life.

One aspect of this novel that has been basically ignored by critics is the gender issue, which should be of great interest to modern readers. Early critics discussed the personality differences between Per Hansa and Beret, including the fact that Beret goes insane because she misses her homeland and is unable to adjust to new ways of thinking, but they did not look at the role that gender plays in her mental collapse. Stevens in 1955 is one of the few critics who mentions this aspect, but he does not discuss it in detail. It seems that Rolvaag is much ahead of his time by showing that pioneer women had very confined roles, which contributed to their unhappiness and emotional downfall.

In their struggle on the Dakota prairie, Rolvaag shows that Per Hansa and Beret confront two main types of obstacles: first, there are the physical hardships of taming the wild prairie; and second, there are the psychological hardships caused by moral dilemmas, homesickness, loneliness, and fear. These two protagonists deal with the physical hardships in very different ways. Whereas Per Hansa sees them as obstacles to overcome so he can build his kingdom, Beret fears them and thinks life is impossible in a place that seems forsaken by God. However, the psychological problems are a different matter; even the most valiant hero cannot triumph over them.

For pioneers, the physical dangers and hardships of immigration were immense. They are like the trolls of the fairy tales that need to be conquered. First there was the problem of traveling to their "promised land." Most Norwegian immigrants were poverty-stricken; yet they had to somehow find a way to transport their goods and families west. Furthermore, they had to travel through an unmarked land and find a small Norwegian settlement. If they missed the tiny community, they would be totally isolated, lost on the vast prairie.

Per Hansa faces both of these problems with imagination and courage. Although he is very poor, having a wagon that belonged in the "scrap heap" (4), and lost, not knowing where to find the trail of his former companions, he still possesses a hope for a glorious future: in Dakota Territory he thinks he is going to take up land, build a home, and "do something remarkable" (5). However, he is worried about finding the trail, and even wonders why he left settled Fillmore County, Minnesota, especially before their expected baby was born. But he felt he had to go; an urgent restlessness would not permit him to linger. Not allowing himself to become too discouraged, he sets out to find the trail, and, as a true fairy tale hero should, he succeeds. His future again looks bright and hopeful.

In the contrasting story of Beret, Rolvaag shows another, darker view of pioneer life in which immigrants feel cast into a desolate wasteland, bereft of civilization and even the moral force of God. The many satisfactions and adventures of pioneer life experienced by Per are lost on Beret, who feels unhappy and even terrified from the beginning of her arrival in Dakota. Her fear is both physical and psychological. For instance, she fears they will never see their friends again, and she worries about giving birth in this desolate land. She is also afraid of the surroundings. Even a normally beautiful sight such as the sunset is terrifying. Loneliness and fear are her companions.

After Per Hansa and Beret find their fellow Norwegians, new obstacles await them because they must develop a farm on the prairie, which is not an easy task. They have to break sod, build shelters, grow crops, and get supplies and equipment. Per Hansa confronts these challenges with determination and enthusiasm. When he arrives at the small settlement, he is ecstatic. But it is not always easy for him to remain exuberant. Even that first evening, as the pioneers are visiting together, a mood of depression and fear settles on all of them as they realize that anything could happen to them since they are "so far from the world . . . cut off from the haunts of their fellow beings . . ." (33). Per Hansa, though, determines not to let this negative mood rule him. He rouses himself and sets out to see his land.

Looking over the kingdom he is going to found, he becomes excited and eager to begin working. His mood is indomitable and conquering with a buoyant rest-lessness that will not let him sit still. He thinks, "Isn't it stranger than a fairy tale, that a man can have such things here, just for the taking?" (42). Beret's unhappi-ness and fears he feels he can overcome by telling her about their glorious future, for he wants her to share in his happiness. He dreams about how pleased she will be with the beautiful home and farm he will build for her. However, when she sees the land they are to take, Beret's response is far different. At once she fears that something will go wrong here. She wonders, "How will human beings be able to endure this place?" (29) The emptiness of the land, so unlike Norway, gives no sense of privacy or even a place to seek shelter: "Why, there isn't even a thing that one can *hide behind!*" (29). In such a land, she cannot practice the reserve and poise she had learned in Norway (Rolvaag, "Immigration History").

In spite of Beret's uneasiness, Per Hansa enthusiastically sets about making his farm, or, as a fairy tale hero would call it, "building his kingdom." Dreaming of the future, nothing can daunt him. At first he works fourteen hours a day breaking sod. His days lengthen to sixteen or seventeen hours, and then he won-ders if he can work nineteen hours and get along on five hours of sleep. His energy is boundless when his future looks so bright. Even the building of his sod house thrills him. Per Hansa imaginatively constructs his hut large enough to house both the animals and his family. Although there is plenty of sod, there is no large wood nearby for the rafters. But Per Hansa, like a typical romantic hero, knows how to overcome this obstacle. Like other romantic adventurers, he makes a long solitary trip far away to the Big Sioux River and brings back a load that is "like an incident out of a fairy tale" (59). Per Hansa is happy—he has been able to leave home to find excitement and goods to make a better life.

Beret, on the other hand, senses none of his passion. She tries to make a home for her family in Per's sod hut, but as her life on the prairie continues, her feel-ings of loneliness and terror magnify. It seems to her that people cannot live in this desolate, empty, and endless place where no life exists, but where the air and land stir "with so many unknown things" (42) that trouble her. Because of her loneliness, she does something that would have been unheard of in Norway: she agrees to build one hut to house both animals and humans. The cow, Rosie, she thinks, will be a welcome companion on the long winter nights.

Aspects of pioneer life that Per finds exciting or interesting, such as encoun-ters with the Native Americans, Beret finds heathenish and frightening. When

Per visits their camp, he finds something enchanting that "enthralled and held him captive" (76). Beret, on the other hand, is angry when Per teases her about the scalping done by Native Americans. "Can't you shut up with that talk!" she cries (72). Before in Norway, Beret would never have shamed him before others, but now her terrors have changed her radically.

Beret and Per respond differently to the disappearance of their cows, Per looking for logical explanations while Beret lets her fancies run rampant. Although Per Hansa, like the other Norwegians, is filled with uneasiness when their animals disappear as he remembers "half-forgotten tales . . . about happenings away off in a far country . . . [where] both man and beast would be spirited away by trolls" (96), he refuses to dwell on his fear. Solitarily, he sets out to retrieve the animals and again performs a seemingly impossible task by finding them at another settlement. When the cattle are lost, Beret's fears become more pronounced. She sees the land as a savage place where even cattle cannot live. In her fright, Beret begs Per to let someone else go to look for the animals because she does not want to be left alone. But Per leaves anyway. Alone with only the children that night, Beret, before going to bed, places her heaviest clothes over the windows to shut out the night and the eyes she fears are watching her. Lastly, she places the big immigrant chest, a symbol of home and security, in front of the door. Little by little, she is descending into insanity.

As the summer passes, Beret becomes more and more fearful, but Per Hansa does not see this. That first summer is to him a "wondrous fairy tale—a romance in which he was both prince and king" (110). He envisions the glorious future in which he will have horses, pigs, cattle, chickens, ducks, and geese; there will be houses for chickens and pigs, stables, storehouses, and a barn. But most precious to him is his idea of his "royal mansion" (111–112). He and Beret, he feels, will live in complete happiness on his future farm, which he pictures as the Garden of Eden with Norwegian pine trees.

Sometimes immigrant groups found themselves rivals, and the next obstacle, claim jumpers, a common problem on the lawless frontier, threatens Per's happiness. One day he discovers stakes with Irish names printed on them on his neighbors' lands. "By God!" he thinks. "The trolls must be after him!" (116). Not until he has destroyed the stakes is he able to rest. Back in Norway, he could not have done such a thing, for there it would have been morally wrong to destroy another's landmarks, but as Dittman says, Rolvaag shows that on the frontier, different attitudes allow one to protect oneself and one's friends in any way possible (23). Though Per feels guilty for breaking the old rule, he conquers his misgivings and is full of good cheer about his actions, telling his neighbors what he has done and making it "sound exactly like a fairy tale" (154).

For Beret, however, these actions are a disregard for moral law (Reigstad 118). She finds it "hideous" and "appalling" that Per has committed this black sin against his fellows (124). Even though the Irish have set up the landmarks illegally, this does not matter, because Per Hansa did not know this when he destroyed them. But she does not totally blame her husband for his actions. Rather, she thinks it is the desolation on the plains that calls "forth all that was evil in human nature" (153). Beret is so upset at Per's actions, she finally speaks up and again accuses her husband in front of others, telling him of his "shameful sin" of destroying someone else's landmarks and warning all of them that they are in danger of turning into "beasts and savages out here" (154–155). Once again we see evidence that Beret is losing her mind.

As time continues, Beret's unhappiness becomes religious in nature. She is convinced that this is a land ruled by a merciless, vengeful God, where the devil himself must have great power. According to Parrington, with her dark religion Beret feels that Dakota is "marked by God's displeasure, and life for her becomes a silent struggle of renunciation and atonement. A primitive Norse Calvinist, victimized by a brooding imagination that sees more devils than vast hell can hold, she dwells 'on the border of utter darkness' where the forces of good and evil struggle for the human soul" (xviii). On the prairie, with nowhere to hide, she fears that God will seek her out and punish her.

She clearly understands this when she sees some travelers going farther west, something she thinks is terrible, for more people are going spiritually astray. Wanting to save them from her fate, she cries to God to show mercy on others, for only she, she feels, has sinned so sorely against him. As she is about to warn them to turn back before it is too late, she suddenly remembers that she cannot speak their language. A heavy loneliness gathers about her as she wonders why God is smiting her so heavily that she cannot even talk to other human beings. Rather than life being a fairy tale, it is more of a nightmare for Beret.

Another source of contrast and conflict between Per and Beret is Per's trips into town for supplies. Through his portrayal of Beret's loneliness, Rolvaag illustrates the difference between male and female pioneer experience. Per Hansa finds these trips very exciting, an outlet for his boundless energy, and an opportunity to extend aid to immigrants more needy than him, as when he gives some poor Norwegians potatoes. The trips are also a source of new ideas, such as when he gets the idea to whitewash the inner walls of his sod hut. On the other hand, Beret, left behind to care for the three young children and livestock, accepts these departures with melancholy resignation: "her whole appearance seemed to reflect a never-ending struggle with unreality" (156–157). She cannot respond to any pleasures, and, in fact, overreacts to minor incidents. When she hears her sons fighting and using coarse language, she lashes out blindly at them with a stick, something she, a kind mother, would not have done before. When a neighbor, Tonseten, gives them badger meat, fit only for trolls in Norway, she is shocked. Incidents like this convince her they have left all civilized life behind. Feeling that everything human is leaving them, she determines that they can no longer stay here and starts to pack the immigrant chest. Beret's hanging more and more clothes over the windows at night to protect them from the savagery outside suggests her growing fears and her incipient insanity. Per Hansa's return with his buoyant enthusiasm signals a return to sanity for her, and she stops covering the windows, deciding that her destiny lies here—God knows best.

Rolvaag portrays the elements that the pioneers must conquer as mythological creatures like the trolls from Norwegian folklore. One of the greatest challenges for all the pioneers on the prairie was winter, with its boredom and blizzards. Per Hansa's days are no longer exciting; he is prevented from traveling because a new baby will be born soon, and he feels he cannot leave Beret. With so much time on his hands, he is able to observe Beret and notices that she is eating and sleeping little, appearing shabby and unkempt, losing the most common objects, and crying easily or showing unusual tenderness. Beret, Per sees, is in a world of her own. Her religion becomes darker until her God is solely the God of law. As biographers Jorgenson and Solum say, "The living God of Per Hansa she hardly knew. . . . Her God was not the God of life. . . . A morbid, doleful theology had been taught her from childhood. It had warped her mind almost beyond recognition" (345). She begins to think that God will punish her by killing her in childbirth and therefore plans for her burial to make sure that she will be safe in this alien land. The chest they brought from Norway, which had been in her family since the 1600s, will have to be her coffin, she decides; in it she will be connected with her fatherland.

The anguish of the dismal winter reaches its apex the day before Christmas, when Peder Victorious is born. Here Rolvaag again shows how life on the frontier was especially hard on women. Beret nearly dies on the isolated, snow-covered prairies with no doctor, and only two neighbor women to help her. Out of a kind of prudish custom, Per Hansa cannot remain with her during childbirth. He stays outside the hut, walking and crying, tormented by the fear that he will lose her. But, fortunately, both Beret and the baby live. In his happiness, Per Hansa has the baby baptized as "Peder Victorious," for he believes that he and his son after him will be victorious over the prairie. This, being another departure from Norwegian tradition, is deeply troubling to Beret. She hates the name "Victorious" since it is never used in Norway as the name of a person, and she fears that it is sacrilegious. The devil, she thinks, having tempted her husband to give the boy such a name, now has her baby in his power.

A similar example of how Beret sees this place as bereft of tradition and morality comes again that winter, when the settlers discuss changing their names, as immigrants often did. When Per Hansa thinks that "Peder Hansen" has no distinction in America and decides to change it to "Holm," Beret is filled with anxiety. Because she thinks it terrible to abandon the sacred names given in baptism, she is afraid that they will soon be disregarding other hallowed things. Her terror of the plains increases when she sees that people willingly, even joyfully, disregard sacred, precious matters, becoming more like animals. Nothing here is as it had been in Norway.

Besides boredom, the pioneers wintering on the prairie faced terrible blizzards. These ferocious days-long storms could start suddenly and cause the death of anyone caught in them. When conquering the blizzard, which he does while getting more fuel for the winter months, Per is again the fairy tale hero. The blizzard, seen by Per as a giant troll, strikes, and Per Hansa, with his slow-moving oxen, is left behind as the other men race for shelter. But miraculously, as a typical romantic hero, he is saved by bumping into the wall of the house he is searching for. The Norwegian men spend several festive days there, even going to a dance, but the fun ends quickly, and they have to return to their homes on the desolate Dakota frontier. As usual, Beret must remain home, caring for the children and the cow, worrying whether Per is still alive.

The next obstacle, trying to grow wheat, a crop they have never grown in Norway, Per easily conquers by becoming the clever American entrepreneur. In order to get money to buy seed, he begins trading with the Indians, buying their furs and selling them for high profits in Minnesota, gathering a fortune as easily as any fairy tale hero (and the hero of the American Dream myth). When he speaks of his trips, Beret catches his "note of suppressed excitement" and thinks, "No wonder he was eager to get away! If he would only think of the fact that others felt the same desire" (292). Per, indeed, is happy. His ventures offer excitement, and even more important, wealth, something necessary to build his kingdom. Just as the sales are completed, he has to go to town with the other men to buy wheat, thus leaving Beret once again at home to carry on the monotonous daily work.

Spring field work brings more obstacles from nature. Per is elated to be growing wheat, the king of crops; having his own land and wheat crop is like a fairy tale come true. But his euphoria does not last long, for another blizzard strikes, seemingly freezing his seed. In his frustration over losing his crop, Per seeks work planting potatoes, but once again he is miraculously saved. The wheat crop has not been ruined—it is growing. As a typical romantic hero, Per Hansa cannot be defeated by the trolls! Light-hearted and happy, Per feels life is wonderful! Once again, however, Beret does not participate in his excitement. She is unable to catch the vision for the future, and instead sees only the grim reality of the present, a tedious existence in a sod hut where she feels they live almost like animals. When a settler appears who wants to build a frame house, Beret tells the newcomer that his wife will be happy because she will have walls that block out the fearful things on the prairie and floors that can be cleaned for the Sabbath, things that will make her life fit for a human. She tells the man, "Human beings should not live like beasts! After they have turned into beasts, houses don't matter" (312). A real house, then, may have helped delay or even stop Beret's approaching insanity; life would have been more bearable for her here.

Rolvaag shows that Beret is not the only woman to suffer psychologically on the vast frontier. A traveler, Jakob, drives by with his wife, who has become insane on the prairie after the death of her son. Seeing her, Beret tries to explain to Per Hansa that she cannot tolerate this type of life any longer. She tells him that this life is "impossible" and "beyond human endurance" (323). After the visitors leave, Beret perceives a menacing creature in the sky. At first she discerns it only during twilight, but gradually as her fears become greater, the terrifying object is present even during the day.

Although this terrifying being exists only in Beret's mind, a real menace, a natural disaster, soon comes out of the sky. This time the trolls come in the form of locusts. During the summers of 1873 through 1877 and part of 1878, swarms of locusts destroyed crops and left the people in famine and poverty. Rolvaag says that some became beggars; others went insane; and still others left the plains and went back East (349).

Again, like the fairy tale hero, Per almost miraculously defeats nature itself. When the strange cloud of locusts approach as he is harvesting his wheat, the excited Per Hansa is filled with a nameless fear, but as the plague descends upon the field, he is seized by an angry determination and defiance against a God who threatens to take the crop from him. In a half-mad rage, he fires his gun into the cloud, miraculously changing their movement and causing the grasshoppers to leave his land. His wheat is saved. No one else is as lucky as the fairy tale hero; their crops are destroyed. But the romantic hero is not totally lucky, for he loses his wife; complete insanity finally shrouds Beret when the locusts come. Firmly convinced that they are the devil arriving in the Dakota prairies, she hides from them in the immigrant chest with her two youngest children. The chest, a tangible image of the old country, will protect them, she thinks, because the devil will not dare take it. Thus Beret breaks down completely. Her religious training, her homesickness, her new environment, and her loneliness have all contributed to her insanity. The costs of immigration have been too great for her.

Next seen some years later, Per Hansa is a wealthy landowner, having achieved the American Dream. Neighbor Tonseten tells a minister that Per always had luck with him: he saved his entire wheat crop when everyone else lost theirs; he sold many potatoes that same year; his fur trading with the Indians was extremely successful. He now has three quarters of land and much livestock. Per Hansa has met all the physical hardships of pioneering on the plains and triumphed over all the "trolls." He has founded his farm, built his house, encountered Native Americans, survived blizzards, provided food and fuel for his family, outsmarted claim jumpers, grown crops, and outlasted locusts. His fairy tale kingdom, then, seems to have come true; Per Hansa should be a happy man.

But he is not. Like Beret, he has paid a severe price, and here Rolvaag shows the painful reality of pioneering for men as well as women. No longer is Per the jubilant, joyful man he had been earlier; although his ambitions for material success have been fulfilled, he is aged from strenuous labor and haggard from sorrow. His altered physical appearance portrays his agony, for he does not look like a young man anymore: his hair and beard are "unkempt" and "grizzled"; his face is "deeply furrowed"; his entire body seems " ravaged and broken" (382). Poor Per has anguished over Beret's insanity. He tries to determine what caused her mental collapse, finally realizing that it was because of her hard life on the dismal prairie. As he says to the minister, it is "this business out here—and for the life of me I can't see any sin in it. . . . Is a man to refuse to go where his whole future calls, only because his wife doesn't like it?" (383). But he is tormented by the fear that "it may be *his* fault that she has fallen into that state of mind" (385). Clearly Per Hansa's life is not a happy one. Although he has "founded his kingdom," emotionally he has paid too big a price to "live happily ever after."

It almost looks as if the fairy tale will end happily when Beret regains her sanity through the help of the minister, who reunites her spiritually with her homeland. Unfortunately, this is not to be, for the new Beret is a childlike religious fanatic rather than the kind woman Per married. However, Per's life, although not ecstatically joyous, is endurable as long as he has his work to do and his best friend, Hans Olsa, nearby.

Hans Olsa's imminent death after being caught in a prairie blizzard brings Per's emotional hardships to a head. Convinced by Beret that he needs absolution before he dies, Hans Olsa implores Per to go out on the snow-covered prairie to get a minister, a request that fills Per Hansa with a nameless dread, for he knows such a trip can result only in his death. To Beret, who demands that he go, he questions, "Do you want to drive me out into the jaws of death?" (454). Beret, however, with her dark religion, is convinced that Hans Olsa, like her husband, has forsaken God in this alien land by seeking only material things. Therefore, she wants Per Hansa to save his friend from hell. Surely, she reasons, Per, who always has been able to accomplish impossible tasks, can travel through a blizzard in this time of crisis.

Per is caught in a terrible dilemma. He knows that if he goes, he will die. But he knows that if he does not go, he will be haunted by the imploring face of Hans Olsa and the reproachful face of his wife. He stalls, hoping Beret will change her mind. Time passes as he visits with his two older sons, who seem to represent the future, enthusiastically instilling the dream of the glorious future into their minds and telling them how to manage the farm. When Beret remains adamant that Per Hansa must try to get a minister before Hans Olsa dies, Per decides to face death, for he recognizes he has little left to live for: his best friend is dying; his wife is no longer a soul mate; and his children are old enough to fulfill his vision. He no longer wants to go on living; the emotional hardships are too great. Instead of looking to the rope and cross beam as he has twice earlier, he accepts death on the open prairie. And so he leaves in the whirling, blinding snow. The following spring, his body is discovered by a haystack, his face turned toward the west. One could say that ironically, the fairy tale hero has been defeated, not only by the elements, but by the dark obsessions of his wife, caused by her isolated existence on the plains.

And so the novel ends. The man who began as a buoyant fairy tale hero is dead, while Beret lives, scared, lonesome, and psychologically scarred. Obviously, the ending to this fairy tale is not the traditional one where the heroes "lived happily ever after." Rolvaag does not see that total happiness is possible for immigrants, because there are too many sacrifices and hardships involved. Although he shows that a fairy tale can become a physical reality in America, this transformation comes at a great price. The physical obstacles can be overcome, but the psychological sufferings cannot.

Rolvaag's two protagonists vividly portray the ecstasies and agonies Norwegians experienced as they immigrated to America in the 1870s. The possibilities that lay before them were as rich and as plentiful as those in a fairy tale. In America, Per Hansa does have a much better and more exciting life than he would have had in Norway. Here he fulfills his ambitions and becomes a "somebody." His accomplishments are great: he gains land and wealth to pass along to his sons; he builds his dream farm; he meets new people; he absorbs new thoughts and new ideas; he lives through one exciting adventure after another. Life in America is almost like a fairy tale that comes true.

But Rolvaag demonstrates that the fairy tale is not merely a happy, exciting story. There are severe hardships, or trolls, using fairy tale terminology, that must be overcome. First, there are the physical obstacles recounted here: traveling to the land, developing a farm, providing food and fuel, dealing with Native Americans and claim jumpers, losing livestock, taking strenuous trips to town for supplies, withstanding the physical isolation, and surviving natural disasters. Rolvaag shows through Per Hansa that these can be overcome by living with enthusiasm, determination, vision, and strenuous labor. Second, there are the psychological hardships, which are more difficult to defeat. Beret, particularly, suffers emotionally and mentally. Much of her suffering comes from her own temperament. She is terrified of the alien land—its barren sameness, its ferocious summer storms and winter blizzards, its plagues of locusts, and its native people. Further, she misses her homeland with its rules and sense of stability. She cannot easily abandon the old ways of thinking and wholeheartedly embrace new ideas and new ways of doing things. Thus she broods about such things as her son's unusual name of "Victorious," their new family last name, their eating of badger meat, and their treatment of claim jumpers. In each of these instances, she feels that they are forsaking the old rules and becoming like beasts. Clearly, she loses much when she leaves Norway.

However, Beret's temperament does not account for all of her suffering. Much of it comes because she is a woman in America. Certainly not all pioneer women suffered as Beret does, but many did, and Rolvaag tells their story, which had been neglected in the idealization of the pioneer experience in American culture. Rolvaag shows that because Beret is a female, she is powerless. She does not get to make any decisions about where they will live, when they will travel, or how they will provide for their basic needs. Rather, she, like other women, follows the wishes of her husband. Besides being powerless, Rolvaag shows that Beret is also almost friendless. There are only two other women in the settlement, and they are not her close friends, merely acquaintances. One is the wife of Per Hansa's best friend, Hans Olsa. The male pioneers, although always good and kind to her, cannot be her close friends, for males and females did not associate as equals in the 1870s. Moreover, Rolvaag clearly portrays that because Beret is a woman, her life is extremely boring. Once she arrives at the tiny settlement on the Dakota plains, she never leaves. All of the men take trips to get food, fuel, and farm supplies. They travel over the prairie, visit other settlements, and make trips to town. But the women remain at home throughout the entire novel. The majority of the book takes place from June 1872 to August 1873. During these fifteen months, Beret never travels except by foot, and she goes only as far as her neighbors' houses because it is not safe to travel farther. By 1878 when the novel ends, Rolvaag shows Beret still in her hut on the prairie. For seven years, she has been exiled from civilization, from the rules and stability of Norway, never leaving the tiny Norwegian settlement. She has remained trapped in her little sod house, caring for first three and then four small children, doing the same monotonous chores day after day and year after year.

Although the women, then, face the greatest psychological hardships, the men are not immune. Through Per Hansa, Rolvaag shows the anguish of a man who watches his wife's mind disintegrate. His ardent enthusiasm disappears as he experiences the agony of immigration by losing his "princess," his best friend, and ultimately his own life.

The final two sentences of the book summarize the type of life Norwegian immigrants found in America in the 1870s and also show Rolvaag's ambivalence toward his subject matter. Rolvaag writes that when Per Hansa's body is discovered, "his face was ashen and drawn. His eyes were set toward the west" (465). Obviously, these words describe Per Hansa's physical death, but they are also symbolic. Per has discovered that life is hard physically and psychologically, and therefore his face is "ashen and drawn," but at the same time, he faces the West, where lies an untamed land of adventure and romance, where new fairy tales are waiting to be transformed into reality. Throughout his life on the prairie, Per Hansa has a vision, and he makes it come true. He is like the conquering fairy tale hero, and the novel is clearly optimistic about the possibilities in America for the hard-working immigrant. However, unlike the fairy tale hero, he cannot "live happily ever after" because his material success and marvelous adventures have come at a huge price. Immigrant life in America is not solely a fairy tale in which people can overcome all hardships by defeating all the evil "trolls" and live in total happiness. The grim reality is that there are many physical and psychological sufferings that go with this life. Through Per Hansa and Beret, then, Rolvaag shows the ecstasy and the agony of conquering a new land.

WORKS CONSULTED

Boewe, Charles. "Rolvaag's America: An Immigrant Novelist's Views." *Western Humanities Review* 11 (1957): 3–12.

Boynton, Percy H. "O. E. Rolvaag and the Conquest of the Pioneer." *English Journal* 18 (Sept. 1929): 535–542.

Commager, Henry S. "Human Cost of the West." *Senior Scholastic* 58 (29 Feb. 1951): 10–11.

Dittman, Erling. "The Immigrant Mind: A Study of Rolvaag." *Christian Liberty* 1 (Oct. 1952): 7–47.

Gross, David S. "No Place to Hide: Gothic Naturalism in O. E. Rolvaag's *Giants in the Earth.*" *Frontier Gothic: Terror and Wonder at the Frontier in American Literature.* Ed. David Mogen, Scott P. Sanders, and Joanne B. Karpinski. Rutherford: Fairleigh Dickinson UP, 1993. 42–54.

Hahn, Steve. "Vision and Reality in *Giants in the Earth.*" *South Dakota Review* 17.1 (1979): 85–100.

Homola, Priscilla. "Rolvaag's Beret as Spiritual Descendant of Ibsen's Brand." *South Dakota Review* 24.2 (1986): 63–70.

Hutchison, Percy A. "Norwegian Pioneers in the Dakotas." *New York Times Book Review.* 29 May 1927: 5.

Jorgenson, Theodore and Nora O. Solum. *Ole Edvart Rolvaag, A Biography.* New York: Harper, 1939.

Larsen, Hanna Astrup. "Ole Edvart Rolvaag." *American-Scandinavian Review* 20 (Jan. 1932): 7–9.

Nevins, Allan. "On the Dakota Frontier." *Saturday Review of Literature* 3 (11 June 1927): 896.

Parrington, Vernon Louis. Editor's Introduction. *Giants in the Earth.* New York: Harper, 1929. ix–xx.

Reigstad, Paul. *Rolvaag: His Life and Art.* Lincoln: U of Nebraska P, 1972.

Rolvaag, O. E. "Country and Fatherland." *American Prefaces: Journal of Critical and Imaginative Writing* 1 (April 1936): 109–112.

———. *Giants in the Earth.* New York: Harper, 1927. Text edition by Vernon Louis Parrington. New York: Harper, 1929.

———. "Immigration History." Unpublished class introduction. Norwegian-American Historical Association. Rolvaag Memorial Library, St. Olaf College, Northfield, MN.

———. Letter to Lincoln Colcord. 27 Nov. 1926. Norwegian-American Historical Association. Rolvaag Memorial Library, St. Olaf College, Northfield, MN.

———. "The Vikings of the Western Prairies." *American Magazine* 108 (Oct. 1929): 44–47, 83, 86.

Schultz, April. "To Lose the Unspeakable: Folklore and Landscape in O.E. Rolvaag's *Giants in the Earth.*" *Mapping American Culture.* Ed. Wayne Franklin and Michael Steiner. Iowa City: U of Iowa P, 1992. 89–111.

Sledge, Martha. "Truth and Fact: The Rhetoric of Fiction and History in Immigrant Literature." *South Dakota Review* 29.2 (1991): 159–169.

Steensma, Robert C. "The Land of Desert Sweet: The Homesteader and His Literature." *Rendezvous: Idaho State University Journal of Arts and Letters* 3 (Winter 1968): 29–38.

———. "Rolvaag and Turner's Frontier Thesis." *North Dakota Quarterly* 27 (Autumn 1959): 100–104.

Stevens, Robert Lowell. "Ole Edvart Rolvaag: A Critical Study of His Norwegian-American Novels." Diss. U of Illinois, 1955.

4

Jasmine or the Americanization of an Asian: Negotiating between "Cultural Arrest" and Moral Decay in Immigrant Fictions

Gönül Pultar

One of the significant developments in the United States during the past decades has been the revision of the literary canon, which had once been white, Anglo-Saxon, Protestant and, needless to add, predominantly male. This meant not only the incorporation of female authors as well as writers of various ethnic minorities who were or would have been neglected or undermined previously, but also a radical change of direction in the selection process. The standards, be they aesthetic or philosophical, that had been employed as criteria in the old canon were readjusted, in the belief that literature should "not only address itself to matters of transcendent human and artistic significance but also record . . . the full variety of American life" (Skardal 97). Paralleled with, as well as affected by, the emergence of multiculturalism, this evolution made possible, among other things, the flourishing of a powerful ethnic fiction by non-Anglo authors.

Jasmine, the 1989 novel by the Indian (of the subcontinent) immigrant woman writer Bharati Mukherjee, must be considered among such a fiction. It recounts the Americanization of an Indian first-generation female protagonist and reveals that although living out one's ethnicity is easier nowadays in multiethnic America, the path to Americanization for a non-Anglo is not without thorns. On the one hand, there are restrictions imposed by the ethnic group; on the other hand, the social and spiritual decay presented by the contemporary "puritan" Anglo-American mainstream brings disillusion. As the novel proceeds between flashbacks of contrastive and conflicting portrayals of mutually alien cultures and locales, the tensions inherent in the process of Americanization of the Asians are admirably displayed. It is these tensions that I examine in this essay. I also introduce the term "cultural arrest."

Eric Liu, the "accidental Asian," may argue for the inexistence of such tensions, or against their problematization. However, "what gets covered over in the flurry of change and action [in the Americanization process] is the conflict and the confusion of 'the whole cross-cultural business' as Gayatri Spivak puts it, the trauma of getting used to the idea that one is not going to be completely at home in either place—or burying that idea in a heap of excitement about becoming, and being, 'American,' as Jasmine does so well" (Bose 49). Whether the latter is to be lauded for doing this, or despised for it and for her actions that stem from her idea of "being 'American,'" is the major problem posed by the novel.

As a mirror image of present-day America, *Jasmine* exudes violence from beginning to end (see Dayal for a discussion of the violence in this novel). However, unlike most other ethnic novels, it is not directed against any hegemonic cultural group such as the Anglos, but constitutes, in the candid, pseudo-picaresque narration by the protagonist herself of her Americanization, one of the harshest indictments of nothing less than the American way of life itself. I argue that the mainstream reflected in the novel is a wasteland characterized by moral decay.

Written in the form of a confessional novel, *Jasmine* is the story of an Indian female protagonist, who is given the name Jyoti upon birth, but then is also called Jasmine, Jase, and Jane during various periods of her life that correspond to different men in it, as well as to different stages of it.[1] Born and bred in India, she arrives in the United States as an adult. Since she does not come from an ethnic group victimized by the Anglo-Americans in the past or has not herself undergone discrimination while growing up, she is able to pose an uncomplexed, unburdened "novel" eye where her African-American or Native American counterpart would see nothing but racism and suffering. This is one aspect of the novel that distinguishes it from other ethnic novels, and makes for an entertaining work before all else; it is farcical in a tragicomic way, as when a character chokes to death in a Mexican restaurant because the waiters, instead of helping him, dash off into hiding as soon as they hear police might come: they are all illegals (8).

The novel starts in India. A little girl of seven is told her fortune: she will be widowed and exiled. Although she reacts immediately at the time, a foregrounding of the will and strong-mindedness she will display later, on her way to becoming an American, she believes that she was "nothing, a speck in the solar system. . . . I was helpless, doomed. . . . Fate is fate" (3–4). In fact, Jyoti-Jasmine herself sums up the plot of the novel by referring to "the war between my fate and my will" (12). It ends, with the prophecy enacted, as she is heading "west" to California, with all that the West as a myth symbolizes, "greedy with wants and reckless from hope" (241).

A coming-of-age novel, *Jasmine* equates the course of "heading west" with reaching maturity. Thus, at first her native India is there, symbolized by a belief in "fate," implacably depicted as a backward society that treats girls abominably by denying them education and marrying them off at eleven, denying them existence even: daughters are considered "curses."[2] Jyoti comes out in the midwife's arms with bruises around her throat (40). As she explains later to the American professional woman by whom she is employed, Jyoti's mother loved her so much she had wanted to kill her, because she and her husband would not have been able to provide her with a dowry.

At age fourteen Jyoti gets married to an engineering student, a progressive man who changes her name from Jyoti to Jasmine, making her "shuttle between identities" (77). Parenthetically, this is a marriage of love Jyoti herself engineers, the story of which contradicts her own earlier depiction of women's fate in India.

Her husband, taking the advice of a former professor who has emigrated to the States and who writes that there is electricity there twenty-four hours a day, decides to go to America. While India proves to be "feudal" (76) and therefore stifling for liberal-minded progressive people such as the young man, "America" appears, in its promise of technology and bright lights, a land for moral improvement.

Jasmine's first estrangement from her own people, or the first stage of her Americanization, takes place as husband and wife examine the brochure of an institution in Florida welcoming Indian students. Looking at familiar Indian faces, she sees them, for the first time in her life, as "strange," as "a kind of tribe of intense men with oily hair, heavy-rimmed glasses, and mustaches" (92).

Gurleen Grewal labels this novel an "immigrant *Bildungsroman,*" because it posits, "like most narratives of *Bildung . . .* a norm of self-development." For Grewal, what's more, the entirety of Mukherjee's writing chronicles "the transitions from an expatriate sensibility to an immigrant one." *Jasmine*, in particular, Grewal finds, "is inscribed in what Adrienne Rich has called the 'old American pattern, the pattern of the frontier, the escape from the old identity, the old debts, the old wife, to the new name, to the new life'" (182). Thus, for *Jasmine*'s protagonist, the self-development is to "become" an immigrant in the United States. Seen in that light, although Jyoti-Jasmine herself may not have been aware of it at the time, her shedding of an unproblematic mono-identity (as Jyoti) was the first step in her *Bildung*, in this case and at this early stage, toward exile and an expatriate state, that will in turn lead the way to being an immigrant. Her estrangement from her own people, finding them "a kind of tribe" to be looked down upon—rather than exoticizing them and their Indian-ness as she will later learn to in the United States with Bud—seems to be an almost inevitable second step. The immigration to a land and its culture must perforce entail an affective migration from another one.

However, as her husband is about to complete formalities, some of them illegal, to migrate to the United States, he is killed by a Sikh terrorist. Once over the shock, Jyoti-Jasmine is appalled by the prospect of quasi-immuration she believes her state of widowhood requires in India. Although docile adherence to Indian mores clashes with her "Jasmine" identity, she seems to be implying that without her husband to support her, she is unable to withstand her immediate family's and society's traditionalism. So, she decides to follow in her late husband's steps, to complete his mission (97) and depart for America. Armed with forged papers, she becomes another illegal immigrant, reaching U.S. soil through dubious means.

For Jasmine, a good student at school, learning English had been to want "more than you had been given at birth," it had been to want "the world" (68). Now, leaving India seems another exploit in the same direction. She believes that if she can leave India, she can begin again and create for herself an entirely new destiny (85).

Yet this starting with "new fates" involves at first, not an initiation or purification process, but debasement, with an almost Naipaulian sense of desolation. This is the hidden side of the coin in any glorification of immigration to America, and a foregrounding, for any reader wishing to see it, that the route toward Americanization is far from bringing moral improvement. The rite of passage involves being pushed around and degraded as refugees and outcasts by shadowy airline personnel (100–101). These are experiences that weigh on the conscience of the immigrant, who has to learn to live with memories of them, even when s/he apparently easily sheds the past.

This is seen to be all the more so as Jasmine encounters violence as soon as she lands. On her first night on U.S. soil, she is raped and then kills the rapist.

After having been rescued by a do-gooder, Jasmine eventually joins the professor's family. Thus, after a portrayal of India, we have a portrayal of Indians abroad. Jasmine spends months in their New York home, almost never leaving the apartment, because what business does a young widow have out in the streets! The family lives, with the professor's parents in an extended family setup, in a block in Queens with Indian families as neighbors in thirty-two of the fifty apartments—a distinctive residential segregation they themselves create. They spend their whole free time, when not visiting other Indian families, at home, speaking their native language, watching video-cassettes of Indian movies, "artificially maintain[ing] an Indianness" (145), Jasmine informs the reader, creating the life of Punjab, even if the Punjab of the past is no more (162). The old parents are the unhappiest. Some of the customs that were built-in within the social fabric, and reproduced over generations, cannot be replicated in the United States. For example, in India, a young bride would obey her more-often-than-not tyrannical mother-in-law absolutely, then expect later the same subservience from her own daughter-in-law. However, in New York, this is not possible because young women work and are just not at home physically to cater to the whims of the elderly. The latter now lament: "Our sons are selfish. Our daughters want to work. . . . All the time, this rush-rush. . . . There are no grandchildren. . . . This country has drained my son of his dum. . . . turned my daughter-in-law into a barren field" (147–148).

The professor, learned and dignified in the eyes of his womenfolk, so Americanized in the way he pronounces his name, making it sound like an Anglo-Saxon one, works not in academia, but, as Jasmine has occasion to find out, as a dealer in women's hair in a room he rents in the basement of an Indian barbecue shop.

America, after all, is not conducive to moral elevation. The social degradation the immigrants have to suffer through robs them of their essential dignity: a Pakistani taxi driver tells Jasmine that in Kabul he was a physician, yet in the United States, immigrants must live "like dogs" (140). The depiction of the Indian immigrants trapped in New York, "behind ghetto walls" (145), sad yet so realistic, is one of the most poignant parts of the novel.

A number of points have to be clarified at this stage, before we move from ethnic America to mainstream America. Jozsef Gellen has proposed the term "proto-ethnicity" for the original heritage prior to Americanization, with "ethnicity" coming to mean that culture developed in America (qtd. in Skardal 99). That there is a difference between the two is not only hinted at in the narrator/protagonist's allusions to "artificial Indianness," or the fact that the old Punjab no longer exists anymore, but is also made evident in her observation that in the meantime India is also changing. She recalls that bicycles were giving way to scooters and to cars, and radios were giving way to television, and realizes that the centuries-old social order that encompassed fortune-telling was itself crumbling (229).

Her reminder that India is also changing seems to imply that her fate could have, and probably inevitably would have, changed even if she had not left it. This of course conflicts with the notion that seems to be inherent throughout the narrative discourse that America is the only alternative for a "progressive" life, in the same way that her marriage to the liberal-minded engineer, a union of love, contradicts, as I mentioned above, her statements about women's fate in India. This is one of the tensions that remain unresolved by an unsuspecting Jasmine, and that I believe constitutes one of the important aspects of immigrant experience reflected in the novel. The immigrant has to make him/herself believe that his/her passage was necessary and inevitable in order to live a life that can be called worthwhile, and in parallel fashion, to convince him/herself that this could never be achieved in the homeland.

Another matter to be indicated is the fact that the life led by the professor's family is described by Margaret Mead as a "post-figurative culture," a culture that is unchanging, in which at least three generations are involved and norms are passed on by grandparents to grandchildren. What distinguishes such a society is the absence of consciousness and questioning; the society remains unanalyzed by its members (1–24 passim). For example, as an Indian widow, remarriage is out of question for Jasmine as long as she stays with the professor's family. However, what is amiss is that there are no grandchildren to pass the norms on to. The reference to the daughter-in-law as a "barren field" seems to suggest a pathology both in the ethnicity and in the land, i.e., mainstream America. For Jasmine, the life she is made to lead with the professor's family, generously hospitable in a manner only Orientals are able to be, is nevertheless another sort of immuration (148), and, not unnaturally, she wants out.

The episode with the Indian family in New York City, the Vadheras, is relatively brief, an "incident" in this picaresque novel, functioning at surface level merely to show that Jasmine could not "go back," either to India or to its modified American version.[3] But its importance outweighs its length. In fact, the snapshot brevity of the episode leaves the discerning reader free to go beyond the caricatural characters and the narrative at the surface, and engage in a debate as to what Indian culture, or Eastern cultures in general, as an alternative to Anglo-American culture, would represent and signify for America. Jasmine herself will point out later in her life in the United States that there is more of India and Asia in America than her dismissive "behind ghetto walls," when she remarks that in any important medical center in the United States one will notice many Asian doctors (32).

To illustrate, I would argue that the unproductive "rush-rush" and the axiomatic spiritual impoverishment the Indian mother-in-law complains about can be taken as nothing but a pallid reflection, among immigrants, of what once was the Protestant work ethic and its postmodern sequel, workaholism, within an exhausted Puritanism—displayed by the "white" America the novel later portrays. The binary opposition, afforded by the attitude displayed through the unquestioning hospitality of the Indian family and the culture that is manifest through the many Indian films they watch, is very much there, as the "gap" to be filled by the reader.[4] Indeed, Jasmine herself, without being conscious of it, is aware of the potential of her stay with the Vadheras, which she fails to make use of when she reflects that they had taught her a great deal (161–162).

That Indian culture is very much an intrinsic part of this novel does not escape critics, especially of Indian extraction. Among them, Kuldip Kaur Kuwahara, for example, considers Jasmine "both an Indian mystical journey and an American story of self-making," and finds that Mukherjee uses the structural device of Indian mysticism to write yet another novel of the immigrant experience. In fact, Mukherjee's narrative operates "within the parameters of Indian mysticism and fatalism challenged by American materialism and optimism." The dual story and the blending of the Indian and American elements allow Mukherjee to contrast, according to Kuwahara, "the paradoxical pattern of social limitations and spiritual freedom in India with the social freedom and spiritual limitations of life in the New World." (31, 33)

If *Jasmine* can be treated as an American work of fiction, as in this volume, it can just as well be discussed purely within Indian literary tradition—a trait of immigrant fiction that requires a whole essay to itself, but which must also be highlighted as being very much an aspect of this novel. Accordingly, Kuwahara writes: "Mukherjee plays with two contradictory images of women in Indian literature: images of strength, of women as goddesses; and images of weakness associated with women's limited spaces within traditional social structures. Heroines in Indian literature convey an inner strength. Unlike them, Jasmine is . . . hollow shell. . . . She is a weak echo of Kalidas's Shakuntala or Rabindranath Tagore's Chitra" (32). Yet, Kuwahara's conclusion is that between these two worlds, Jasmine is still able to achieve the possibilities of the American Dream, despite its dangers (33). Indeed, once she leaves her compatriots, Jasmine looks for a job, this time with a forged green card. Nothing demonstrates better the moral rottenness of mainstream America than the unlawful dealings concerning Jasmine's eventual entry into it.

Her introduction into "white," "Anglo" America corresponds to her shedding of her "ethnicity," disclosing another facet of the expatriate-to-immigrant experience: "Once we start letting go—let go just one thing, like not wearing our normal clothes, or a turban . . . —the rest goes on its own down a sinkhole" (29). She starts working for the family of a Columbia professor, only to find that Americans are just as barren. The WASP intellectual is unable to father; thus the couple have adopted a daughter for whom Jasmine will act as "caregiver," as they put it.[5]

Just as there are two Indias presented in the novel, there are two Americas: the

New York of the professional couple, then a small town in Iowa. Naturally, there is an immense contrast between the two Indias and the two Americas, and Jasmine will remain "shuttled" in between, wavering up to the last minute, up to the last page of the novel, between "the promise of America and old-world dutifulness" (240). But then, while the two Indias exhibit the divergence mentioned earlier, the two Americas, in their respective order, only seem to become more deeply steeped in moral and social deterioration. In fact, *Jasmine* is a chilling account and a harsh indictment of the American way of life.

The Indians cling heroically and pathetically to an Indian dream that is static; what characterizes Americans, finds Jasmine, is "fluidity": "the fluidity of American character and the American landscape" (138). She states that immigrants arrive eager to participate in the American Dream, not realizing that "in America, nothing lasts" forever—not buildings, not agreements between people. Everything is impermanent (181).

The American Dream has been trivialized by men and women who have had it too easy, taking too much for granted. Throughout the novel there is a contrast with the hardships in India, underscoring without seeming to the duality of spirituality versus freedom, Kuwahara remarks. In the United States, individual freedom appears to have been reduced to instant gratification of an almost animalistic nature: the WASP professor's wife has no scruples about breaking up her marriage and leaving behind the little girl she adopted for a man himself married with three children. The couple is unable to procreate, have no sense of family, and prove incapable of manifesting any affection for their child: the adopted daughter knows this, and calls the *au pair* Jasmine mummy. "Truly there was no concept of shame in this society," as Jasmine herself puts it (171).

This is the school where Jasmine is broken into Americanization. Not unexpectedly, she falls for the young WASP professor Taylor Hayes, not so much for what he is but what he represents, the democratic employer serving his servant. She falls into the pattern in an amoralistic fashion, replacing in his bed the wife who left. Although this is another step forward in her Americanization, it must be remarked that this is again of an illicit nature.

Taylor calls her Jase, giving her a new identity. Jasmine believes that the change in her is her choice, not Taylor's, and that to change identities is absolutely necessary for survival: "To bunker oneself inside nostalgia, to sheathe the heart in a bulletproof vest, was to be a coward" (185–186).

Grewal criticizes the representation of "the retention of ethnic identity as cowardice or failure" on the part of first-generation immigrants. She writes that in so doing "the novel seems obtuse to their condition of existence," and quotes Sucheta Mazumdar, who explains that "Asian ethnic ghettoes are a genuine response to the needs of new immigrants who live, work, or find support services there" (190).

Grewal's critique raises an important issue concerning both expatriate-to-immigrant experience and the fiction that reflects it mimetically, uncovering another of the major tensions I argue are found in the novel. For one thing, if we are to take Jasmine-Jase's admonition at face value, then all the Pilgrims and Puritans who came to America and failed to adopt the ways of the Native Americans were evidently cowards, even more so when they labeled the latter as "savage Indians." It is interesting that this point should come up in an immigrant *Bildungsroman* and not (as far as I know) in fiction written by the Native Americans themselves. It is also noteworthy that it comes up in a novel written in the last quarter of the twentieth century, when globalization has rendered the culture ante to immigration, not any more food for nostalgia, but an item of consumption that is readily accessible, both through the Internet and the relative ease of travel, cheaper and shorter than ever. The affective distance that is needed is there in these instances.

But of course that is not what Grewal had in mind. The ethnic identity in question is one that is "ethnic" in relation to mainstream Anglo-Eurocentric identity, and Grewal articulates a sentiment shared by many in America, not least by the Latinos. Taken to the extreme, this stance would call Jasmine-Jase herself a coward; further opposing the privileged position that Anglo-Eurocentric culture possesses within the mainstream, acquired just because it preceded others to America by a few centuries. Any student of literature pondering immigrant fiction needs to confront these considerations.

This does not mean that everybody would agree. For Liu, the self-confessed "accused banana" (36), as obviously for many others at the opposite end, there is a certain "American-ness," negotiated over the years, where "whiteness" (entailing perforce such "black" elements as jazz, Native American ones as "moccasin" and Chinese ones as "take away") prevails. It is a way of life and a mental attitude rather than a matter of skin color. The question then becomes, Would Liu's ethnically white wife take a mere acquaintance of the Liu family back from China into her home for months on end? Or would he be too ashamed to suggest it to her, the way he was ashamed, while he was growing up, of his table manners when dining in white classmates' homes? Are there absolute and universal codes of ethical behavior? And, more specifically to do with immigrant experience and mimetic fiction reflecting it, To what extent should the immigrant incorporate the ontological/cultural world of the society of arrival, now that the melting pot is not any more imperative, or perhaps not even feasible?

The last question is the one that should preoccupy us. Whatever will eventually be the contributions of the multiculturalist paradigm, and there are many, I predict that this question ultimately will be its major legacy. It is to *Jasmine*'s credit and to its author's that this question is being posed.

Without undue idealization of any of the attitudes above and the attendant rhetoric that might ensue from them, I would like to suggest that it is a fact that "to bunker oneself inside nostalgia, to sheathe the heart in a bulletproof vest" is an indication of stasis and stagnation. Jasmine-Jase is aware that this "cultural arrest," as I would like to term it, of the expatriate/immigrant signifies also an arrest in personal growth and leads to stultification, as she witnessed among the Vadheras. Collective cultural arrest can only lead to ghettoization beyond the provision of lifesaving "support services."

However, there is an anomaly in *Jasmine* in that although it is the story of a peasant girl from India whose education stopped in her early teens, it is narrated by an intelligence that incorporates all the culture and worldly wisdom of the British-educated Canadian, then American, university professor Bharati Mukherjee. I find that that is what bothers the reader—there is something that just does not coincide or cohere; or, as Anindyo Roy puts it, at this point "the novel appears to be no longer seamless" (135). Thus, it is not that blind, wholesale retention of ethnicity and imperviousness to the culture of arrival is without criticism, because it is very much so. The criticism is well-founded in the case of the Vadheras, and the reader with any sensibility concerning the expatriate/immigrant experience finds her/himself, as s/he progresses in the novel, engaged in a debate on a possible well-dosed negotiation between retention and shedding. The negotiation becomes necessary because it is obvious that Jyoti-Jasmine-Jase's wholesale rejection and change are just as misplaced as the Vadheras' retention. There would have been no hot dogs and no pizza in America had German-Americans and Italian-Americans acted as she does. That the Puritans, who built this country, could have upon arrival denied and obliterated their culture and identity is unthinkable if not almost sacrilegious.

As to "adventurous Jase," as she calls herself, one lesson she learns from Taylor is to "pull down an imaginary shade" (186). By a chance encounter—an act of coincidence that mars the overall tenor of the novel—Jasmine comes across her husband's murderer, who has somehow also migrated to New York. Afraid that he might want to kill her if given the chance, she "pulls an imaginary shade" on her life with Taylor and the little girl, and flees to Iowa.

In Iowa, she starts working in a bank as a teller and before she knows it, has the fifty-year-old owner of the bank fall in love with her. Bud Rippelmeyer divorces his wife of twenty-eight years and they start cohabiting. He calls her Jane. "Me Bud. You Jane" (26).

But violence catches up to Jyoti-Jasmine-Jase-Jane. Bud is shot by a discontented client. He becomes an invalid, an apt symbol for the America that is unveiled in the novel. He can have an erection only with the help of machines. When he and "Jane" decide to have a child, it can only be through artificial insemination. The barrenness is chronic.

What Jasmine encounters in Elsa County, Iowa, and the reader through her is the American Despair. Most people in Elsa County, Iowa, have lost "discipline, strength, patience, character" (23). Instead there is despair. Her companion tells her, "Things weren't always this ugly, Jane" (158). There are daughters-in-law who want to put their aged but perfectly healthy mothers-in-law in the Lutheran home; women who start sobbing suddenly; men in debt, unable to keep up payments, blaming bank owners for it and shooting them; youngsters overburdened by their heritage who commit suicide. "Something's gotten out of hand in the heartland," as the Elsa County Mental Health Center consultant puts it (155). A farmer digs a trench around his banker's house with stolen backhoe equipment and on TV says, "Call it a moat of hate." A man beats his wife with a spade, then hangs himself (156). Land developers come and offer huge prices for nonagricultural use of traditional agricultural land. They want to build golf courses where there has been farmland for generations, and they tempt with their offers the young offspring who have inherited the land. These, however, feel uneasy if they acquiesce. Such a youngster is their next-door neighbor Darrell, who dreams of leaving the region and starting anew elsewhere, but who cannot let go of a tragic sense of guilt at forfeiting his parents' heritage. Consequently, he cannot depart, and takes his life instead. It is "a way of life coming to an end" (229).

Bud, on meeting Jasmine, decides to make up for "fifty years of selfishness" (14). He thinks he can "atone" for something—for being "American, blessed, healthy, innocent," thinks Jasmine-Jane. Bud's former wife explains: "This is puritan country; we're born with guilt or quickly learn it. Guilt twists a person" (228).

So, although he already has two married sons, Bud decides to adopt a Vietnamese child. The newcomer is Du, a survivor from a refugee camp. His parents and his brothers have been killed. One sister, staying in another camp, used to come and feed him insects to make him survive. He did. Now, his new mother, Jasmine, reflects that in some ways his new land is just as violent and confused as his old: "In the America Du knows, mothers are younger than sisters, . . . illegal aliens, murderers, rape victims; . . . parents are unmarried, fathers are invalids" (224). Despite all this, Du appears to have become the all-American teenager, refusing to talk Vietnamese, watching science fiction movies on television, hoarding gadgets, making friends, getting good grades in school.

And then suddenly, one day, he leaves. His sister has arrived in California. He leaves with a Vietnamese man, speaking Vietnamese with him. Although Jasmine considers her own transformation as being "genetic," she sees Du's as "hyphenated." Recalling how fast he became American, she realizes he is a "hybrid" (222). Henceforth, the key concept for immigrants, as well as any engagement with fiction on immigrants, will be the magical word "hybrid," not "melting pot" or "assimilation" anymore. Israel Zangwill's play has become outdated.[6]

Du leaves, saying that he will never forget them. But his adoptive mother knows very well that for Du, "abandonment, guilt, betrayal" means nothing; the boy would see them as "banal dilemmas" (221).

Du's departure is the foregrounding for Jasmine's own going away. When Taylor comes with his daughter to Elsa County to reclaim "Jase" and take her "West," this time it is her turn not to have any qualms deserting an aging invalid who left his long-standing wife for her. She is carrying his child, although illegitimate, a child who, conceived for once, although artificially, will not know its own father and will have only a surrogate father to raise it, just like the other, adopted little girl.

Fakrul Alam writes that

the character of Jasmine . . . has been created to depict Mukherjee's belief in the necessity of inventing and re-inventing one's self by going beyond what is given and by transcending one's origins.

For Mukherjee, immigration—specifically immigration to America—is a crucial step to be taken in any move to remake oneself in the light of one's desires. Clearly, . . . Jasmine . . . is someone who is ready to go beyond conventional morality to seek fulfillment. (109)

"Going beyond conventional morality" is perhaps Jasmine's most salient trait. Kuwahara says that Jasmine's journey is a symbolic as well as a literal journey (31). Even so, the reader is left to wonder if such "going beyond" is a must in the path from expatriate to immigrant, which inheres essentially going beyond "what is given," as Alam puts it. What's more, any symbolism in this novel connected with transcending conventional morality can have negative connotations only: Jasmine's desertion of the elderly invalid also goes beyond carving herself a niche in the new country, which purportedly is the implicit goal, alongside the shedding of expatriate identity, of the immigrant *Bildungsroman*. If the form, whether literal or symbolical, that Jasmine's journey takes is what becoming American is all about, then American-ness has become untypically immoral.

In conclusion, although it is impossible for Jyoti-Jasmine-Jase-Jane to go back either to India or to the ethnic Indian group in New York, her integration into an American mainstream in moral decay appears to be just as problematic.

Leaving behind rape, murder, suicide, violent shooting, and betrayal, heading toward a West that is more mythical and symbolical than real, Jasmine pulls an imaginary shade on her life with Bud, believing she is acting as an American, shedding "old-world dutifulness" in a "free country" (239). Her utter insensitivity to the sense of guilt, in tune with the general rottenness, yet so essential to Puritan teaching, shows that she herself has yet a long way to go before she can become truly American, in the sense that white Americans of an earlier period were. Yet her further Americanization can only signify her being irreversibly engulfed in the social malaise, swamped by the wasteland laid bare in the novel. Within that universe, Jasmine's identification with it can in turn serve only as endorsement and bolstering.

The "coming of age" in the novel has a hollow ring to it, sardonic almost in the Swiftian black humor with which it is recounted. The moral improvement secretly hoped for before immigration has been stood on its head.

Mainstream society takes on the form of a dystopia in the fictionalized America of Mukherjee. The alternative, the multicultural society, offers a picture no less hellish. Vacillating between definitions of identity, Jasmine and the likes of her, such as Du, are doomed to remain in a sort of limbo, hyphenated "lost souls" unable to find anchor, unable to make commitments, reckless with a hope that is much more vacuous than it sounds. The reader is not told whether Du has reached his West and whether Jasmine will be able to reach hers. Yet even if she does attain it, she is bound to wonder why, in the words of Walt Whitman in "Enfans d'Adam":

having arrived at last where I am—the circle almost circled; For coming westward from Hindustan, from the vales of Kashmere, from Asia— . . . Now I face the old home again— looking over to it, joyous, as after long travel, growth, and sleep; But where is what I started for, so long ago? And why is it yet unfound?

NOTES

1. For literary history, Mukherjee's earlier published collection of short stories *The Middleman and Other Stories* (1988) already contained a short story entitled "Jasmine." The story is about a Trinidadian girl who becomes an illegal immigrant who comes to love being in America. According to Fakrul Alam, the author of a volume devoted to Mukherjee, the writer later developed the story's plot so that it could make for "a more compelling work about inventing and re-inventing a self through immigration" (100).

2. Such a depiction of India is much critiqued by critics themselves of Indian extraction. Anindyo Roy criticizes Mukherjee for having reduced "the complexities of immigration to the simple dream of escape from a confining world" (134), and Gurleen Grewal finds that "in the portrayal of her immigrant heroine, Mukherjee reinforces images of the Third World Woman . . . in short a victim awaiting rescue" (187). For Chandra Mohanty, what such an image of the Third World woman does is to posit "western women as secular, liberated, and having control over their own lives" (qtd. in Grewal 187). Debjani Banerjee openly accuses Mukherjee of "catering to a First World audience while still mining the Third World for fictional material" (173).

3. Grewal writes that "in her haste to Americanize Jasmine and dress her up in the images of dreams, Mukherjee neglects a significant immigrant story, that of the Vadhera family in Flushing that provides her a home, no questions asked, on the strength of old connections in the homeland. . . . Mukherjee allows her [Jasmine] little empathy for the Vadheras, . . . little solidarity on the basis of their shared predicament as immigrants" (189).

4. This Oriental hospitality is so unquestioning that Jasmine herself does not question it and never feels any gratefulness. Yet Oriental hospitality and all its ramifications also necessitated a more extensive treatment in the novel, as it is the antithesis of the Western conceptualization of the alien and especially of the Oriental as the "other." Oriental hospitality posits the alien and therefore the Westerner as first and foremost a "guest" to be well treated, before and above one's equals and oneself.

5. "Because Jasmine's employers, the liberal New York couple, call her a 'caregiver,' not a maidservant, we are led to assume there are no class boundaries or distinctions [in American society]," writes Grewal (192), intimating that the novel gives a false and idealized image of America with regard to class and race relations.

6. Israel Zangwill's play *The Melting Pot: A Play in Four Acts*. New York: MacMillan, 1911 (c. 1909).

WORKS CITED

Alam, Fakrul. *Bharati Mukherjee*. Twayne's United States Authors Series No. 653. New York: Twayne, 1996.

Banerjee, Debjani. "'In the Presence of History': The Representation of Past and Present Indias in Bharati Mukherjee's Fiction." *Bharati Mukherjee: Critical Perspectives*. Ed. Emmanuel S. Nelson. New York: Garland, 1993. 161–180.

Bose, Brinda. "A Question of Identity: Where Gender, Race, and America Meet in Bharati Mukherjee." *Bharati Mukherjee: Critical Perspectives*. Ed. Emmanuel S. Nelson. New York: Garland, 1993. 47–63.

Dayal, Samir. "Creating, Preserving, Destroying: Violence in Bharati Mukherjee's *Jasmine*." *Bharati Mukherjee: Critical Perspectives*. Ed. Emmanuel S. Nelson. New York: Garland, 1993. 65–88.

Grewal, Gurleen. "Born Again American: The Immigrant Consciousness in *Jasmine.*" *Bharati Mukherjee: Critical Perspectives*. Ed. Emmanuel S. Nelson. New York: Garland, 1993. 181–196.

Kuwahara, Kuldip Kaur. "Bharati Mukherjee's *Jasmine.*" *Journal of American Studies of Turkey* 4 (1996): 31–35.

Liu, Eric. *The Accidental Asian: Notes of a Native Speaker*. New York: Random, 1998.

Mead, Margaret. *Culture and Commitment*. New York: Doubleday, 1970.

Mukherjee, Bharati. *The Middleman and Other Stories*. New York: Fawcett Crest, 1988.

———. *Jasmine*. Ontario: Viking Penguin, 1989.

Nelson, Emmanuel S., ed. *Bharati Mukherjee: Critical Perspectives*. New York: Garland, 1993.

Nye, David E. and Christen K. Thomsen, eds. *American Studies in Transition*. Odense, Den: Odense UP, 1985.

Roy, Anindyo. "The Aesthetics of an (Un)willing Immigrant: Bharati Mukherjee's *Days and Nights in Calcutta* and *Jasmine.*" *Bharati Mukherjee: Critical Perspectives*. Ed. Emmanuel S. Nelson. New York: Garland, 1993. 127–141.

Skardal, Dorothy. "Revising the American Literary Canon: The Case of Immigrant Literature." *American Studies in Transition*. Eds. Nye, David E. and Christen K. Thomsen. Odense, Den.: Odense UP, 1985.

5

Developing Negatives: Jamaica Kincaid's *Lucy*

Jacqueline Doyle

"I am not an artist," Lucy asserts, "but I shall always like to be with the people who stand apart" (98). A person who stands apart both in her native Antigua and her newfound New York City, Lucy cultivates distance as a way of seeing and as the basis of self-expression and self-exploration.[1] Repeatedly confronted by the cultural and historical assumptions of her liberal white employers in the United States, she seeks a way to assert her own experience and ground her own shifting identities—as an emigrant from an island still suffering the ravages of slavery and colonialism, as an immigrant to a country complicit in that history and its power relations, and, as a newly independent, self-possessed, "invented" self-in-progress (134).

When her employer Mariah insists that Lucy enjoy the spring daffodils despite their association with her oppressively British colonial schooling, Lucy starts and stumbles, at first cannot find the words for her alienation, cannot describe the complexity and difference of her political and historical situation. Every time she tries to talk about this, she becomes tongue-tied (29). Significantly, she achieves her voice in distance. When she moves away, she seems to get her voice back (30).[2]

Jamaica Kincaid's *Lucy* charts the nineteen-year-old's first year in New York, from bleak January to bleak January, from her new life as an immigrant *au pair* under Mariah and Lewis's roof, through the gradual collapse of their marriage, to Lucy's departure for an apartment with a girlfriend—where she has a bed and a roof over her head that are her own (144). She says the leave-taking from Lewis and Mariah, in some respects a set of surrogate parents, began when she heard of her father's death, and also when she made her final break with her mother, posting a last letter with a false return address (138, 140). Her mother had written her earlier about her father; the letter, marked "URGENT," joined the growing stack of unopened envelopes in Lucy's room.

From the moment she left home, Lucy aspired to disentangle herself temporally and spatially from history and place, to achieve what she calls her first real past, one that was her own and over which she had control (23). Early in her first spring in the United States, she describes her reaction to her mother's letters as a desire to put as much distance between herself and the events written about in her mother's letter as she could manage; with this separation from both her colonized mother and her motherland, she would be free to leave behind the mind-set of her mother's, her people's, and her nation's historical bondage. She would, in essence, be free to see the world as it is, not as a descendant of slaves and colonial subjects sees it (31).

Distance from homeland, history, her father, and above all from the mother she feels betrayed her propels Lucy forward, allows her to develop and give form to herself. Separation seems to suggest an art form to her, for the very day she ignores the "URGENT" letter from home, Lucy decides to buy a camera.

Indeed, Kincaid's slender chronicle of Lucy's year might be read as a variation both on the *Bildungsroman* and the *Künstlerroman*. Lucy arguably is an artist, who fashions and articulates her developing identity in her first-person narrative and perhaps in print, for she begins to write in a blank book at the close of the novel. Her photographs, and her aspirations for them, capture her way of seeing as well.[3] It is the unexpected perspective on the ordinary that fascinates her in the black-and-white museum prints she emulates, the reality behind the appearance, the clarity of the detached image. Lucy dwells on the pictures of her Caribbean home that do not make it into the glossy travel brochures, and the pictures of American home life that do not make it into the smiling family albums. Through distance and keen observation, she reverses the imperialist gaze and moves toward her own distinctive, postcolonial vision of the world and her place in it. The process of "inventing [her]self" parallels her developing of "negatives" in the darkroom; she says she did not have anything exactly in mind, but when the picture was complete she would know (134).

Lucy arrives at the airport on a "gray-black and cold night," disappointed that she's unable to "see anything clearly . . . even though there were lights everywhere" (3). She finds a picture-perfect family—blond-haired, nearly identical in her eyes—a husband, wife, and four daughters, whose Manhattan apartment is filled with artfully displayed family photographs and souvenirs from their foreign travels. Lucy sees the pictures as smiling out at the world, giving the impression that they found everything in it "unbearably wonderful." Each photo seemed to be a memento of places they had visited whose history they could relate from its beginnings (12–13).

In time, the pictures come to suggest an unexamined self-satisfaction in the family, and the construction of an appearance steadily being eroded by the reality of Lewis and Mariah's crumbling relationship. The collection of souvenirs suggests a similar complacency. Lewis and Mariah are at home wherever they go; they appropriate "things," tourists taking possession of each place they visit much as their earlier counterparts colonized these places. Like their colonial predecessors, they construct a history for each object, which revolves around themselves and the circumstances of acquisition—in their eyes, the beginning of that place or thing.[4]

This equation between tourist and colonist is underlined in Kincaid's *A Small Place,* published directly before *Lucy.* "You" the tourist in the first chapter becomes "you" the British colonist in the second: "You came. You took things that were not yours. . . . You murdered people. You imprisoned people. You robbed people" (35). As the early explorers and colonists brought "souvenirs"—human beings, along with exotic flora and fauna—back to the courts of Europe, the tourist takes home souvenirs, trinkets, picture postcards, and rolls of film to be developed. In *A Small Place,* Kincaid illuminates the dark background and missing scenery in these tourist snapshots. She opens her account by emphasizing vision: "If you go to Antigua as a tourist, this is what you will see" (3). The white North American or European vacationer sees constant sun, charmingly bad roads, beautiful beaches, sparkling blue water, comfortable hotels. Shifting from "you" to "we" and "I"—"we Antiguans, for I am one" (8)[5]—Kincaid produces a photographic negative of the visitor's picture: drought, beaches for tourists only, hotel sewage spewing into the ocean, and Antigua's hidden history—"the number of black slaves this ocean has swallowed up" (14), the oppression of the British, the disarray of Antigua after emancipation.

Lucy unfolds as a series of verbal snapshots of Lewis and Mariah and their liberal friends, Antigua's tourists viewed in their own habitat.[6] They all have names she associates with British colonials like Peters, Smith, Jones, and Richards, names that were easy to pronounce, and that, Lucy concludes, "made the world spin" (64). She finds they have all been to the islands—meaning the place where she was from—and they had fun there. Because of that, she decides not to like them (64–65). In Antigua, the tourists and resident North Americans are oblivious to the contempt of the natives for their manners, appearance, accents, prejudices, and ignorance (*A Small Place,* 17–18, 27). For the most part, Lewis and Mariah and their friends also remain completely unaware of Lucy's perspective on them. Mariah's best friend Dinah arouses Lucy's fury by saying what so many do: "So you are from the islands?" (57) Ignoring Lucy's history and origins, Dinah ignores the name of her birthplace and Lucy's own name as well. Lucy explains that to a person like Dinah, someone in her position is merely "the girl," the *au pair.* She believes it would never have occurred to Dinah that she had likewise sized her up and labeled her with certain stereotypes (58).

Even before she buys the camera, Lucy reverses the relation of tourist to native by turning her viewfinder on her employers. Mariah in particular becomes the focus of her scrutiny of this world, whose inhabitants fail to see both their own privileges and the contradictions in their political assumptions. Why is Mariah so proud of her self-named "Indian blood," which she announces to everyone as if in "possession of a trophy"? "How," Lucy asks, "do you get to be the sort of victor who claims to be the vanquished also?" (40–41). Lucy is amused to observe Mariah's efforts to preserve the farmlands around her summer house. Does Mariah see that the things she wants to conserve are the very same things that make her and her family's life so comfortable? (73). Does she examine her own complicity with what she opposes—the relation between Lewis's conferring with his stockbroker about investments and corporations that threaten the world's natural resources? (73). Mariah has politically correct objections to fairy tales for her daughters (45), but she herself seems to live a fairy tale, for she has never doubted (26), and she expects they will live happily ever after.

Lucy sees aspects of Mariah's world and marriage that Mariah is comfortably blind to (14). In the dining car on the train Lucy sees black and white where Mariah sees nothing: Mariah doesn't seem to notice what she has in common with other diners, or what Lucy has in common with the waiters (32). Yet even this appearance is deceptive, for the dignified black waiters are in reality quite different from the people back home; Lucy concludes that they are not at all like her relatives, even if they look like them (32).

Long before Mariah acknowledges the problems in her marriage, or discovers that Lewis is having an affair with Dinah, Lucy sees it. The parallel scenes take the form of paired snapshots. First she sees Lewis in the kitchen licking Mariah's neck as she leans back in ecstasy, as though they were putting on a show for each other (47). Then she sees Lewis in the living room licking Dinah's neck—not a show, according to Lucy, but something real (79). The shelves of photograph albums chronicling the history of Lewis and Mariah's meeting, their marriage, their happy family life, their vacations, their birthday parties and holidays suddenly become an artfully constructed appearance masking the reality of this missing image. Lucy sees irony in that this was a picture that no one would ever take and one that would never end up in one of those photo albums, but was a "significant picture all the same" (80). When Lucy later begins her experiments with photography, she pursues the reality behind appearances, the ordinary illuminated by truth. Walking in on Lewis and Mariah just after a fight, she impulsively snaps a photo for a reason that she cannot fathom. "I said, 'Say "cheese"' and took a picture. Lewis said, 'Jesus Christ,' and . . . left" (118).

Lucy's own photographs, tacked up on the walls of her room, embody what Susan Sontag terms a "new visual code" or "ethics of seeing" (3). The shots are casual, tentative, her subjects ordinary, such as people walking on the street or some of the things she had acquired in America, the children, and Mariah. Her interiors reflect everyday clutter, not the formality of carefully cleared surfaces. So she exposes to public view what is usually unseen, as in her picture of a dresser top with her dirty panties and lipstick, an unused sanitary napkin, and an open pocketbook (121). Her playful image of the children, too, reverses the smiling faces of the photo albums. She shows their bottoms facing the camera—their mooning her a sign of their disgust when she requests more smiles for the photos she is taking.

Sontag observes that photography is less often practiced as an art than as "a social rite, a defense against anxiety, and a tool of power" (7). Lucy's photography arguably functions in all of these ways. Her picture taking becomes a "social rite" and "defense against anxiety" that allows her to fix her own impressions of a reality that Lewis and Mariah would define differently. Seeking to leave her past behind and start a new history, she begins a visual chronicle, deciding what is worth looking at and what she has a right to observe. Her photography is also an art form, for she labors for hours in the darkroom, where she tries to make a print that exaggerates the beauty of the thing she thinks she has seen (160). Her art form is intimately connected to power relations. No longer the seen, Lucy seeks to reverse the imperial gaze. Her employer has been raised to believe that her vision is universal. Lucy believed that Mariah wanted both the children and her to see things the way she did. Now Lucy will discover and capture what *she* sees.

In *The Rhetoric of Empire*, David Spurr outlines twelve rhetorical strategies characteristic of colonial discourses over the centuries and around the globe. Lucy neatly reverses most of them, most prominently "aestheticization," "surveillance," "appropriation," and "negation."

"Aestheticization" or what Spurr subtitles "Savage Beauties": When Mariah helpfully sends Lucy off to a Paul Gaugin exhibit at the museum, it is the artist whom Lucy identifies with, not the "savage beauties" in their tropical settings.[7] Lucy explains that she is not sure Mariah meant her to, but she immediately identifies with Gaugin's yearnings (95). Probably Mariah did not intend this identification, but saw bright colors, exotic tropical foliage, and brown-skinned "island" girls "just like" her Antiguan *au pair*. When Mariah's friends ask politely if Lucy is from "the islands," she wishes she could ask indignantly which islands specifically they mean. The Hawaiian Islands or perhaps the islands that are part of Indonesia (56)? Yet even while identifying with the artistic subject rather than generalized, interchangeable artistic objects, Lucy herself sees obvious contrasts between this white man at the center of European culture, his history chronicled in books, and herself, a young woman from a small place in the world working as a servant. Gaugin fled to a tropical island to realize his artistic vision. Lucy reverses this movement from center to margin: she has fled a tropical island to cultivate a private artistic vision. Yet to the degree that she claims the role of the artist, the one "who stand[s] apart" (98), she makes her own vision behind the camera central, while those she views are aestheticized as "other."

"Surveillance" or "Under Western Eyes": Taking on the "privilege of inspecting, of examining, of looking at," Lucy usurps the Western eye and reverses colonial power relations (Spurr 13). She openly stares at Lewis and Mariah and the children as they eat (13). She observes their friends, their parties, their possessions, their appearances as a family, negating in her mind the happy family they appear on the surface to be. She walks the city streets trying to observe everything. It is no longer the gaze of the colonist or of the tourist that selects, frames, and defines the native and her setting. Instead the tourists and their setting are under Lucy's surveillance.

"Appropriation" or "Inheriting the Earth": From the beginning Lucy objects to Mariah's casual assumption of ownership of the people and things around her. She is offended by the way Mariah talks to Gus, the family retainer at their summer home. She wants to ask him if he hates the way Mariah says his name, as if she owns him (34). She's not sure if she hears Mariah correctly when she says "minions" ("a word like that would haunt someone like me"), but the *mys* that define Mariah's world view and complacent sense of inheritance are unmistakable. Mariah says things such as "Gus and I went out in *my* old boat," or "*my* very, very old boat" or "*my* fish" (37, italics added). Although she comes to appreciate Mariah's good qualities, she begins to feel like a dog on a leash in her home (110). Later, Lucy resolves to leave her lover Paul, not because he may be seeing her roommate Peggy, but because he seems to think he "possesses" her (155). Lucy, who comes from a people descended from slaves, values self-possession and a life of her own over happiness (110), and concludes near the end of the book that being alone and independent was in itself an accomplishment. Being happy would seem to be too much to ask for (161).

"Negation" or "Areas of Darkness": If the colonial powers conceived of unexplored territories as "negative spaces," vast blanks ready to be filled by the colonial imagination (Spurr 92–93), Lucy embraces erasure, darkness, and the negative as part of her developing identity. Decolonizing the self entails resistance to colonial discourse and awareness of what it obscures. At age fourteen, Lucy refused to sing "Rule, Britannia! Britannia, rule the waves; Britons never, never shall be slaves," for it was clear to her even then that she was not a Briton and that until not too long ago, she would have been a slave (135). If Britons erased native cultures, now she vows to erase from her mind every word of the Wordsworth poem about daffodils she was compelled to memorize (18). Refusing to identify with the values of the colonizer, Lucy reverses British cultural terms, identifying with the dark Lucifer in *Paradise Lost,* for example, and other "stories of the fallen" (153).[8] She is pleased to see that Mariah's daughter uses bad words (13), and finds power in negation. By defining herself and the person she wants to be as the negative of Mariah, Lucy gains strength and identity. Mariah is one of the "blessed" ones with no "blemish" or "mark" anywhere; Lucy, however, associates a mark with genuine living and is certain she will end up with a mark (27, 25). Mariah smells "pleasant," but her fragrance is "just that—pleasant." Lucy aspires to be powerful, not pleasant; she knew even then she wanted to emit a powerful odor, even if it was offensive to others (27).

Colonial negation, Spurr argues, involves the power to erase the past and replace it with a new past defined by the colonizer: "The discourse of negation denies history as well as place, constituting the past as absence, but also designating that absence as a negative presence: a people without history is one which exists only in a negative sense; like the bare earth, they can be transformed by history, but they cannot make history their own" (Spurr 98). In *A Small Place* and *Lucy,* Kincaid reverses this negation on political and personal levels. She complains of the effect of British schools and libraries in Antigua, repositories of British books, British culture, and British ideas: "in both of these places you distorted or erased my history and glorified your own" (*A Small Place* 36). Lucy seeks to make history her own by establishing a personal life not controlled by her mother, and beginning her own clean slate in America, where everything she sees won't resonate with hundreds of years of historical association (31). At the end of her first winter in the United States, she looks back at the past over which she had felt in control (23). By the following January, when she again begins a new life, with a new job and new apartment, she has accumulated not only a new past of her own but things of her own: new clothes, books, a camera, and prints of the photographs she had taken, prints she had made herself (143).

The negations involved in Lucy's new independence are complex and recipro-cal. She defines herself as the negative of Mariah and her world, but also as the negative of her mother and her motherland. One of Lucy's photographs in particu-lar reflects this double displacement. Presumably it is one of her earliest, for she takes it during her first summer, with a camera belonging to her first American lover. What she sees in the picture is a void: a lake where she had spent the summer with no signs of life—no boats, no people, nothing except water that was dark and treacherous and inviting (149).

The scene exhibits all the blankness, darkness, and negation that Spurr delin-eates in the colonial vision of landscape; Lucy, it would appear, has turned the imperial gaze back on its own setting to create a blank space for her own self-development.

However, as she continues to reflect on the image, it becomes more compli-cated, for she defines the lake in opposition to the water of her childhood, which, in turn, she had "cursed." She saw it as the opposite of the water on her island home which "was three shades of blue" and invitingly calm and warm. She cursed it because it was something she had taken for granted (148).

Embracing the negative—the cold, the "dark," the "uninviting"—in this for-eign body of water, Lucy leaves the "calm, inviting, warm" waters of her child-hood behind to explore "treacherous" but perhaps exhilarating new territory. Moira Ferguson suggests that water throughout Kincaid's fiction "cleanses, fertilizes . . . and opens up new radical possibilities" (255). As a mirroring or re-verse image of Antiguan waters, Lucy's lake bears traces of past associations. However, the purity of the image and its negations (a picture of "nothing"—"no boats," "no people," "no signs of life") clearly nourish her imagination.

Lucy lies in bed on a Sunday morning in her new apartment, meditating first on this photograph on the wall, then on the official documents spelling out her iden-tity, then on her name, on her face in the mirror, and finally on the view from the front window (148–53). Each might be said to function as the "place of indetermi-nacy" that Ferguson describes. The photograph of the lake purifies, renews, clears a space for new life. For Ferguson, Kincaid's recurrent images of water signify a "return to amniotic fluid and new beginnings" (255). Lucy calls the lake a "body of water," hinting perhaps at new birth—or at the possibility of new birth to come, for now there are "no signs of life" visible in the picture beyond the movements of the waves.

Her passport, her immigration card, her work visa, birth certificate, and lease "showed everything" about her and "yet they showed nothing," nothing of conse-quence but her name, which perhaps shows too much. "Everything" and "nothing," her name, as she conceives it, contains both painful past associations and what Ferguson terms "new radical possibilities," a negative space for dissent and self-invention. Lucy Josephine Potter: she used to hate all three of those names, Lucy because it seemed "slight, without substance," Josephine because her uncle Mr. Joseph failed to pass on his rumored, but false sugar plantation riches, Potter because it probably came from the Englishman slave owner of her ancestors (149). Later she comes to "embrace" the name Lucy, which she associates, by way of her mother, with the fallen Lucifer, and thus with power and self-knowledge. She undergoes a change from feeling "burdened and old and tired to feeling light, new, clean. . . . It was the moment I knew who I was" (152).

The gaze she turns on herself and her surroundings is distant, critical, and also open to knowledge and experience. Hugging herself in the cold, Lucy looks at her negative or mirror image in the bathroom. She notices that at twenty, she has not even a little bit of innocence left on her face. She concludes that if life were cold and hard, it would not surprise her (153). From her front window, she sees only a few people, no trees, a gray winter scene where everything looks unreal, which makes her feel she will "never be part of it," a sense of distance intensified rather than diminished when her Irish immigrant roommate joins her. Lucy questions whether her roommate is seeing the same things as they look out on the same view and concludes, "probably not" (154).

Despite her self-scrutiny, Lucy does not produce a photographic self-portrait. Among the many black-and-white photographs tacked to her bedroom walls at Mariah's, she tells us she had no photographs of herself (120). She studies her image carefully, however, and finds that much has changed since she left Antigua, even though her image in the mirror is the same. Her familiar self has been replaced by someone she doesn't know very well (133).

This erasure remains part of the figurative picture she painstakingly develops. As in her photographs, she seeks hidden truths about herself, the reality behind the appearance. From the beginning of her narrative, that first night when she "could not see anything clearly" (3), Lucy tries to bring herself and her new world into focus. She at first envisions her future as "a gray blank," then as "a large gray patch surrounded by black, blacker, blackest" (6). Adapting to the cold, pale light of New York, she achieves images of great clarity, but remains unsatisfied with her vision. In the darkroom, she tries and tries to make a print that makes things she saw more beautiful than the thing she thinks she has seen, so that they will reveal to her the unseen, but she doesn't succeed (160). Unsure what picture of herself will emerge, "not hav[ing] anything exactly in mind," Lucy is nevertheless sure that "when the picture was complete I would know" (134).

She sums up her year's development clearly. She is now living a life she had always wanted to live. She is living apart from her family in a place where no one knows much about her and is free more or less to come and go as she pleases (158). She has achieved separation and freedom, but not happiness, "the feeling of longing fulfilled that I had thought would come with this situation" (158). Her future is no longer "gray" or "black," but is figured instead as a series of empty white pages. Mariah's gift of a leather-bound book is prompted by Lucy's comment that her "life stretched out ahead of [her] like a book of blank pages" (163). At the close of her narrative, Lucy takes up her "fountain pen full of beautiful blue ink" and opens the blank "blood red" book, its pages "white and smooth like milk" (162). She writes her full name at the top of the page: Lucy Josephine Potter. When she looks at it, among her many thoughts, she chooses to write down only this one: "I wish I could love someone so much that I would die from it." Looking at these words, she feels a great wave of shame and begins to weep so that the words become "one great big blur" (263–64).

As in many novels of artistic development, the beginning of the book Lucy writes is simultaneously the end of the narrative charting her progress to that point. However, for a *Bildungsroman* or novel of development, her assertion of self seems oddly blurred and incomplete. As a *Künstlerroman* tracing the development of an artist, be it photographer or writer, the narrative seems similarly incomplete. *Lucy* closes in a visual blur and apparent act of erasure.

Lucy remains in the state of "in-betweenness" that Homi Bhabha describes as the postmodern condition. Bhabha envisions such border territories peopled by migrants, refugees, exiles, the colonized as a "space of intervention": "These 'in-between' spaces provide the terrain for elaborating strategies of selfhood—singular or communal—that initiate new signs of identity, and innovative sites of collaboration, and contestation, in the act of defining the idea of society itself" (9, 1–2).

In *Lucy,* Kincaid traces a negatively impelled *Bildung* to define a radically provisional selfhood. Indeed, what propels Lucy from her homeland is the denial of *Bildung* in a society where she desired only to "erase from [her] mind, line by line" all traces of colonial culture, and where she desired more than a female could aspire to. Her hatred of her mother was born with her mother's dreams for her sons—that they would journey to England and study to become doctors or lawyers or "influential" in some way. These dreams are tainted both by colonial power relations and gender relations, a double denial of Lucy's future. She believes her father did not know her at all, and that therefore she would not expect him to imagine a life of excitement and triumph for her. But since her mother did know her well, she should have had expectations for her (130). Faced with her mother's betrayal, Lucy secretly names her "Mrs. Judas" and begins to plan a separation from her mother even though she suspects she will never complete the schism (130–31).

"Lucy Potter Richardson," written in her book, would call up all the hateful past associations of her name, the history of Antigua and her family, the power and shame she feels as Lucy/Lucifer in rebellion against her mother, motherland, and colonial "mother" country (see Ferguson interview 176–77). Her separation, as she long ago suspected, is not complete. The associations of blood, milk, and tears with this book from her surrogate mother, Mariah, suggest a connection with her birth mother as well.[9] The line she writes about wishing she could love someone so much that she would die from it resonates with her unresolved love-hate bond to her mother. Earlier she says of their relationship, that for ten of her twenty years, half of her life, she had been mourning the end of a love affair, that her feelings for her mother were perhaps the only true love in her life (131).

A number of recent critics have suggested radical transformations of the *Bildungsroman* and *Künstlerroman* among contemporary women writers.[10] Whereas the male hero embarks on a journey of separation and self-definition, the development of the female hero exhibits a more complex interplay of separation and attachment, particularly to her mother. Rachel Blau DuPlessis suggests a remothering in the female *Künstlerroman,* one strategy for "writing beyond the ending" of "social scripts" and plots confining women.[11] "To compose a work is to negotiate with these questions," DuPlessis writes: "What stories can be told? How can plots be resolved? What is felt to be narratable by both literary and social conventions?" (3) In the twentieth-century female *Künstlerroman,* the maternal muse and reparenting motifs (here, Lucy's mother and surrogate parents, Mariah and Lewis) undermine and displace socially sanctioned "narratives of heterosexual love and romantic thralldom" (94). Resistance to "thralldom" takes on added significance and resonance in postcolonial women's writing. Trinh T. Minh-ha, among others, stresses the urgency of "unlearning" the dominant languages and forms imposed by invading colonial powers in the name of "civilization": "tie/untie, read/unread, discard their forms . . . shake syntax, smash the myths" (148, 20). If dominant narrative patterns not only define what is socially possible for male and female characters, they also establish what is impossible for the "native," male or female. Subversion of these forms by self-described "guerrilla writers" such as Kincaid is to be expected (Muirhead 45).[12] New stories demand new ways of telling and new resolutions. Joanne S. Frye suggests that the strength of the "female growing-up novel" lies in its dismantling of cultural assumptions of gendered identity and "its ability to subvert narrative teleology, to resist and redefine the power of the conclusion toward which a narrative moves" (Frye 110).

"Certain things were expected" of Lucy and her future in Antigua, above all "obedience to the law and that she follow convention" (133). Kincaid's novel, like Lucy herself, moves beyond inherited assumptions, narrative expectations, and constricting forms to establish a site of indeterminacy and freedom, the "great big blur" from which new forms may emerge. Kincaid herself in an interview claims such hybrid territory as her own. She was brought up to believe that English traditions were right and hers were wrong, that the life of an English person and his or her culture was characterized by clarity. Her life and her culture, however, were full of ambiguity. For example, in England when a person was dead, he was dead, but where she came from, a dead person might not be dead. She was taught to think that the ambiguity of her culture was illicit, not the rational stuff of Western civilization. As a result of this colonial illogic, she developed a unique perspective on its effect on her writing: "The thing that I am branded with and thing that I am denounced for, I now claim as my own. I am illegitimate, I am ambiguous" (Bonetti 29–30).

Kincaid now claims the right to both ambiguity and clarity. Lucy claims both as well, achieving the "mark" she desires in the process of development and self-invention, a mark signifying "the beginning of living, real living," on her own premises (25).

NOTES

1. Neither Antigua nor New York City are named in the novel. Kincaid said in an interview: "It is New York, but it could be anywhere. I didn't want to specify because I didn't want any preconceptions about the place. She doesn't even name the island she comes from" (Perry 508). The locations are named here for ease of reference, and because they can be indirectly induced from the text.

2. See Helen Tiffin for a useful discussion of recitation, colonial repression, and the postcolonial "tongue." Tiffin points out that "the gap between the lived colonial or post-colonial experience and the imported/imposed world of the Anglo-written has often been referred to by Commonwealth post-colonial writers and critics as 'the daffodil gap'" (920n7).

3. In interviews with Selwyn Cudjoe and others, Kincaid mentions that she herself studied photography at the New York School for Social Research (215). Her discussion with Cudjoe of light and truth might almost be a photographer's aesthetic. The blinding light of Antigua, illuminating but also "hellish," influenced her early "obsession" with the idea of one truth: "I think that at some point I became obsessed with things being not that unclear, that things could not just vanish, that there could be some light that would show the reality of a thing, that this was false and this was right" (231).

4. Susan Sontag suggests that the family photographs and tourist photographs both give people the illusion of possessing a "past that is unreal" (8). The family constructs "a portrait-chronicle of itself—a portable kit of images that bears witness to its connectedness," and the tourist converts "experience into an image, a souvenir" (8).

5. Kincaid writes from somewhere between the "I" of Antigua and the "you" of North America. Although she explains that she is "incapable of the consciousness of the tourist," she also cannot "claim" to be in "the position of the natives." It is her very in-betweenness that releases her voice. "If I had stayed in Antigua," she explains, "if I had stayed the native, I believe I would not have been able to write" (Muirhead 40).

6. In an interview with Moira Ferguson, Kincaid described the intimate relation between her photography and her first writing. At a time when she thought she would become a photographer, she used to write down everything about a photograph before taking it, including what she wanted it to feel like. Then referring to these notes, she would snap the picture (163).

7. Kincaid has described her own reactions to Gaugin by saying that she doesn't find it easy to say that she identifies with him, but that when she read one of his journals *The Intimate Journal of Paul Gaugin*, she "found it a great comfort" because Gaugin was very selfish and very determined and he wasn't afraid to use "someone's negative view of his work. He wore it as a badge. I rather admire that" (Vorda 103). Elsewhere she calls Gaugin's *Journal* "inspiring" and a "recent influence." "You know he's another dissenter rebel" (Muirhead 47).

8. Allan Vorda asked Kincaid whether she would "apply Lucifer's comment from *Paradise Lost* that it's 'Better to reign in Hell, than serve in Heav'n' to Antigua's colonial situation." She answered, "Yes, . . . It's better to be dead than live like this. It's better to risk dying than to live as a slave" (94).

9. Ferguson points out that the red, white, and blue of the book, its pages, and ink

"enables her to reverse the colonial project since the notebook visually signs patriotism in its red, white and blue composition" ("Lucy and the Mark" 254). Lucy's independence parallels the partial independence of Antigua in 1967. Oczkowicz even suggests that the attraction of the United States for Lucy is that it is a "former colony" where "she has an opportunity to create a personal space in which she can choose how to exist" (145).

   10. See Rachel Blau DuPlessis, Suzanne Jones, Joanne Frye; on the *Bildungsroman* and Kincaid's *Annie John,* see Louis F. Caton and Donna Perry.

   11. It is interesting that the two "ends" DuPlessis defines for the female character in the nineteenth-century novel are marriage and death. Lucy's longing to "love someone so much that I would die for it," might in this respect be seen as a longing for the impossible narrative closure of the traditional novel. Looking back at *Lucy,* Kincaid has suggested that her character has a view of the world shaped by nineteenth-century thought as interpreted by colonial educators in the Caribbean. She is very moral and very judgmental (Vorda 100).

   12. Elsewhere she elaborates on her sabotage of literary traditions by noting that whatever a short story or a novel is, "I'm not it." She is interested in breaking the forms, and not to do so, she claims, would obstruct her writing (Bonetti 28). "The whole point of the existence of someone like me is I'm not an English [literary] person," Kincaid explains in her interview with Ferguson, "so I don't really care. When people think of falling standards, they must be thinking of people like me who just sort of usurp all the boundaries and just mix them up and just cross borders all the time" (166).

WORKS CITED

Bhabha, Homi K. "Introduction: Locations of Culture." *The Location of Culture.* London: Routledge, 1994.

Bonetti, Kay. "An Interview with Jamaica Kincaid." *Missouri Review* 15.2 (1992): 124–42., 1997.

Caton, Louis F. "Romantic Struggles: The *Bildungsroman* and Mother-Daughter Bonding in Jamaica Kincaid's *Annie John." MELUS* 21.3 (1996): 125–42.

Cudjoe, Selwyn R. "Jamaica Kincaid and the Modernist Project: An Interview." *Caribbean Women Writers: Essays from the First International Conference.* Ed. Selwyn R. Cudjoe. Wellesley: Calaloux, 1990. 215–32.

DuPlessis, Rachel Blau. *Writing Beyond the Ending: Narrative Strategies of Twentieth-Century Women Writers.* Bloomington: Indiana UP, 1985.

Ferguson, Moira. "A Lot of Memory: An Interview with Jamaica Kincaid." *Kenyon Review* 16.1 (1994): 163–88.

———. *"Lucy* and the Mark of the Colonizer." *Modern Fiction Studies* 39.2 (1993): 237–59.

Frye, Joanne S. *Living Stories, Telling Lives: Women and the Novel in Contemporary Experience.* Ann Arbor: U of Michigan P, 1986.

Jones, Suzanne W., ed. *Writing the Woman Artist: Essays on Poetics, Politics, and Portraiture.* Philadelphia: U of Pennsylvania P, 1991.

———. *Lucy.* New York: Penguin, 1990.

Kincaid, Jamaica. *A Small Place.* New York: Penguin, 1988.

Muirhead, Pamela Buchanan. "An Interview with Jamaica Kincaid." *Clockwatch Review* 9.1–2 (1994–5): 39–48.

Oczkowicz, Edyta. "Jamaica Kincaid's *Lucy:* Cultural 'Translation' As a Case of Creative Exploration of the Past." *MELUS* 21.3 (1996): 143–57.

Perry, Donna. "Initiation in Jamaica Kincaid's *Annie John.*" *Caribbean Women Writers: Essays from the First International Conference.* Ed. Selwyn R. Cudjoe. Wellesley: Calaloux, 1990. 245–53.

————. "An Interview with Jamaica Kincaid." *Reading Black, Reading Feminist: A Critical Anthology.* Ed. Henry Louis Gates, Jr. New York: Penguin, 1990. 492–509.

Sontag, Susan. *On Photography.* New York: Farrar, 1977.

Spurr, David. *The Rhetoric of Empire: Colonial Discourse in Journalism, Travel Writing, and Imperial Administration.* Durham: Duke UP, 1993.

Tiffin, Helen. "Cold Hearts and (Foreign) Tongues: Recitation and the Reclamation of the Female Body in the Works of Erna Brodber and Jamaica Kincaid." *Callaloo* 16.3 (1993): 909–21.

Trin T. Minh-ha. *Woman, Native, Other: Writing Postcoloniality and Feminism.* Bloomington: Indiana UP, 1989.

Vorda, Allan. "I Come from a Place That's Very Unreal: An Interview with Jamaica Kincaid." *Face to Face: Interviews with Contemporary Novelists.* Ed. Allan Vorda. Houston: Rice UP, 1993.

6

Speaking and Listening: The Immigrant as Spy Who Comes in from the Cold

June Dwyer

> How does one stop reading the exterior signs of a foreign tribe and step into the inwardness, the viscera of their meanings? Every anthropologist understands the difficulty of such a feat; and so does every immigrant.
>
> —Eva Hoffman
> *Lost in Translation* (209)

> What did I know? I didn't speak English very well, and like anyone who doesn't I mostly listened.
>
> —Chang-rae Lee
> *Native Speaker* (195)

The inability to speak English in the United States is viewed by many members of the monolingual populace not as an obstacle that an immigrant must overcome, but as a downright fault. Senator Harry Byrd, complaining about the flood of immigrants in 1992, told his colleagues: "I pick up the telephone and call the local garage. . . . I can't understand the person on the other side of the line. I'm not sure he can understand me. They're all over the place, and they don't speak English. Do we want more of this?" (Sontag, "Calls to Restrict Immigration" E5). Byrd's indignation seems to suggest that his mechanic's inability to speak English is tantamount to his not having any linguistic ability, and further that he lacks the desire to learn English. This is simply not true. The number of English classes offered around the country is woefully inadequate to meet the demand. Slots in the Riverside Church English classes in New York City are determined by lottery, with ten times as many applicants as there are spaces. Says one spokesperson from the city's Community Development Agency, "There's not a single English-language program in the city that isn't inundated, and waiting lists go into years, not months" (Sontag, "English as a Precious Language" 34). Immigrants want to learn English because they know their chances of more than modest success in this country are virtually nil without it.

But the practical element constitutes only part of the immigrant desire to master English. The other component is psychological; not to speak English is to be ignored. As Eva Hoffman observes in *Lost in Translation*, "because I'm not heard, I feel I'm not seen" (147). The fact that silence is tantamount to invisibility both disturbs and undermines the confidence of the immigrant. Henry Park, the protagonist of Chang-rae Lee's novel *Native Speaker*, observes that this virtual invisibility on the part of immigrants, because it is nonthreatening, causes established Americans generally to discount them: "[I]f I just kept speaking the language of our work the customers didn't seem to see me. I wasn't there. They didn't look at me. I was a comely shadow who didn't threaten them. I could even catch a rich old woman . . . whispering to her friend right behind me, 'Oriental Jews'" (53). Established Americans are quite comfortable with such an arrangement. They want an immigrant who is able to understand, but who will not speak up or speak out; they want a "comely shadow" to serve them at the grocery or the garage, but not bother them. What the rich old lady and the rest of established America do not understand is the power in the immigrant's silence. Immigrants who are not brought into the American conversation instead watch and listen, picking up valuable, and sometimes damaging, information. To consider them "comely shadows" is to underestimate them and overvalue ourselves.

In *Native Speaker* the Korean-American protagonist Henry Park has a strikingly unusual, but altogether appropriate job for an immigrant. He works for a Westchester County-based private spying agency called Glimmer & Company, an organization that numbers among its clients foreign governments, domestic agencies, and powerful private companies. Uniquely fitted for such a career by dint of his second-generation American status and his Asian cultural heritage of reticence and self-control, Henry initially is "thrilled" when he is recruited right after college to do this work. Feeling a "bizarre sanction" for the "secret living" (175) he has known throughout his life as the child of an immigrant family, he is able to gain power without exposure to the ridicule experienced by immigrants in more public positions.

In *Native Speaker*, readers must confront a totally new vision of the marginalized immigrant. Alongside the childlike waifs of Emma Lazarus's poem at the base of the Statue of Liberty and the awkward yet spunky greenhorns of so many other novels, we must now factor in the vision of the immigrant as domestic spy. Although Henry is literally a spy, his work metaphorically adds a new level to our understanding of what immigrants do for their adopted country. Specifically, they find out and tell us things about ourselves that we would rather not have known. Henry says as much, near the end of the book. He begins by wondering whether his father would have approved of the work he has done:

If anything, I think my father would choose to see my deceptions in a rigidly practical light, as if they were similar to that daily survival he came to endure [as an owner of a number of small grocery stores], the need to adapt, assume an advantageous shape.

My ugly immigrant truth, as was his, is that I have exploited my own, and those others who can be exploited. This forever is my burden to bear. But I and my kind possess another dimension. We will learn every lesson of accent and idiom, we will dismantle every last pretense and practice you hold, noble as well as ruinous. You can keep nothing safe from our eyes and ears. This is your own history. (319–20)

Henry's tale of adaptation, deception, and exploitation is not just American immigrant history, but American history itself—"your own history" as Henry tells his readers. Being outsiders, immigrants are in a special position to observe and reflect. Seeing so much, they may pick and choose what to emphasize, and so they wield great, if hidden, power in the society. Some of it is helpful; some of it is dangerous; some of it is self-destructive.

The amoral nature of the immigrant's power is embodied in Henry's boss Dennis Hoagland, a second-generation Irish-American. Totally devoid of what we like to valorize as immigrant idealism and optimism, Dennis articulates another philosophic strain, a hard-boiled immigrant realism. As he tells Henry:

There's no real evil in the world. It's just the world. Full of people like us. Your immigrant mother and father taught you that, I hope. Mine did. My pop owned three swell pubs but he still died broke and drunk. The Jews squeezed him first, then the wops, then people like you. Am I sore? No way. It doesn't matter how much you have. You can own every fucking Laundromat and falafel cart in New York, but someone is always bigger than you. If they want, they'll shut you up. They'll bring you down. (46)

Although part of him knows that Dennis has a point, Henry is unable to maintain such cynicism, and the book traces his movement from outsider/spy to willing participant in the American family with all its attendant sadness and hope. When Henry's friend and co-worker Jack Kalantzakos calls their spying organization a "family," although a "sad excuse for one," Henry corrects him: "It's an orphanage, Jack. . . . And there's a Fagin" (292). Glimmer is an enterprise of questionable integrity, and its leader is no father figure.

Fortunately, in his growing disenchantment with living like an "orphan," Henry finds solace in two genuine families: one personal, the other political. And although both are troubled with grave difficulties, he chooses to invest his devotion and his future in them. His immediate family—his wife, Lelia, and young son, Mitt—initially seem to embody the American Dream and the validity of the idea of the melting pot. Lelia, a red-haired, open-minded speech therapist of Scottish ancestry, represents all that the dominant group is supposed to be in America. She bears no prejudice against newer ethnic groups that have come to this country— indeed, she falls in love with Henry, marries him, and has a child with him. Lelia's vocation is to help people fit in by teaching them to speak English easily. She welcomes and respects newcomers and, by dint of her attitudes and line of work, speeds their acculturation.

Mitt, whom Henry first worries will look too much like an Asian and so experience prejudice, is a splendid mix, an articulate and self-assured little boy. During the first summer that he spends at his Korean grandfather's house in Westchester County, Mitt is subjected to some unkind name-calling on the part of the neighborhood kids, but by the following summer, they are all great friends. Yet at his birthday party that second summer, he is accidentally smothered by these same friends when they are making a "dog pile" of bodies and Mitt finds himself on the bottom. Mitt's death is truly an accident—the kids were only playing. But symbolically, such an event warns that the American melting pot is not a viable concept. Mitt's life, so well-adjusted and such a seemingly healthy mix of old and new America, is unwittingly snuffed out by overly boisterous members of the established group.

Henry's dreams for Mitt were born of the melting pot ideology. He had wished his son to grow up, not confused by two cultures but rather "with a singular sense of his world, a life univocal, which might have offered him the authority and confidence that his broad half-yellow face could not. Of course, this is assimilist sentiment, part of my own ugly and half-blind romance with the land" (267). Henry understands, even before Mitt's death, that his "assimilist sentiment" is both romantic and ugly—romantic because assimilation is never smooth, and ugly because it entails the betrayal of his past and his roots.

When he is assigned to gather information on a Korean-American politician named John Kwang, Henry finds that he must confront both the romance and the ugliness of his assimilist notions. In doing so, he is introduced to another family—a political family of many different immigrant groups—and a more multicultural notion of American-ness. Although he is supposed to be spying on Kwang for an unknown "client," Henry instead finds himself drawn to him because Kwang's life choices as an immigrant have been so atypical. Unlike the average immigrant who stays in private life and thinks small, Kwang has an expansive, truly American vision: he has gone into politics and aspires to become mayor of New York. He wants to help more than just himself; he wants to help the entire immigrant community. Kwang seems to be able to handle his dual identity, appearing, as Henry observes, "effortlessly Korean, effortlessly American" (328). Without forgetting his mother tongue, Kwang has mastered the many cadences of the English spoken in America. At one point, Henry admiringly describes him:

He was how I imagined a Korean would be, at least one living in any renown. He would stride the daises and the stages with his voice strong and clear, unafraid to speak the language like a Puritan and like a Chinaman and like every boat person in between. I found him most moving and beautiful in those moments. And whenever I hear the strains of a different English, I will still shatter a little inside. Within every echo from a city storefront or window, I can hear the old laments of my mother and father, and mine as a confused schoolboy. . . . They speak to me, as John Kwang could always, not simply in new accents or notes but in the ancient untold music of a newcomer's heart, sonorous with longing and hope. (304)

Kwang's relationship to the language and his polyvocality represent an alternative to Henry's assimilist dreams for Mitt. Kwang proceeds on the assumption that he may create a multiethnic "family" of all the immigrants in Queens. He bonds them to him emotionally and politically by the formation of a Korean money club—a *ggeh*. Although such clubs operate informally all over the Korean community—Henry's father belongs to one when he first arrives—Kwang's is transethnic and on a much grander scale. Since it operates like a bank, but is not regulated, such an organization is illegal. Kwang, however, has no desire to profit from it, except by gaining political loyalty from its members.

Unfortunately, Henry's political family, like his private one, suffers the loss of its center. John Kwang's career falls apart through "events both arbitrary and conceived" (141). Using a Korean concept of the money club to help other immigrants is only part of what destroys John Kwang's career. Kwang's easy Americanization plays a role as well. Although he appears to Henry as "such a natural American, first thing and last" (326), Kwang has taken too much advantage of the power and freedom that America offers, cutting corners and indulging himself personally. Not only is the *ggeh* illegal, so are many of its immigrant members. Kwang himself, notwithstanding his profession of loyalty to the concept of family and to his own family, is not above spending time with other women. And finally, he feels great affection for one of his staffers, a Dominican named Eduardo Fermin, but when he finds that Eduardo is "disloyal" and giving information about his doings to the outside world, Kwang betrays him to a Korean gang. The gang kills Eduardo by bombing Kwang headquarters late at night. The ensuing uproar and revelations about the money club, the illegals, and Kwang's private life effectively end his political career. Kwang has been too optimistic about his ability to make a difference in America. Unlike Dennis Hoagland, he never subscribes to the hard-edged dictum that in this country, "someone is always bigger than you. If they want, they'll shut you up. They'll bring you down" (46). And so he is brought down.

Kwang's downfall immediately turns him into a "foreigner" whose home is picketed by whites carrying signs saying "AMERICA FOR AMERICANS" and chanting that they want to kick every last one of the illegals "back to where they came from . . . let them drown in the ocean with 'Smuggler Kwang'" (331). Imperfect though John Kwang turns out to be, Henry takes sides against the picketers, seeing himself as part of Kwang's immigrant family. John Kwang is his hero because he has dared, for better and for worse, to act like an American—the messages of the picketers notwithstanding. Kwang has charted his existence "on the public scale when the rest of us," says Henry, "wanted only security in the tiny dollar-shops and churches of our lives" (328).

Henry, with the picketers and the photographers, keeps the vigil outside Kwang's house, dreading to see his hero broken and hoping to be of some help. When Kwang does appear, the crowd bears down on him, grabbing at him and shouting at him in a magnified and ugly replay of the crush that caused Mitt's death. Here at least, Henry is present—this time sensing danger. He interposes himself:

And when I reach him I strike at them. I strike at everything that shouts and calls. Everything but his face. But with every blow I land I feel another equal to it ring my own ears, my neck, the back of my head. I half welcome them. And at the very moment I fall back for good he glimpses who I am, and I see him crouch down, like a broken child, shielding from me his wide immigrant face. (343)

Even as Henry sides with his hero against the representatives of the dominant group and defends him, he sadly recognizes Kwang's diminished stature. His self-sufficient American hero has become a broken immigrant child, ashamed of his failure. Kwang does not literally die, but he dies politically, leaving Henry once more bereft. For Henry, Mitt was the personal, private image of the possible fulfillment of the American Dream; John Kwang was the public image of that hope. Mitt was the melting pot; Kwang the image of polyethnic America: both have been destroyed.

Henry's mention of Mitt's "broad half-yellow face" (267) and Kwang's "wide immigrant face" (343) as he remembers their destruction, serves as a reminder of the use of the immigrant body as a site of difference. The fate of the two also recalls the violence that attends American immigrant life. The book, however, does not end in despair but instead finds Henry carrying on, appreciating other immigrant children (even though he has lost Mitt) and other adult immigrants (even though he has lost John Kwang). What bonds him to them is not their specialness and seeming perfection—those qualities he attributed to his son and his hero—but their ordinariness.

The essence of their ordinariness is located in their speech. Unlike Mitt and John Kwang, who spoke so perfectly, the people Henry now feels so close to are marked by their incomplete mastery of English. The complex role of language in the life of the American immigrant and in Henry's final vision of America is reflected in the book's title: *Native Speaker*. A native speaker is not someone who speaks the language perfectly so much as it is someone who uses it comfortably and expressively. Lelia and Henry discuss this when they first meet:

"People like me are always thinking about still having an accent," [Henry tells her]. . . .

"I can tell," [she answers]. . . . "You speak perfectly, of course. I mean if we were talking on the phone I wouldn't think twice."

"You mean it's my face."

"No, it's not that. . . . Your face is part of the equation, but not in the way you're thinking. You look like someone listening to himself. You pay attention to what you're doing. If I had to guess, you're not a native speaker." (12)

Lelia understands not only the sounds, but the psychology behind an immigrant's speech. She recognizes in the non-native speaker's self-consciousness the awareness that an incomplete mastery of English is a convenient excuse for prejudice and exclusion.

Perfection in immigrant speech reflects the greenhorn desire to fit in and the belief that if all the externals are properly in place—the voice, the clothes, the manners—that somehow one will be accepted. But it is not that easy. Henry remembers his embarrassment at his parents' imperfect English, knowing that it branded them as foreigners. But he also recognizes that John Kwang's excellent English—like his own—seems incongruous: "I kept listening for the errant tone, the flag, the minor mistake that would tell of his original race. . . . I couldn't help but think there was a mysterious dubbing going on, the very idea I wouldn't give quarter to when I would speak to strangers, the checkout girl, the mechanic, the professor, their faces dully awaiting my real speech, my truer talk and voice" (179).

The English language is thus a double bind for the American immigrant: speak it poorly and you are discounted; speak it well and you are suspected.

Perfect speech is guarded speech. Politicians, like immigrants, often speak this way because of their desire for acceptance. Henry makes this connection, observing that John Kwang's staffers are "Careful with the tongue" (176). But this is not the norm: the average American generally is not a careful speaker. As the cynical Dennis Hoagland points out, because Americans are inclined to "run off at the mouth" (172), they make terrible spies. In contrast, Henry's reticence and careful English make him a good spy, but not a comfortable or confident American. His guarded words, which Lelia refers to as "the Henryspeak" (6), infuriate her, and he slowly has to learn the value of language as an outlet for the feelings, and to use "all that burning language that I once presumed useless, never uttered and never lived" (285). But speaking out and saying what one feels leave a person vulnerable, and this is what the immigrant fears.

Lelia believes—and the story seems to bear her out—that it is not the thumb, but the mouth that makes us human. Speaking too carefully undermines this humanity: the careful speaker is, as Lelia points out, a "false speaker of the language" (6). The validity of this observation starts to dawn on Henry when, at Kwang's behest, he visits the parents of the slain staffer, Eduardo Fermin. Eduardo's grieving mother speaks of the aspirations of her much-loved son. Says Henry:

She brings me an album of pictures. We look at pictures together, and she keeps talking about him. I know what she means, despite her tenses. She's not acting out, acting crazy. I know this Mrs. Fermin. Half the people in Queens talk like her. Half the people I knew when I was a child. And I think she's saying it perfectly, just like she should. When you're too careful you can't say anything. You can't imagine the play of the words in your head. You can't hear them, and they all sound like they belong to somebody else. (257)

Felt words rather than grammatical words are real speech, and these are the words that are listened to.

The idea that speech is an expression of the self, rather than a method of replicating the self in the image of the "other," is an important lesson Henry learns in *Native Speaker*. Toward the end of the story, he and Lelia listen to a Korean and a Hispanic worker conversing during their break at an all-night deli:

We listen to the earnest attempts of their talk, the bits of their stilted English. I know I would have ridiculed them when I was young: I would cringe and grow ashamed of those funny tones of my father and his workers. . . . Just talk right, I wanted to yell, just talk right for once in your sorry lives. But now, I think I would give most anything to hear my father's talk again, the crash and bang and stop of his language, always hurtling by. I will listen for him forever in the streets of this city. (337)

The adult Henry is very different from the little boy who saw correct English as a requirement for acceptance. Now he recognizes in his father's and in other immigrants' speech, not their inferiority, but their vitality and their ardent desire to live and work and make something of themselves in America.

After John Kwang's downfall, when Henry has given up spying, Lelia suggests that he help her with her speech work. She needs another pair of hands, she says, but Henry corrects her, "Another mouth" (337). They work with immigrant children, making them feel comfortable speaking English, not emphasizing correctness, but instead joking around and interacting. At the end of one class, Lelia gives the children stickers with their names—not Americanized names, but their given names in their native languages—printed on them. She pronounces them "as best she can, taking care of every last pitch and accent," and Henry notes, "I hear her speaking a dozen lovely and native languages, calling all the difficult names of who we are" (349). This respectful gesture of speaking other languages in an English class suggests that everyone is a native speaker of some language and that we all have "difficult" names to those who do not know our language. In Lelia's class, not being able to speak English well is no bar to being respected as an individual. Lelia's attitude supplies an important corrective to that of Henry's youth, as well as to the adult attitudes of people such as Senator Byrd who see not speaking correct English as a deficit rather than a difference.

The difficulty of speech for the American immigrant lies in its two seemingly different functions: in this country, it is both a mode of expression and a method of inclusion or exclusion. The two are, however, not totally unrelated, for those who cannot or do not express themselves in English are ignored and therefore excluded. Henry, in describing the phenomenon of John Kwang's presence on the political scene, refers to his having become "part of the vernacular" (139). It is not just that Kwang speaks well that makes him part of the language of America—it is his willingness to speak out. His language is both correct and expressive.

John Kwang doesn't "seem afraid," says Henry, "like my mother and father, who were always wary of those who would try to shame us or mistreat us" (139). His becoming a public figure has forced his inclusion; it not only means that he speaks the language, but it also means that his name becomes a word in the vocabulary. As Henry's friend Jack says of Kwang, "He's a very public figure . . . people think of John Kwang. *He is in the language now* [my italics]. The buildings and streets there are written with him. In this sense, he exists" (169).

Kwang's outspokenness also serves as a critical commentary on Henry's silent spying. Kwang's behavior is rare in an immigrant, not because he works hard—most immigrants work extremely hard—but because he is not afraid to draw attention to himself as he works; as a politician John Kwang is willing to openly commit himself to the life of the country, rather than to stay safely on the margins as Henry and many other immigrants do. Describing his immigrant colleagues at Glimmer & Company, Henry notes, "We pledged allegiance to no government. We weren't ourselves political creatures. We weren't patriots. Even less, heroes" (17). In contrast, John Kwang makes that commitment—he buys into America. His story has a familiar ring: he comes to the country as an orphan houseboy for an American military officer, sets out on his own, gives himself the common American name of John, is stolen from, does some stealing himself, sleeps in doorways. Eventually, he is picked up by a Catholic priest and sent to school. Somewhere along the way, he begins "to think of America as a part of him, maybe even his" (211).

Unlike Henry and his colleagues, he pledges allegiance.

As a spy, Henry is an outsider, committed to neither the subjects of his investigation nor to his country. As he writes up his "unauthorized biographies," he refers to himself as "the most prodigal and mundane of historians" (18), suggesting that his work lacks both focus and vision. However, once he begins to admire John Kwang and to participate in his political activities, Henry finds himself to be a totally different kind of historian. Having become the person in charge of the huge list of participants in Kwang's money club, Henry realizes that

I have steadily become a compiler of lives. I am writing a new book of the land. Like John Kwang, I am remembering every last piece of them. Whether I wish it or not, I possess them, their spouses and children, their jobs and money and life. And the more I see and remember the more their story is the same. The story is mine. (279)

These people are not subjects written up by an impersonal third party: "This is a family," John Kwang reminds Henry, and Henry feels himself a part of it.

Because Kwang's immigrant family is composed of many nationalities, English is their common language. It is their ticket to inclusion into his friendly and sympathetic organization, just as it is their ticket to inclusion into the chillier business world outside. Henry muses upon the multiplicity of languages spoken in New York City and on the necessity for a common tongue: "Ancient Rome was the first true Babel. New York City must be the second. . . . Still, to enter this resplendent place, the new ones must learn the primary Latin. Quell the old tongue, loosen the lips. Listen, the hawk and cry of the American city" (237). Although English has been used as a bar in America to exclude and diminish the stature of immigrants, it is also a bond between them in an increasingly multicultural America. By the end of the story, Henry's preoccupation has shifted from worry about acceptance by the increasingly small, although still powerful, dominant group, to an appreciation of and an identification with the increasingly diverse group of new Americans. He stands on the streets of Queens and observes:

This is a city of words.

We live here. In the street the shouting is in a language we hardly know. The strangest chorale. We pass by the throngs of mongers. . . . Everyone sounds angry and theatrical. Completely out of time. They want you to buy something, or hawk what you have, or else shove off. The constant cry is that you belong here, or you make yourself belong, or you must go. (344)

This is expressive English—ungrammatical and unsentimental, but full of enterprise and vitality.

Henry's realignment with the hard-working speakers of broken English and their children suggests that there are no grand solutions and no quick fixes for the problems of immigrant acceptance and assimilation into American society. Neither intermarriage with the dominant group, nor bold political action on behalf of the immigrant constituency will provide a smooth transition—as the bright but brief lives of Mitt and John Kwang show. And going the route of the silent, nonparticipating immigrant-spy, although it is certainly the position many newcomers are thrust into when they come here, is not a viable alternative. Rather than advocating immigrant withdrawal or championing those paradigms that require perfection on the part of the immigrant, Henry ends up taking a more realistic stand. He acknowledges the rocky road that immigrants must travel. He celebrates not their perfection, but their humanity, epitomized in the slow and difficult process of their learning the language of American society. It is not their eventual assimilation that moves him, but rather the transitional state itself. Their halting immigrant English is the emblem of their struggle, for it indicates their desire, in the face of great difficulties, to make their way in the society. In its roughness there is the music of ambition, emotion, and commitment.

Native Speaker, in an odd way, enlarges and thereby transforms the picture of the greenhorn trying to fit into America. Instead of highlighting the embarrassments of the awkward and vulnerable newcomers, the book celebrates them. It asks us to listen to immigrants' incorrect but highly expressive English and to find in it the cry that they "belong here" (344). In their different English we may hear "the ancient untold music of a newcomer's heart, sonorous with longing and hope" (304). Their attitude is earnest and, though their constructions are stilted, they express their feelings perfectly.

WORKS CITED

Hoffman, Eva. *Lost in Translation*. New York: Penguin, 1989.

Lee, Chang-rae. *Native Speaker*. New York: Riverhead, 1995.

Sontag, Deborah. "Calls to Restrict Immigration Come From Many Quarters," *New York Times* 13 Dec. 1992: E5.

————. "English as a Precious Language," *New York Times* 29 Aug. 1993: B31, 34.

7

Repositioning the Stars: Twentieth-Century Narratives of Asian American Immigration

Qun Wang

In the study of Asian American literature, the issue of "authenticity" is as problematic as the definition of the term Asian American itself. Although the racial boundary of the Asian American community is historically and geographically delineated by the origin of its immigrants and ontologically dictated by the commonality in people's struggle for dignity and social justice, Asian American literature's cultural configuration is controversial. Nineteen ninety-one, for instance, saw the publication of *The Big AIIIEEEEE! An Anthology of Chinese American and Japanese American Literature*, edited by Asian American writers and critic Frank Chin et al. The selections in the anthology are as debatable as Chin's introductory article, "Come All Ye Asian American Writers of the Real and the Fake," in which Chin divides Chinese and Japanese American writers into two groups: Asian American authors and Americanized Asian authors.

In the article, Chin posits that only those Asian American writers who are not susceptible to "Christian conversion" (18) and who uphold traditional Chinese and Japanese values such as Confucianism, "the Japanese sense of honor," and "the samurai sense of nobility" (69) can be considered as the real voices in Asian American literature. This group includes Chinese American writer Louis Chu (*Eat a Bowl of Tea*, 1961) and Japanese American writers Toshio Mori (*Yokohama, California*, 1949) and John Okada (*No-No Boy*, 1957). But Chinese American writers such as Pardee Lowe (*Father and Glorious Descendant*, 1943); Jade Snow Wong (*The Fifth Chinese Daughter*, 1945); Maxine Hong Kingston (*The Woman Warrior*, 1975; *China Men*, 1980; *Tripmaster Monkey: His Fake Book*, 1989); and Amy Tan (*The Joy Luck Club*, 1989; *The Kitchen God's Wife*, 1991), Japanese American writer Bill Hosokawa (*NISEI: The Quiet Americans*, 1969), and Asian American writers who use the exclusively Christian form of autobiography (11) and revise Asian "history, culture, and childhood literature and myth" (29) are the fake. In their depiction of the "Christian yin/yang of the dual personality/identity crisis" (26), these writers not only misrepresent their own cultural heritage, but betray its values.

Chin's article raises an interesting question concerning the issue of how to integrate Asian histories and cultures into Asian American literature. A noticeable phenomenon in Asian American literature is that most "successful" works are produced by American-born Asian American writers. These writers do not have any language problem; some of them are more ideologically in tune with American mainstream culture than with their own cultural heritage (as is demonstrated in Shawn Hsu Wong's *Homebase*, 1979, Tan's *The Joy Luck Club*, and Gish Jen's *Typical American*, 1991); and because of their language capability, many of these writers have adopted the role as translators for their ethnic cultural heritage. In Maxine Hong Kingston's *The Woman Warrior* and *China Men*, Amy Tan's *The Joy Luck Club*, and Fae Myenne Ng's *Bone* (1993), the narrators are second-generation Chinese Americans (people who are born to parents who are first-generation immigrants). They not only tell stories about their own lives, but also serve as "narrators" and "translators" (Part III of *The Joy Luck Club* is titled "American Translation") of traditions with which they are struggling, as the narrator in *Bone* describes:

We know so little of the old country. We repeat the names of grandfathers and uncles, but they have always been strangers to us. Family exists only because somebody has a story, and knowing the story connects us to a history. To us, the deformed man is oddly compelling, the forgotten man is a good story, and a beautiful woman suffers. (36)

Comparing works by first-generation Asian immigrants published in the United States with those by second- and third-generation Asian American writers also shows a divergence in thematic concerns, in tone, and in the use of traditional materials such as myths and legends. In "Ethnicizing Gender: An Exploration of Sexuality as Sign in Chinese Immigrant Literature," Chinese American scholar Sau-ling Cynthia Wong calls for "in-depth comparisons" of the "intriguing contrast between the thematic preoccupations of the foreign- and American-born Asian American writers" (123). In her study of Asian American female writers' works, Wong notices that whereas immigrant writers such as Yu Lihua, Nie Hua-ling, Chen Ruoxi, Li Li, Shi Shuqing, and Cong Su "are especially interested in issues of heterosexual courtship, marriage, jilting, celibacy, divorce, widowhood, extramarital affairs, and child rearing, a consequence of sexual union," American-born authors seem to favor "the coming-of-age story in which sexual initiation is conspicuously absent: the canonical pattern shows an adolescent or young adult seeking a healing reconnection to his/her ethnic culture and a viable place in American society" (123). Indeed, whereas the main thematic preoccupations in Vietnamese American writer Le Ly Hayslip's autobiography, *When Heaven and Earth Changed Places* (1989) and *A Child of War, A Woman of Peace* (1991), and Korean American novelist Ronyoung Kim's *Clay Walls* (1987) revolve around issues such as survival and the fight for respect and dignity, characters in Chinese American writer Gish Jen's novel, *Typical American*, David Wong Louie's collection of short stories, *Pangs of Love* (1991), and Amy Tan's *The Kitchen God's Wife* (1991) are more concerned about individual development and social and economic mobility; whereas the voices behind Filipino American writer Carlos Bulosan's autobiography, *America Is in the Heart* (1943), Asian American Indian writer Bharati Mukherjee's novel, *Jasmine* (1989), and Korean American writer Mary Paik Lee's autobiography, *Quiet Odyssey* (1990), are painful, bitter, and sometimes sarcastic and angry, the ones behind Chinese American writers Pardee Lowe's *Father and Glorious Descendant* (1943) and Jade Snow Wong's *Fifth Chinese Daughter* (1950) are reconciliatory and appeasing.

It is also interesting to notice that although works by both first-generation Asian immigrants and those by second- and third-generation Asian American writers are celebratorial of the writers' cultural heritage, the two groups' treatment of their cultural and literary traditions is quite different: the use of traditional materials by the first group of writers is usually sincere, faithful and respectful, whereas the use of the same materials by the second group is more creative and symbolic. In Hayslip's much-celebrated autobiography *When Heaven and Earth Changed Places*, traditional Vietnamese legends are incorporated not so much to symbolize individual characters' struggle to find their identity as to suggest the importance of familial and social harmony. *When Heaven and Earth Changed Places* ends with a Vietnamese legend about a boy-turned-soldier who made peace with his enemy after realizing that revenge would throw both into a vicious circle. At the end of the legend, the two men, "no longer boys, parted and began new lives. To commemorate the breaking of the circle of vengeance, the temple bell rings twice each day and reminds the people to arrest their passions long enough to think; and having thought, to hear the song of enlightenment" (365). The legend is apparently used to reflect the traditional Vietnamese values placed on forgiveness, reconciliation, and peace. On the other hand, second-generation Chinese American writers' use of Chinese myths and legends is more liberal and symbolic. Kingston's autobiographical novel, *The Woman Warrior*, portrays a second-generation Chinese American's struggle to redefine her relationship with her ethnic cultural heritage. Structurally, the novel follows a circular movement that eventually brings the narrator to embrace ontologically what she cannot culturally change. *The Woman Warrior*, therefore, relies heavily on the use of ancient Chinese myths and legends to generate thematic power as well as aesthetic appeal. In "Come All Ye Asian American Writers of the Real and the Fake," Frank Chin uses *The Woman Warrior* as an example to suggest that Kingston, (David Henry) Hwang, and (Amy) Tan are the first writers of Asian ancestry, "to so boldly fake the best-known works from the most universally known body of Asian literature and lore in history" (93). Chin argues that, in *The Woman Warrior*, Kingston mixes two famous Chinese legendary characters, Fa Mulan and Yue Fei, from two different stories:

In *The Woman Warrior*, Kingston takes a childhood chant, "The Ballad of Mulan," which is as popular today as "London Bridge Is Falling Down," and rewrites the heroine, Fa Mulan, to the specs of the stereotype of the Chinese woman as a pathological white supremacist victimized and trapped in a hideous Chinese civilization. The tattoos Kingston gives Fa

Mulan, to dramatize cruelty to women, actually belong to the hero Yue Fei, a man whose tomb is now a tourist attraction at West Lake, in Hanzhou city. (3)

Although Chin's arduous effort to defend the purity of Asian cultures is laudable and his attempt to delineate the cultural configurations of Asian American literature useful to developing a healthy critical discourse, his definition for Asian American literature is too narrow and arbitrary. Kingston's combining of the legendary female character, Fa Mulan, and the historical male figure, Yue Fei (a general who lived in the Song Dynasty: 420–479) in *The Woman Warrior* reveals a dialogic richness: it is intended to destroy both the traditional Chinese gender line, which was ignominious in placing women at the bottom of the social totem pole, and the line that separates imagination and reality. Besides, as Amy Ling in *Between Worlds* (1990) suggests, the transportation of the carving on the back from the life of Yue Fei is appropriate to the story of Fa Mulan, "for it effectively symbolizes the physical tortures that Chinese women have endured" (160). Rather than to rewrite "the heroine, Fa Mulan, to the specs of the stereotype of the Chinese woman as a pathological white supremacist victimized and trapped in a hideous Chinese civilization," as Frank Chin charges, Kingston's is an effort to reclaim Chinese American women's sense of history and identity by creatively using Chinese lore and legends.

In the "Foreword" to *Reading the Literatures of Asian America* (1992), Korean American scholar Elaine H. Kim acknowledges that the pioneering work of the members of the Combined Asian Resources Project (CARP)—Frank Chin, Jeffrey Paul Chan, Lawson Fusao Inada, Nathan Lee, Benjamin R. Tong, and Shawn Hsu Wong—played an important role in helping define the identity of the Asian American community and establish Asian American literary voices. But Kim also points out that "the terms of our cultural negotiations have changed and are changing over time because of differences in historical circumstances and needs" (xiii). To (re)vision Asian American literature is to "traverse the boundaries of unity and diversity," to make "our rootedness" enable us "to take flight," and to "'have it all' by claiming an infinity of layers of self and community" (xvi). Chin's argument for maintaining the "purity" and "authenticity" of Asian cultures and literary traditions in Asian American literature is, indeed, flawed in two respects. First, his argument is built on the assumption that tradition is autocratic and stagnant. In *An Introduction to Chinese Literature*, Chinese scholar Wu-chi Liu acknowledges Confucianism's strong impact on Chinese civilization and literature. He notes: "A practical moral philosophy that teaches the rules of personal cultivation and the virtues of human relationship, Confucianism has molded the Chinese national character and pervaded every aspect of Chinese society, the family, literature and the arts" (4). But the author also challenges Confucianism's orthodox rule by suggesting that in Chinese literature it was usually "the rebels from Confucianism who deviated from the norm and carved out new paths in literary fields," rebels who "found their inspiration sometimes abroad but oftener among the common people." For the latter's "spring of native wit and emotion replenished constantly the dwindling reservoir of literary sources and materials depleted by long periods of use" (4–5).

In *Marxism and Literature* (1977), British writer Raymond Williams posits that the most accessible counter-hegemonic works have often been historical, but the rigorously selective process that defines "tradition" is always linked to "explicit contemporary pressures and limits." Whereas "history" may seem recoverable as "tradition," tradition's hegemonic impulse is always the most active: "a deliberate selective and connecting process which offers a historical and cultural ratification of a contemporary order" (116–17). Williams's theory suggests that to dehegemonize tradition as an autocratic historical force is to recognize its arbitrariness and the possibility of change. But Chin's argument for the importance of maintaining the "purity" of a cultural tradition not only confuses the relationship between tradition and history, it also threatens to remove the dynamics from the critical process of historical interpretation and reconstruction, a process that has always been responsive to social, political, and cultural changes.

The contents of the cultural traditions that Chin wants to maintain are as question begging as the way Chin wants to maintain them. It is true that Confucianism, with its emphasis on courtesy and familial and social harmony, played an important role in stabilizing China, which for centuries was torn by endless wars and meaningless deaths. But the kind of "harmony" Confucius envisioned was built on the feudal ethical code of the so-called three cardinal guides (ruler guides subject, father guides son, and husband guides wife) and the five constant virtues (benevolence, righteousness, propriety, wisdom, and fidelity) and its infrastructure supported by patriarchy and primogeniture.

The second flaw in Chin's argument is that it does not acknowledge that many Asian American writers are trying to identify a voice that can best describe the Asian American experience; they are not in search of a mouthpiece that, at its best, is capable of echoing what has already been expressed and described in Asian literatures. Given the fact that a person cannot achieve self-actualization without first identifying the person's relationship with her/his own cultural heritage, to be a hyphenated American also means that we are blessed with two cultures and can have the freedom and luxury to be selective. Or as Brave Orchid, the dynamic mother in Maxine Hong Kingston's *The Woman Warrior* puts it: "When you come to America, it's a chance to forget some of the bad Chinese habits" (139). In *Articulate Silences*, Chinese American scholar King-Kok Cheung suggests that it is the distrust of inherited language and of traditional myth with patriarchal ethos that brings Asian American writers, especially Asian American female writers, to the conclusion that they must cross cultural borders in search of ways to not only "revise history," but also "transfigure ethnicity," for "the point is never to return to the original but to tell it with a difference" (170). Thus, Cheung's "two-toned language" (16) concretely objectifies a large group of Asian American writers' effort to negotiate a ground on which they can find their own identity, an effort demonstrated in works by first-generation Asian immigrants as well as by second-generation Asian American writers.

Twentieth-century narratives of Asian American immigration generally raise more questions than provide answers. Although many writers have remained faithful to their cultural heritage, they also see the necessity of negotiating a ground on which they can embrace their newly created identity. Dissimilar to works by second-generation Asian American immigrants whose search for identity is ontologically connected with their attempt to reclaim their sense of history and culture, in a sense, looking backward, works by first-generation Asian American immigrants look forward to building connections with the mainstream American culture as well as maintaining the one they have brought with them. In Korean American poet Myung Mi Kim's poem "Into Such Assembly," the narrator discusses her ambivalent feelings about becoming a naturalized American citizen. As the narrator participates in the naturalization oath taking ceremony, scenes from her past keep invading her mind: a cable car riding across a pond, a red lacquer chest in a slate blue house, and blooming chrysanthemums are powerful images that lead the narrator to questions such as who is mother tongue and who is father country (*The Forbidden Stitch* 18–19). The poem, however, ends with the narrator's envisioning the naturalization assembly of people from different cultures and nationalities; it is a gathering of the human race just like when the rain dissolves land and ocean, making them one (19).

Asian Indian American writer Bharati Mukherjee's novel *Jasmine* (1989) also revolves around the main character Jasmine's confusion about and search for identity. Mukherjee's thematic preoccupation with the search for and creation of identity is revealed and accentuated by the different names Jasmine is given and uses: she was born Jyoti; but to Prakash, her husband in India, she is Jasmine; to Half-Face, the ruthless smuggler of illegal immigrants, she is Kali (according to Indian mythology, Kali is a fearsome goddess who is a destroyer); to Taylor, her employer and friend in New York City, she is Jase; to Bud, her partner in Iowa, she is Jane. After going through the struggle in search of her true identity, Jasmine comes to the conclusion that possibilities lie in the process of making, unmaking, and remaking of her identity. At the end of the novel, Jasmine realizes that she has "stopped thinking of" herself "as Jane," but has accepted the life of "adventure, risk, transformation: the frontier is pushing indoors through uncaulked windows." She is ready to "reposition the stars" (214).

Other Asian American writers also are concerned with resolving ambivalent feelings and building connections between two cultures. For example, Korean American writer Mary Paik Lee's autobiography *Quiet Odyssey: A Pioneer Korean Woman in America* (1990) describes her own and her family's struggle after they immigrated to the United States in the beginning of the twentieth century. The hardships the author had endured as a child in both Korea and in the United States did not diminish her hope for a better future; nor did they shake her determination to fight for dignity. As Lee recalls in the book, when her parents first came to America, "they had expected life to be difficult—but they had put their faith in God and were determined to survive whatever hardships came their way" (132). From the fact that Lee knew neither the names of her maternal grandparents nor the social origins of her paternal ones but was familiar with the names of several American missionaries in Korea (137) to the fact that when Lee became an American citizen in 1960, she immediately decided to change her name from Kuang Sun Paik to Mary Paik Lee, the reader senses a flexibility and adaptability demonstrated by many first-generation immigrants in the United States and their willingness to change. In the appendix, Chinese American scholar Sucheng Chan, the editor of *Quiet Odyssey*, suggests that Lee's desire to write and publish her autobiography is "a retrospective attempt to come to terms with the tensions of being a Christian and Asian immigrant in America" and that her story is "an act of reconciliation rather than a full disclosure" (137). It is a reconciliation built on the possibility of bridging two worlds.

Filipino American social activist and writer Carlos Bulosan's autobiography *America Is in the Heart* (1973) is a work that portrays the pernicious impact of social stratification on the Filipino American community and the narrator's ambivalent feelings about his experience in the United States. Hoping for a new beginning in life, Bulosan came to the United States as a teenager. As the ship was arriving in Seattle, his first sight of the approaching land was an exhilarating experience, as he recalled:

Everything seemed native and promising to me. It was like coming home after a long voyage, although as yet I had no home in this country. Everything seemed familiar and kind— the white faces of the buildings melting in the soft afternoon sun, the gray contours of the surrounding valleys that seemed to vanish in the last periphery of light. With a sudden surge of joy, I knew that I must find a home in this new land. (99)

His dreams were soon shattered by the smell of the fish canneries in Alaska, by the hostile tone behind people's cold comment, "Why don't they ship those monkeys back where they came from?" (99), and by the brutality of the Filipinos he had never seen in the Philippines. He migrated from city to city on the West Coast, looking for jobs and security. While he was staying in a hospital to take care of his friend José, who was injured trying to run away from railroad detectives, he was puzzled by the treatment they had been receiving in America:

Walking down the marble stairway of the hospital, I began to wonder at the paradox of America. José's tragedy was brought about by railroad detectives, yet he had done no harm of any consequence to the company. On the highway, again, motorists had refused to take a dying man. And yet in this hospital, among white people—Americans like those who had denied us—we had found refuge and tolerance. Why was America so kind and yet so cruel? Was there no way to simplifying things in this continent so that suffering would be minimized? Was there no common denominator on which we could all meet? I was angry and confused, and wondered if I would ever understand this paradox. (147)

Unlike some of his compatriots who responded to racial oppression with hatred and violence, Bulosan was determined not to be consumed by anger and frustration. After being introduced to concepts such as the "war between labor and capital" (186) and "the dynamic social struggle in America" (187), he decided to "fight the world with his mind, but not with his hands" (224). Together with José, they started the first Filipino American magazine, *The New Tide*, joined the Filipino Workers' Association, and became activists in the labor movement. At the end of the book, Bulosan expressed his appreciation of the opportunities America had offered him, opportunities he would not be able to explore in the Philippines. He realized that "the American earth was like a huge heart unfolding warmly to receive" him and nothing "could destroy his faith in America." For it was something that had grown out of his "defeats and success, something shaped by . . . struggles for a place in this vast land" (326). It was then he realized that "no man could destroy" his "faith in America that had sprung from all our hopes and aspirations, *ever*" (327).

The controversy surrounding literature by first- and second-generation immigrants—whether such writing should maintain traditional cultural purity or incorporate some of the adopted culture—is illuminated by postcolonial discourse, which focuses its attention on the study of power structure and relations. In a 1983 interview with University of California-Berkeley Professor Paul Rabinow, et al., French philosopher Michel Foucault responded to the criticism that his critical study of modern power structures lacked an overall theory and, therefore, was anarchistic in nature. Foucault argued that he believed that the forms of totalization offered by politics are always very limited. What he attempted to achieve was "apart from any totalization—which would be at once abstract and limiting—to open up problems that are [both] concrete and general"; he was interested in studying "problems that approach politics from behind and cut across societies on the diagonal, problems that are at once constituents of our history and constituted by that history" (375–76). It is interesting to notice that in discussing postcolonial theory in general and Edward W. Said's *Orientalism* in particular, scholars such as Raman Selden and Peter Widdowson raise questions that resonate with the criticism of Foucault's theoretical approach. In *A Reader's Guide to Contemporary Literary Theory,* Selden and Widdowson observe that while warning against "the danger that anti-dominant critiques will demarcate separatist areas of resistance and struggle," Said calls "for a critical 'decentred consciousness' and for interdisciplinary work committed to the collective libertarian aim of dismantling systems of domination." However, since Said's credentials do not "reside in the presumed authenticity of ethnic or sexual identity or experience, or in any purity of method, but elsewhere," where and what this elsewhere is, "is the major problem of postcolonial criticism, and of other differently directed forms of radical 'ideology critiques'" (191).

Since both Foucault and Said's argument is built on a decentralizing that leaves no privilege to any center, to suggest that they develop a new theory to replace those that they challenge is to misunderstand the very basic premises of their arguments. In "The Subject and Power," Foucault states that the key issue "is not to discover what we are, but to refuse what we are." For "the political, ethical, social, philosophical problem of our days is not to try to liberate the individual from the state, and from the state's institutions, but to liberate us both from the state and from the type of individualization which is linked to the state" (qtd. in Rabinow, Introduction, 22). Similarly, in the closing chapter in *Orientalism*, Said makes it clear that his "project has been to describe a particular system of ideas, not by any means to displace the system with a new one." He has attempted to raise a whole set of questions that are relevant in discussing the problems of human experience, questions such as

How does one *represent* other cultures? What is another *culture*? Is the notion of a distinct culture (or race, or religion, or civilization) a useful one, or does it always get involved either in self-congratulation (when one discusses the "other")? Do cultural, religious, and racial differences matter more than socio-economic categories, or politicohistorical ones? How do ideas acquire authority, "normality," and even the status of "natural" truth? What is the role of the intellectual? Is he there to validate the culture and state of which he is a part? What importance must he give to an independent critical consciousness, an *oppositional* critical consciousness? (325–26)

Said's questions reveal the basic premises on which postcolonial criticism builds its tenets. The questions are intended not so much to search for what Raymond Williams calls the "recognition of the essential" and "through this recognition" "its desirability and inevitability, according to the basic laws of reality" (102) as to bring our attention to the dynamics of a constitutive and constituting process that challenges the very foundation on which modern power structures are established. In other words, what is so debatable about Selden and Widdowson's criticisms of Said's critical methodology is that they follow the approach of what King-Kok Cheung calls "either/or binarism" (170). The approach not only fails to recognize the immense plurality of human experience (the word "purity" used in Selden and Widdowson's statement is itself question begging), it also threatens to remove the dynamics from "the constitutive and constituting" process of literary criticism.

In his critically acclaimed book *Imagined Communities*, American scholar Benedict Anderson uses San Martin's edict to baptize Quechua-speaking Indians as "Peruvians" as an example to demonstrate that the concept of "nation" was, from the start, "conceived in language, not in blood, and that one could be 'invited into' the imagined community" (145). To recognize the limitations of the concept of nation is therefore to accept language as a dynamic process by which meaning is created. Chinese American scholar Amy Ling's article, "Creating One's Self: the Eaton Sisters," also suggests that "the self is not a fixed entity but a fluid, changing construct or creation determined by context or historical conditions and particularly by power relationships" (306). By using the example of the Eurasian American Eaton Sisters, who had adopted identities of their choice in creative writing (one Chinese and the other Japanese), Ling convincingly demonstrates the dialectical relationship between creation and re-creation and between the permeability of the boundaries of the self and the influence of historical conditions. This willingness to cross borders to recreate one's identity and to come to terms with being a hyphenated American is reflected in the twentieth-century narratives of Asian American immigrants, many of whom have demonstrated a willingness to cross borders and to negotiate a ground on which they can create and embrace their true identity.

It is true that many works by first-generation Asian immigrants portray their ambivalent feelings about their experience in the United States. Their attachment to the cultures they have brought with them is as strong as their eagerness to embrace the new ones. They demonstrate a flexibility that is built on their willingness to bridge the old world with the new one and their determination to help reshape the ideological and cultural contours of the country. This willingness to cross borders and bridge two cultures is one of several thematic preoccupations that have demonstrated their recurrent power in second- and third-generation Asian American writers' works as well. To understand the ethos of Asian American immigration literature, thus, we need not only to recognize traditions' hegemonic impulse, but also use traditions to broaden rather than to restrict our understanding of the dialectical relationship between the Asian American experience and our cultural heritage. Instead of taking an essentialistic approach to the study of culture, as Frank Chin suggests, we need to appreciate both the indelible impact of Asian cultures on Asian American literature and Asian American writers' readiness to cross borders.

WORKS CITED

Anderson, Benedict. *Imagined Communities*. New York: Verso, 1983.

Bulosan, Carlos. *America Is in the Heart*. Seattle: U of Washington P, 1973.

Cheung, King-Kok. *Articulate Silences: Hisaye Yamamoto, Maxine Hong Kingston, Joy Kogawa*. Ithaca: Cornell UP, 1993.

Chin, Frank. "Come All Ye Asian American Writers of the Real and the Fake." *The Big AIIIEEEEE! An Anthology of Chinese American and Japanese American Literature*. Ed. Jeffrey Paul Chan, Frank Chin, Lawson Fusao Inada, and Shawn Wong. New York: Meridian, 1991. 1–92.

Chu, Louis. *Eat a Bowl of Tea*. New York: Carol, 1990.

Hayslip, Le Ly. *When Heaven and Earth Changed Places*. New York: Plume, 1989.

———. *A Child of War, A Woman of Peace*. New York: Plume, 1991.

Hosokawa, Bill. *NISEI: The Quiet Americans*. New York: Morrow, 1969.

Hwang, David Henry. *M. Butterfly*. New York: Plume, 1989.

Jen, Gish. *Typical American*. New York: Plume, 1991.

Kim, Elaine H. Foreword. *Reading the Literatures of Asian America*. Ed. Shirley Geok-lin Lim and Amy Ling. Philadelphia: Temple UP, 1992. xi–xvii.

Kim, Myung Mi. "Into Such Assembly." *The Forbidden Stitch*. Ed. Shirley Geok-lin Lim, Mayumi Tsutakawa, and Margarita Donnelly. Corvallis: Calyx, 1989. 18–19.

Kim, Rongyoung. *Clay Walls*. Seattle: U of Washington P, 1990.

Kingston, Maxine Hong. *Tripmaster Monkey: His Fake Book*. New York: Vintage, 1989.

———. *China Men*. New York: Vintage, 1980.

———. *The Woman Warrior*. New York: Vintage, 1975.

Lee, Mary Paik. *Quiet Odyssey: A Pioneer Korean Woman in America*. Seattle: U of Washington P, 1990.

Lim, Shirley Geok-lin and Amy Ling, eds. *Reading the Literatures of Asian America*. Philadelphia: Temple UP, 1992.

Ling, Amy. "Creating One's Self: The Eaton Sisters." *Reading the Literatures of Asian America*. Ed. Shirley Geok-lin Lim and Amy Ling. Philadelphia: Temple UP, 1992. 305–18.

———. *Between Worlds*. New York: Pergamon, 1990.

Liu, Wu-chi. *An Introduction to Chinese Literature*. Bloomington: Indiana UP, 1966.

Louie, David Wong. *Pangs of Love*. New York: Plume, 1991.

Lowe, Pardee. *Father and Glorious Descendant*. Boston: Little, 1943.

Mori, Toshio. *Yokohama, California*. Seattle: U of Washington P, 1985.

Mukherjee, Bharati. *Jasmine*. New York: Fawcett Crest, 1989.

Ng, Fae Myenne. *Bone*. New York: Hyperion, 1993.

Okada, John. *No-No Boy*. Seattle: U of Washington P, 1979.

Rabinow, Paul. Introduction. *The Foucault Reader*. New York: Pantheon, 1984. 3–29.

———. "Politics and Ethics: An Interview." *The Foucault Reader*. New York: Pantheon, 1984. 373–80.

Said, Edward. *Orientalism*. New York: Vintage, 1979.

Selden, Raman, and Peter Widdowson. *A Reader's Guide to Contemporary Literary Theory*. 3rd. ed. Lexington: UP of Kentucky, 1993.

Tan, Amy. *The Kitchen God's Wife*. New York: G. P. Putnam's Sons, 1991.

———. *The Joy Luck Club*. New York: Ivy, 1989.

Williams, Raymond. *Marxism and Literature*. London: Oxford UP, 1977.

Wong, Jade Snow. *Fifth Chinese Daughter*. Seattle: U of Washington P, 1989.

Wong, Sau-ling Cynthia. "Ethnicing Gender: an Exploration of Sexuality as Sign in Chinese Immigrant Literature." *Reading the Literatures of Asian America*. Ed. Shirley Geoklin Lim and Amy Ling. Philadelphia: Temple UP, 1992. 111–29.

Wong, Shawn Hsu. *Homebase*. New York: Plume, 1991.

8

Borderland Themes in Sandra Cisneros's *Woman Hollering Creek*

Katherine Payant

For a writer with quite a small *oeuvre*—a novella, a volume of poems, and a book of short fiction—Chicana feminist Sandra Cisneros has become widely read and known. Cisneros blurs lines between genres, calling her fiction, often vignettes rather than structured narratives, "lazy poems" ("Do You Know Me?" 79). Her *Bildungsroman, The House on Mango Street*, is read both as a young adult novel and as a work of adult fiction, and her most recent book of short stories, *Woman Hollering Creek and Other Stories* (1991), includes prose poems similar to those in *Mango Street*, and longer works. Most of her fiction is composed as first-person narratives told to us by the central protagonist. She speaks for people like herself or whom she has known—Mexican and Chicana girls and women who grew up "on the borderlands." According to Cisneros, "If I were asked what it is I write about, I would have to say I write about those ghosts inside that haunt me" ("Ghosts and Voices" 73). Part of those ghosts are the myths and legends of the borderlands, which can hold women back in their quests for self-identity, or, when creatively adapted, can offer possibilities for constructing new cultural motifs.

In *The House on Mango Street*, like Cisneros's childhood home, located in Chicago's barrio, the protagonist Esperanza says, "Mexicans don't like their women strong" (10). One could say that all of Cisneros's female characters either struggle to be strong and succeed, thus transcending culturally dictated gender roles, or are defeated in their struggle (Lewis 69). The fact that they live "on the borders," straddling two or three cultures, requires them to combine several ways of thinking and being, a stressful situation that also has great potential for empowerment. Though some of her characters seem to fail in effectively creating a healthy hybrid identity that works for them, several others find new insights and strengths.

It may be useful to place Cisneros in the history of Mexican American writing. Mexican Americans are the most numerous of all immigrant groups and are also one of our oldest ethnic groups, many having come here at least as long ago as people with Anglo roots. Therefore, it is a stretch to call these Mexican Americans immigrants. Until recently, it has been argued that they were an "invisible" or forgotten minority, and certainly their literature received little attention from mainstream culture (Leal and Barron 10). Going back to the earliest accounts of explorers and settlers in the Southwest, moving on to early folklore and legends to the nineteenth-century *corridos* (narrative ballads) of the borderlands, to the first literature written in English in the twentieth century, to the flowering of Chicano literature in the 1960s, Mexican Americans have long been writing of their experiences. Though some of the early modern literature was, according to literary historian Raymund A. Paredes "tentative and subdued, even submissive," rather than "proud and defiant" (45) from the earliest days much of the popular literature dealt with conflicts with the dominant Anglo culture (36–39). Certainly this animosity Chicanos feel for the "arrogant, ruthless, and avaricious" Anglo culture dominates much Mexican American writing of the last several decades, whether by males or females (Paredes 36).

As pointed out in the introduction, the Chicano political movement of the 1960s was in some sense an outgrowth of the civil rights movement of those times. At first the fiction coming out of this movement was predominantly male (Savin 354). Critical of Anglo culture as sterile, materialist and prejudiced, it documented the experiences of Mexican American men. Fiction writers such as Rudolfo Anaya, (*Bless Me, Ultima*, 1972) and Tomas Rivera (. . . *Y no se lo trago la tierra*, [*And the Earth Did Not Devour Him* 1971]), and poets such as Rodolfo Gonzales (*I Am Joaquin*, 1967) set the themes and tone of Mexican American literature for future decades. Liberally combining English and Spanish, including Chicano slang, sometimes drawing on Native American folklore, they told the stories of the barrios, the migrant workers, and restless young male seekers, trying to find identity in an unaccepting gringo world.

The 1980s and 1990s, however, have been the decades of the Chicanas. Left out of the political debates of the earlier decades, women of Mexican American heritage are now documenting their experiences and those of their Chicana sisters. Until this time, women had either been portrayed traditionally, as mothers or healers, or as Ada Savin says, *la chingada* [the violated one] by their *carnales* [brothers] (354). Though Cisneros is perhaps the best known of these Chicana writers, others include Bernice Zamora, Gloria Anzaldúa, and Cherríe Moraga.

A central theme in much of this Chicana writing, including Cisneros's, is "life on the borderlands," an idea that is elaborated by poet Anzaldúa in her seminal work *Borderlands/La Frontera* (1987). In this multigenre work—part essay, memoir, and poetry—Anzaldúa discusses what it means to be a *mestiza*—a hybrid creature, not Mexican, not Anglo, not Indian, but something different than all three, a person at the crossroads, full of energy whose "future depends on the breaking down of paradigms" (80). A *mestiza* must know her history; she must cross linguistic barriers and straddle several cultures, in fact, creating a new culture. She must not be bound by rigid, linear ways of thinking and behavior, by traditional subject-object dualities, or prescribed methods of reaching her goals. A *mestiza* copes by "developing a tolerance for contradictions, a tolerance for ambiguity. She learns to juggle cultures. . . . Not only does she sustain contradictions, she turns the ambivalence into something else" (79).

The goal should not be articulated, because there are endless possibilities for the future for such a person, but if it were, Anzaldúa envisions a world where people of all nations, races, classes, genders, and sexual preferences would be united in a pluralistic vision of respectful humanity, eventually even a new, blended race of humanity.

As L. M. Lewis, says, all the stories in *Woman Hollering Creek* are interrelated and form a continuum. The stories can be grouped into three types: those concerning pre-adolescent girls; those dealing with adolescents who undergo some kind of initiation, and the third group of longer stories describing the efforts of adult women to break away from culturally determined roles. In the process, some of these characters seem to create a comfortable space for themselves on the borders of cultures.

In the first group of stories, actually vignettes, girls seem secure in poor, but happy and warm homes. The opening piece, "My Lucy Friend Who Smells Like Corn," celebrates that phenomenon of girlhood, "best friends," girls so close they "could be sisters, right?" (5) Another story, "Mexican Movies," describes the fun of eating popcorn in the darkened theater, indulging in horseplay in the aisles, and sleepily being carried to bed by one's parents. There are sad moments, when the cruelty of the Anglo world intrudes, as in "Eleven" when a mean teacher makes the protagonist wear a ratty old sweater that doesn't belong to her. Jeff Thompson points out (417) that there is social satire in Cisneros's description of the stereotyped Mexicans in the movies who wear big sombreros and "never tear the dresses off the ladies" (12). The borderlands' theme appears when the family pays a visit to Mexico to the grandparents (Cisneros's family made extensive visits across the border). Some American tourists take the children's picture outside the cathedral where their grandmother is praying to the Virgin de Guadalupe. Disappointed, they discover that these cute Mexican kids speak English; the protagonist tells us she understands Spanish only when she "pays attention." We're "Mericans" says the girl's little brother, an inadvertent combination of Mexican and American, reflecting the children's hybrid status (19–20).

There are some suggestions of gender restrictions in these early pieces: for example, the brothers' cry "'*Girl*. We can't play with a *girl*,'" her "brothers' favorite insult now" (18), and in "Barbie—Q," where the protagonist and her sister learn, like all little girls, about appearance and fashion, by dressing their somewhat damaged Barbie dolls acquired at a fire sale. The distortions of these dolls suggests both the poverty of the girls—that they must play with damaged goods—and also possibly the damage done to females by the culture. According to Thompson (417), the damage emphasizes the lengths to which society will go in concealing woman's flaws, especially her lack of a penis. If the doll is dressed for the prom who's to know she has a damaged foot "so long as you don't lift her dress, right . . . ?" (16). Though the adult reader can detect the barriers and social restrictions already surrounding these children, as in most *Bildungs* of girls, self-awareness or knowledge of limitations does not come until adolescence in the next two stories, "One Holy Night," and "My *Tocaya*" (Namesake).

As many feminist psychologists have pointed out, adolescent girls who flourish and even excel in childhood come up against traditional role restrictions and expectations with the onset of puberty. Some rebel, but many unconsciously restrict their hopes for themselves. In "One Holy Night" the protagonist tells of her sexual initiation at the hands of Boy Baby Chaq Uxmal Paloquin, a thirty-seven-year-old drifter (who just may be a serial killer) who tells the naive girl he is descended from Mayan kings. Here Cisneros wryly combines traditional native myth with the harsh realities for a teenager growing up in an American barrio, where the threat of shame doesn't stop a girl from "doing devil things" (28), as would have been the case in Mexico. Unlike in the title story and "Bien Pretty," where native myth is a source of empowerment, here it is falsified and used to seduce. The girl tells us she fell in love with Chaq, with the mysterious spell he wove of tales of "the people of the sun . . . of the temples," and the "strange language" he spoke. Chaq tells the girl, who sells produce from a pushcart in front of the Jewel supermarket, he is destined to father a savior who will bring back the grandeur of his people (29), and he seduces her, the Virgin, his queen, in his messy room in the back of a garage. The ironic symbolism of the parallel with the Incarnation in Christian myth is obvious, but Chaq is no god, only a dangerous drifter trying to take advantage of a naive young girl.

The protagonist is not only seduced by the romance of the myth, she seeks sexual experience to possess the knowledge of adult women. After her defloration, it seems she has become "part of history" and the drama of love, that perhaps other people can spot her new identity as an experienced woman, but soon she realizes that she appears no different to anyone. Cisneros emphasizes the universality of the disillusionment of sexual initiation for women. The protagonist feels a commonality with other women now, all of whom wait to find out what sexual love is like and find it is a "big deal over nothing" (30).

As time passes, she is pregnant and "the truth started to seep out like a dangerous gasoline" (31). Her angry family burns the pushcart, a symbol of their daughter's shame, and begins searching for Chaq. A letter finally arrives at the garage from the seducer's sister, who, ironically, is a nun; his family are just common Mexican people and are not Mayan royalty. The protagonist is then exiled to a Mexican village where her own mother came from, having been sent from there to the United States to escape the shame of being pregnant with the protagonist. Thus, the cycle of female oppression continues. At the end of her story, the girl is waiting stoically for her baby to be born: "I don't think they [people] understand how it is to be a girl. I don't think they know how it is to have to wait your whole life" (34). Efforts to join the sisterhood of adult women have led to stasis and entrapment.

The other adolescent story, "My *Tocaya*," concerns Patricia Benavidez, told to us in scornful tones by her *tocaya*, Patricia. Patricia is trapped by the patriarchy in her father's taco shop, "bored, a little sad," who acts out by wearing rhinestone earrings and glitter high heels to school. The narrator says she dislikes her because she affects a phony English accent and calls herself "Trish." In the narrator, however, one detects a certain envy for Trish's attempts to create a new identity, to break out of her dull life, and perhaps sympathy—"Maybe her father beat her," says the other Patricia (37), who has heard the father beats Trish's brother. One day Trish disappears, and after a few days, she seemingly turns up dead in a drainage ditch. The community turns her into a saintly, murdered virgin, shedding buckets of tears for a girl they had no use for when alive. "She was my little princess," says the child-beating father, and the narrator finally truly feels sorry, recognizing the insincerity. At the anticlimatic end, a defeated Trish returns home to the renewed scorn of the *tocaya*: "She couldn't even die right" (40). However, although Trish does not escape her oppressive situation, she does have her fifteen minutes of fame by having her face in all the city newspapers. In fact, though Thompson feels that Trish's story emphasizes the dangers (rape and death) faced by young women and the impossibility of escape (419), one could see the story more positively—that in fact, the gutsy Trish is a kind of *doppelganger*, an alter ego for the critical narrator, a girl who dared to do something the narrator never would.

The last group of stories, "There Was a Man, There Was a Woman," occupying more than three-fourths of the book, concern the struggles of women of varying ages to escape the restraints of their gender roles and to find an identity on cultural borders. These stories focus on relationships with men, with protagonists attempting to define themselves through men. In one of these, "The Eyes of Zapata," Inés, the mistress of Emilio Zapata, never leaves the small villages of her homeland; another, Cleófilas, briefly immigrates to the "other side" (*en el otro lado*) with her husband, and others are educated, "liberated" Chicanas who can't speak Spanish well, and who are searching for some understanding and comfort with a heritage they understand only superficially.

Though it doesn't deal overtly with cultural borders, the longest story, "The Eyes of Zapata," does relate to the theme of border crossing. One could see Inés as a typical female victim. Zapata never marries her, in fact, having at least two other wives; he also takes away her son to be with him. She is a victim of the continual violence that sweeps over the villages of Mexico as the *Zapatistas* and the *federales* struggle for supremacy. Yet, as two critics have pointed out, Inés is a powerful figure of feminine strength (Thompson 415; Lewis 75). First, because she defies her father to live with Zapata, she resists patriarchal authority; she refuses to reject the memory of her mother, who was killed because she broke a cultural taboo— she was unfaithful to Inés's father. Second, because Inés lives most of her life apart from Zapata, she faces her pain of her past and that of her countrymen and women honestly and alone. According to Thompson, it is her acknowledgment of male suffering as well as female—"We are all widows" (87), says Inés—that makes her one of Cisneros's stronger women (416). Though suffering greatly from Zapata's treatment, she acknowledges her responsibility for their affair. Forced to retreat to her father's home, Inés "claims that same identity with all the women of her family and demonstrates it by naming her daughter after her mother" (Lewis 100). Not fully independent because she can escape only through leaving her body in nightly dreams, she has gained power through association with her past (her mother) and her daughter. Thus, though she never leaves the villages of Mexico, like some other Cisneros characters, Inés transcends traditional gender borders.

The title story, "Woman Hollering Creek," has received the most attention from critics. Narrated mostly in third-person limited perspective, it is the story of a contemporary Mexican girl, Cleófilas, who marries Juan and moves with him to the "other side," a little Texas town named Seguin. Cisneros describes this marriage as the traditional patriarchal arrangement of a daughter being given by her father, Don Serafín, to Juan. As in some of the other stories, Cisneros stresses the influence of community mores and popular culture. As a teenager, Cleófilas finds her home town boring, with nothing to do but visit with female relatives, attend the one movie playing in town, or watch the *telenovelas* (soaps). The *telenovelas* have steeped Cleófilas with a desire for "passion," the desire to find "the great love of one's life," and to do whatever one can do, at whatever cost to find that love. The soap stars love their men above all else, and for them, love is the most important thing, even if it involves suffering. In fact, the suffering is somehow "sweet," because it proves the depth of one's passion (44–45).

Cisneros suggests that for young immigrant woman without education or perspective, immigration to "the other side" can be just as restrictive as life in Mexico. Cleófilas had felt that the name of the Texan town "Seguin" had sounded romantic and like the "tinkle of money," not ugly the way the names of Mexican villages sound. With the fine job Juan has, they will live in a nicer house, and she will be able to wear the lovely clothes of the women on the *tele*. One is reminded of the immigrant stories of the turn of the century, when Jews and Italians came seeking the good life in America, or the "Golden Mountain" of the nineteenth-century Chinese, who found only discrimination and poverty. Not surprisingly, the reality of Seguin is Juan's modest job with a beer company, a dilapidated house, no *zocalo* (town square) to congregate in, and few female neighbors to provide the warm community bonds of the Mexican village. Her two closest neighbors are lonely older women, Dolores and Soledad (sorrow and solitude), who have lost their husbands. As Oscar Handlin pointed out in his study of the immigrant experience, the loneliness and alienation of the uprooted can be profound (94).

For women immigrants, confined to the home by children and lack of English, alienation and loneliness can be even greater than for men. When the children begin to come, Cleófilas realizes she is trapped. Observing that American towns are built so that one must depend on husbands, Cleófilas suffers the boredom and restraint of more affluent suburban housewives. Juan is not at all like the handsome men in the soaps, but rather as dull as Seguin. Cleófilas is also embarrassed to discover she does not know the American customs, when she lets her baby run around the Laundromat without his diaper and is reprimanded by the proprietor. The only thing she finds of interest in Sequin is the lovely, mysterious arroyo in the back of their property—a deep, wide creek called La Gritona, "Woman Hollering." Cleófilas wonders if the voice in the creek she hears calling to her "in a high silver voice" is La Llorona, the Weeping Woman, a figure in Mexican myth, who, in one version of the story, suffers because she killed her own children. As she observes her own child playing on a blanket in the backyard, she wonders if the quiet "drives a woman to the darkness under the trees" (51).

Juan, too, is trapped—Cisneros's feminism does not prevent her from seeing the suffering and suppressed longings of the working-class men in her stories. He gathers to drink in the evenings with his friends, and whatever thoughts and longings they wish to express become strangled in their drunkenness and perhaps in the restraints that prevent men from baring their souls. Thinks Cleófilas, "They want to tell each other what they want to tell themselves. But what is bumping like a helium balloon at the ceiling of the brain never finds its way out" (48). Sometimes at the end of the evening their "fists speak" what their lips cannot, and they fight with each other, or, in the case of Juan, their rage and confusion are expressed in wife beating.

As Jean Wyatt has suggested, Cisneros's portrayal of Juan Pedrito and Cleófilas's disintegrating marriage reads like a textbook case study of domestic violence (256). Though Cleófilas has always told herself she would strike back if a man ever struck her, she is paralyzed the first time Juan hits her, the epitome of female passivity. She had never ever seen her father strike her mother and this is outside any frame of reference she has. And Juan is so penitent and ashamed each time it happens. Other troubles intrude too, because after she comes home from the hospital with her second son, her personal things seem somewhat disarranged in the house, and a "slender doubt" appears. Is there another woman? Cleófilas by now has developed a good amount of self-awareness. Juan is a tyrant: "the man, this father [a telling description], this rival, this keeper, this lord, this master, this husband till kingdom come" (49–50). According to Jacqueline Doyle, the use of wording from the Christian "Our Father" emphasizes the hierarchical nature of patriarchy, established early in the church by the words of St. Paul telling wives to submit themselves to their husbands' rule (63).

Cleófilas has no recourse but to go back to the other patriarchy—the home of her father and brothers, whom she was expected to serve. She realizes this is a sort of defeat and disgrace, but can think of nothing else for herself—she has no skills, no English, no money. Her new motherhood causes her to remember her familial bonds, specifically when her father reminded her that he would never abandon her (Doyle 61–62). The patriarchy can be constricting, but it does offer security.

Help comes in the form of two strong Chicana women, Graciela and Felice (grace and felicity), who show Cleófilas what aware, powerful Mexican American women can be, and provide a contrast with the two traditional neighbors. They are comfortable on Anzaldúa's border, moving easily from Chicano to Anglo culture and even from female to male culture. Seeing Cleófilas's bruises, Graciela, a nurse at the prenatal clinic, arranges with her friend Felice to drive Cleófilas to the bus station in San Antonio. Cleófilas is full of admiration and amazement for these women, who speak "Spanglish," an English laced with Spanish phrases, drive their own pickup trucks, and don't seem to have husbands to define them. For their part, these two *comadres* find Cleófilas a quaint, pitiful creature whose life ironically seems like a soap opera; they think she may be named after one of those Mexican saints, "a martyr, or something" (54).

On the way out of town, as they cross over the arroyo, here a border between Anglo and Mexican culture and traditional female and male culture, Felice lets out a yell that startles the fearful Cleófilas (Wyatt 245). Felice explains she always yells when she goes over the creek; since there are so few things named for women, except for the suffering Virgin, she likes to affirm a different sort of woman—one who can holler in joy at being alive and strong and free, "like Tarzan." The story ends with Cleófilas surprising herself by laughing in pleasure as she tells this story to her father and brothers back in Mexico. Does this laugh at the end suggest, as some critics have said, that Cleófilas has achieved self-awareness, a transformation that will enable her to someday cross borders at will, like Felice (Wyatt 243; Doyle 61; Fiore 71)? One could argue that realistically, Cleófilas has been defeated in her struggle for self-realization. She is going back to a static life, now tied down with two children, and it is hard to see much future for her. Nevertheless, in the story, the voice of La Llorona is not crying, but laughing as is Cleófilas.

Doyle argues that the key to a full understanding of "Woman Hollering Creek" is the image of La Llorona, a traditional Mexican icon, which Cisneros adapts to fit her thematic purpose. Doyle points out that La Llorona of myth is an ambiguous, multifaceted creature (58). In one version of the story, she is a poor girl who marries above her station, then is rejected by her aristocratic husband, who takes a wealthy mistress. In revenge she kills her children; some say that she is precolonial, based on an Aztec goddess to whom babies were sacrificed. These versions of the tale see La Llorona as a fearsome mother (*mujer mala*), but others portray her as a more passive figure, a *Mater Dolorosa*, the Virgin of the Pieta, weeping for her lost child. On one hand, La Llorona cries for all the violated women and girls; on the other, she is a dark, powerful, terrifying figure of depravity (58). However, in "Woman Hollering Creek," La Llorona is not calling to Cleófilas to kill her children or to submit passively to her female fate. For Cisneros, La Llorona is a female figure whose cry is not a feeble weeping, but a *grito*, a yell or shout signifying womanly strength and joy in that strength. In this interpretation, Cleófilas's laugh at the ending of the story becomes her own *grito* of independence (Doyle 65). Jean Wyatt provides a different twist on this interpretation, saying the masculine "Tarzan" yell of Felice suggests the desirability of sometimes crossing gender boundaries, as well as the boundaries of culture such as language (261). Cleófilas has, briefly, truly been to "the other side."

In *From the Other Side: Women, Gender, and Immigrant Life in the U.S. 1820–1990*, Donna Gabaccia criticizes writers who portray Third World women as pitiful creatures fleeing their patriarchal cultures—the oppression of violent males in their lives—who need the help of empowered American feminists. "Criticism of patriarchy in other cultures remains an important prop for American ethnocentrism" (112) says Gabaccia. She also points out that some scholars "deny the existence or at least the uniqueness of Latin machismo, seeing it as a value-laden mis-

understanding of Latin gender relations" (73). Does Cisneros, a second-generation (maybe 2.5-generation since her mother was born in the United States) writer
contribute to this view of the superiority of American culture? Perhaps if one ex-
amined only "Women Hollering Creek," one would have to say yes, but other
stories in the collection give a more complex picture of the effect of their culture
on these women.

"Never Marry a Mexican" deals with living on boundaries and cultural inter-
stices that are not crossed comfortably, but instead bring profound loneliness and
bitterness. The protagonist, Clemencia, is a second-generation Chicana artist, translator, and substitute teacher who years ago was involved in an affair with her married Anglo professor, Drew. She has also been involved with other married men
(never Hispanic men), and sees herself as a betrayer of other women, as powerful,
vindictive, and cruel. Like Drew, she ironically calls herself "Malinche," (traitor)
after Dona Marina, the Aztec woman who became Cortéz's lover and translator;
Drew sees himself as Cortéz, being attracted by the dark beauty of Clemencia.
According to folklore, Malinche betrayed the Aztecs to the Spanish, had a son
with Cortéz, and is seen by Mexicans to this day as a symbol of *chingada* (the
violated one) as well as female treachery, an abused victim, who is yet somehow
responsible for her violated state, According to many Chicano feminists, icons
such as La Llorona and Malinche are so deeply embedded in the thinking of Mexican women as to be unconscious (Alarcón 184). Clemencia fails to see the ironic
parallel: just as Cortes violated and abandoned Dona Marina, Drew has used and
abandoned her. Though she appropriates for herself the active, even violent male
role (the *chingón* or violator) in her memories of their relationship, using language
such as "I leapt inside you and split you like an apple" (78) and sees herself as
violating the wives of the men with whom she sleeps, in fact, Clemencia is powerless and a "disabled" pathetic, lonely, and disturbed person. Here negotiations
between borders, as Wyatt says, create "only confusion and finally, a newly rigid
gender definition" (243).

"Never Marry a Mexican" also reveals the ambiguity of linguistic borders. The
title of the story is double-edged since it refers to Clemencia's mother's warning to
"never marry a Mexican" and Drew's statement at their last meeting that he would
never marry a Mexican woman. Clemencia's mother had warned her off Mexican
men because Clemencia's own father had been Mexican, from a middle-class family with traditional ideas about women's roles, the sort of boy who would get off a
bus if a girl acquaintance boarded and he couldn't pay her fare (70). Her father's
family constantly criticized her mother because she did not know to keep house
properly and was of a lower social class. After her father's death, Clemencia's
mother remarried to an Anglo man, having begun the affair with the new husband
while the father lay sick in a hospital bed, in a weird parallel to Clemencia's sleeping with the husbands of women giving birth. After her mother's remarriage,
Clemencia feels she neglects Clemencia for her new Anglo family. Though
Clemencia is angry with her mother at being rejected for Anglos, one suspects that
she has turned racial prejudice against Mexicans toward herself and toward other

women. Outrageous acts such as sleeping with men when their wives are giving birth give her a sense of "crazy joy," but seem to suggest a deep self-hatred. At one point near the end of her story, Clemencia says that on bad nights when her blood is full of poison, if she were "to kill someone," she herself might get in the line of fire (76).

Clemencia tells Drew's young son, with whom she is having an affair to spite his father, of a night when she slept at his house when his mother, Megan, was away. The next morning she obsessively explores the other woman's turf, her personal items and clothing, saying to herself, *"Calidad.* Quality" (81). Ironically, Megan's lifestyle proclaims a kind of gentility in the same way that her stylish Mexican father's had and reinforces Clemencia's self-loathing. Megan's lipsticks are coral and pink, what one would expect of a light-skinned redhead, and all the clothing seems clean and utterly chic, in a way that Clemencia feels she could never be. Finally, in an act she sees as revenge, she sticks gummy bear candies into various personal items of Megan's such as her makeup case and her diaphragm in an attempt to torment her with the knowledge of another woman. She hides one in the nesting babushka dolls, identical to the ones that Drew had given her, and keeps the tiniest one (she calls it the baby) for herself. Later, on the way home she throws it into a filthy ditch. This could be seen as an attack on Megan's sexuality or Clemencia's own self, the inner core of her being. As Wyatt suggests, this action could be the childless Clemencia's appropriation of Megan's maternity (252), and then rejection of that maternity. At the end of the story, the supposedly masculine Clemencia, who has rejected her femaleness by giving others so much pain, wishes to mother the suffering people she sees on the streets: "There, there, it's all right, honey" (83).

Clemencia certainly does not present an image of a strong, self-actualized Chicana woman. Although she is outwardly liberated, with middle-class occupations and a comfortable lifestyle, she hates both her Mexican and female side, allows gringo men to use her and obviously derives no pleasure from her relations with them or in her cruelty to others by taking on the negative aspects of the male role. Cisneros has spoken of the difficulty of living as a Mexican woman in American society, of often feeling like a foreigner, even though she was born here (Aranda 66). Wyatt feels that Clemencia shows this "double unbelonging" in her inability to master Anglo idiom. Clemencia says, "that's . . . water under the damn" (73). In a more dangerous way, by misunderstanding the full implications of the Malinche/ Cortéz story for Mexican women, she has allowed herself to be violated. Clemencia seems to misunderstand the several different elements in her background and is unable to combine them into a healthy identity. Lewis, however, believes that the obvious defects of Clemencia's character suggest that a successful combination might be found (71).

Lewis believes, and I agree, that Lupe in "Bien Pretty," the last story in the collection, represents a character who achieves synthesis and emerges from her experience a strong Chicana woman. As such, her story presents a fitting end to the volume. In some respects, Lupe is like Clemencia. She is an artist and a tough cookie who has just moved to San Antonio from the Bay Area, where years ago she was an activist student and a participant in the first grape strike. Recently dropped by her long-time boyfriend, Eduardo, for a blonde financial consultant, she has gotten a job as a director at a community arts center and intends to get back to creating her own art, which she has neglected. Her *comadre* Beatriz tells her that Texas is full of rednecks, and not a place for a "Meskin" woman; later, Lupe says she had no idea she would run into trouble from a Mexican man.

The theme of this story is not so much gender relations as it is achieving an understanding of one's roots and learning to live comfortably on the border between cultures. Ironically, Lupe achieves this through being rejected by her lover. From the beginning, Lupe knows she has a weak connection to her Mexican roots, but longs for a stronger one. She is not fully comfortable with Spanish and admires those who are. She is renting the home of a Texan poet of Mexican American descent that is just crammed full of "Southwestern funk," folk-art objects from Mexican/Aztec/Spanish and even Middle Eastern origins. When she moves from San Antonio, she brings with her a hodgepodge of belongings including a futon, a wok, some *rebozos*, some flamenco shoes, a Tae Kwon Do uniform, crystals, and a bunch of Latin tapes of all her favorite groups. These multicultural objects, plus her newly acquired home, seem to represent her lack of a firm identity.

The success of "Bien Pretty" is in large part due to the marvelous character of Flavio Munguía Galindo, Lupe's pest exterminator, who is almost her downfall. The story is preceded by a series of passionate love messages from a "Rogelio Velasco," the pen name of this rat, who teaches Lupe some important lessons about who she is. He is the sort of guy who thrills one's soul with romance, and has "Romelia. Forever," tattooed on his arm, and "Elsa" above his left nipple. Flavio is a pretty man, says Lupe, and she tells him this, which is a big mistake. Though he has the soul of a poet, he is actually a common *chaparrito*, short and stocky, with a flat, wide face that to Lupe appears as the sleeping face of an Olmec warrior, a perfect man made of red clay by the hands of God. When Flavio comes to her house to exterminate her roaches, not only is she powerfully attracted to him, she sees him as a subject for a romantic painting of an Indian prince from myth, kneeling beside his sleeping princess with volcanoes in the background, so she hires him as a model.

In addition to his exotic looks, Lupe is attracted to Flavio's strong sense of Mexican identity. He murmurs "real" Spanish to her when they make love and knows all the contemporary Latin dances. When Lupe prattles New Age jargon about yin and yang, how all forces of nature come in pairs, how one must get oneself in balance, Flavio connects it to a myth he learned not from a book, but from his peasant grandmother. When Lupe says if she can let go of the present and return to her roots, she will recover her destiny, he tells her, "You Americans have a strange way of thinking about time. You think old ages end, but that's not so. . . . American time is running alongside the calendar of the sun" (149–150). The past is not a dead thing to return to; it still exists with the present, and each affects who we are.

Flavio is not a person who must search for long-dead roots. When he teaches Lupe the contemporary dances, she wants to be taught "indigenous dances," a request that Flavio finds amusing. When she scolds him for wearing name brand American clothes, annoyed, he tells her, "I don't have to dress in a serape and sombrero to be Mexican, I *know* who *I* am" (151). Angry and hurt, Lupe wants to punch him, but she realizes he is right: she "was not Mexican" (152). Eventually, over tacos in the local diner, Flavio tells Lupe of his two "wives," (actually only one is legal) and four sons who need him in Mexico. He tells her that one "can love many people," that it (him leaving) is part of the "yin and yang" of life. Recognizing that he means this in a way she doesn't, Lupe watches him slide out of the booth and her life.

Lupe's anger and hurt over Flavio's rejection first lead her to ineffectual New Age crystals, incense, visualizations of positive images, and conjurings of loving thoughts and forgiveness, accompanied by folk music tapes of Amazon flutes, Tibetan gongs, and Aztec ocarinas. This conglomeration of cultural symbols gives her nothing but "an uncontrollable desire to bash in Flavio's skull" (157). She goes to her local voodoo shop and buys magic folk powders and herbs, along with an image of the Virgin de Guadalupe, so all spiritual bases, ancient and Christian, can be covered.

Healing and self-knowledge begins with burning Flavio's "Rogelio" poems in the Weber grill (though she does save one, pretty in Spanish, but just plain "goofy" in English). At first, she regresses, obsessively watching *telenovelas*, telling herself she is doing "research." She wishes somehow to wake up all these suffering women by slapping them (like she needs slapping) and helping them to become "women who make things happen, not women who things happen to." She wishes these TV women were fierce like her *comadres* and female relatives, passionate and powerful women (161). Earlier, Flavio had told her an instructive tale about his own grandmother, a woman with five husbands, who, with their baby, left the second husband the minute she found out he had been unfaithful. She went to Cheyenne, Wyoming, with her sister and stayed there fourteen years. The stereotypes of long-suffering Mexican women tormented by love are the fantasies of the media that many Mexican women overcome.

The primary source of Lupe's new knowledge is art—her own work and the myths of both ancient and contemporary culture—and also the example of other women. Buying a Mexican women's magazine, like the *telenovelas* perpetuating traditional images of women, Lupe recognizes herself in the angry-sad working-class cashier, who says she is waiting to rush home to her favorite soap. Later, Lupe thinks that she was not created to live vicariously in the soaps or to suffer for love. She will not sing the lyrics of the sad girls, but of pop singer Daniela Romo: "*Ya no. Es verdad que te adoro, pero más me ador yo.* I love you, honey, but I love me more" (163). She will enjoy life—its pain and grief, as well as its joy, and above all she will *live*. Lupe begins her painting of the Indian prince and princess again, but this time the prince sleeping under the volcano will be awakened by the princess.

Like many second-generation ethnic women writers, Cisneros has altered the themes of traditional folk art to create a new, truly hybrid context for the character's search, and in this case she has added to the old images positive images from contemporary culture. Even though Flavio has awakened Lupe, she is now an actor, not a passive "princess" waiting for her man. The end of her story finds her rushing home from work to paint on the roof, as she watches flocks of birds swoop and soar powerfully through the twilight sky, squawking their joy in the moment. This theme of cultural combination is also found in the earlier vignette "Little Miracles, Kept Promises," where college student Chayo combines the traditional long-suffering Virgin de Guadalupe with powerful Aztec goddesses; this syncretism will give her strength to resist family pressures to marry (128).

In *Chicano Narrative: The Dialectics of Difference*, Ramón Saldívar says that Chicano literature, by its nature rooted in conflict will not show characters who have fixed, centralized identities but rather characters who exist on the "unstable borderline" between several identities. There will always be unresolved dialectical tension (174). Certainly, this tension of unresolved ambiguity is present in most of the stories in *Woman Hollering Creek*. However, by being the last story in the volume "Bien Pretty" does seem to partially resolve this tension for the entire work. In this final story, Cisneros suggests that the children of the early stories, whose growth toward strong, joyful adulthood was sidetracked by rigid gender or social expectations, through personal struggle, through the help of their *comadres*, and through adapting images from the several cultures that surround them, can find a place on the border. By recognizing the restricting aspects of their cultures and capitalizing on their powerful pleasures and strengths, Chicana women can become comfortable with "life in the borderlands."

Although Cisneros does criticize the patriarchy of traditional Mexican culture and says that women must overcome its influence, she does not reinforce white Anglo ethnocentricity. Continually celebrating her Mexican heritage, she suggests all that would be lost through total assimilation: the language, the music, the folkways and arts, the warmth and security of community. The borderland is an ambiguous, risky, confusing place, but with thought, care, and much strength, a woman can be secure and even happy there.

WORKS CITED

Alarcón, Norma. "Chicana Feminist Literature: A Re-vision through Malintzin/or Malintzin: Putting Flesh Back on the Object." *This Bridge Called My Back: Writings by Radical Women of Color*. Ed. Cherríe Moraga and Gloria Anzaldúa. New York: Kitchen Table, 1983. 182–190.

Anzaldúa, Gloria. *Borderlands/La Frontera: The New Mestiza*. San Francisco: Aunt Lute, 1987.

Aranda, Pilar E. Rodríguez. "On the Solitary of Being Mexican, Female, Wicked and Thirty-Three: An Interview with Writer Sandra Cisneros." *The Americas Review: A Review of Hispanic Literature and Art of the USA*. 18.1 (1990): 64–80.

Cisneros, Sandra. "Do You Know Me?: I Wrote *The House on Mango Street*." *The Americas*

Review 15.1 (1987): 69–79.

____. "Ghosts and Voices: Writing from Obsession." *The Americas Review: A Review of Hispanic Literature and Art of the USA* 15.1 (1987): 69–73.

____. *The House on Mango Street*. New York: Vintage, 1991.

____. *Woman Hollering Creek and Other Stories*. New York: Vintage, 1991.

Doyle, Jacqueline. "Haunting the Borderlands: La Llorona in Sandra Cisneros's 'Woman Hollering Creek.'" *Frontiers: A Journal of Women's Studies* 16.1 (1996): 53–70.

Fiore, Teresa. "Crossing and Recrossing 'Woman Hollering Creek.'" *Prospero: Rivista di culture anglo-germaniche* 1 (1994): 61–75.

Gabaccia, Donna. *From the Other Side: Women, Gender and Immigrant Life in the U.S., 1820-1990*. Bloomington, Indiana UP, 1994.

Handlin, Oscar. *The Uprooted: The Story of the Great Migrations that Made the American People*. Boston: Little, 1951.

Leal, Luis, and Pepe Barron. "Chicano Literature: An Overview." *Three American Literatures: Essays in Chicano, Native American, and Asian-American Literature for Teachers of American Literature*. Ed. Houston A. Baker, Jr. New York: MLA, 1982. 9–32.

Lewis, L. M. "Ethnic and Gender Identity: Parallel Growth in Sandra Cisneros's *Woman Hollering Creek*." *Short Story* 2.2 (1994): 69–78.

Paredes, Raymund A. "The Evolution of Chicano Literature." *Three American Literatures: Essays in Chicano, Native American, and Asian-American Literature for Teachers of American Literature*. Ed. Houston A. Baker, Jr. New York: MLA, 1982. 33–79.

Saldívar, Ramón. *Chicano Narrative: The Dialectics of Difference*. Madison: U of Wisconsin P, 1990.

Savin, Ada. "Mexican-American Literature." *New Immigrant Literatures in the United States: A Sourcebook to Our Multicultural Literary Heritage*. Ed. Alpana Sharma Knippling. Westport: Greenwood, 1996: 341–365.

Thompson, Jeff. "'What is Called Heaven': Identity in Sandra Cisneros's *Woman Hollering Creek*." *Studies in Short Fiction* 31 (1994): 415–24.

Wyatt, Jean. "On Not Being La Malinche: Border Negotiations of Gender in Sandra Cisneros's 'Never Marry a Mexican,' and 'Woman Hollering Creek.'" *Tulsa Studies in Women's Literature* 14.2 (1995): 243–271.

9

Crossroads Are Our Roads: Paule Marshall's Portrayal of Immigrant Identity Themes

Toby Rose

It is almost formulaic that African-American and other ethnic women writers imbue their characters' conflicts with tropes of race, class, and gender. In her trilogy of novels and short stories, Paule Marshall has been no less concerned with aspects of identity for blacks, for women, and for the powerless. However, her portrayal of identity issues through her characters has always been more multifarious and layered than many of those who were born and brought up in one cultural milieu, however diasporan. Marshall sets out to find a home in the heart for her fictional descendants of African slaves and Caribbean colonial subjects in places where race, class, and gender are only the tip of the iceberg, problematizing already complicated journeys toward self-understanding.

My understanding of her characters' dilemmas has been made easier by my family history. Being a third-generation American Jewish female growing up amidst the old world expressions and ethnic perspectives of my grandparents, I could easily understand the dilemma of my American-born parents trying to assimilate and yet maintain the cultural links and familial ways of their immigrant parents. Not the least of these mores was the use of Yiddish as a language and the perspective of eastern Europeans as a worldview. Raised in a Jewish ghetto neighborhood that was fast becoming a stewing pot gathering of minorities and ethnicities of all stripes, I spent my early years surrounded by ethnic minorities and sheltered from mainstream America, a situation that was radically altered by my parents' flight to an all-white, upper-middle-class WASP suburb, where I soon learned the politics of difference and of choosing between my family's habits of the heart and those that oiled the way for acceptance by my peers' families.

Marshall's protagonists thrash through these complexities initially but go on to wrestle with tougher decisions involving not just acceptance of self vis-à-vis the dominant culture, but also straddling the increasingly global worlds and issues

sues that insinuate themselves into the lives of contemporary immigrants, migrants, and expatriates.

As a child of an immigrant family from the Caribbean growing up in a close-knit West Indian Brooklyn community, Selina Boyce, the protagonist of *Brown Girl, Brownstones*, must negotiate not only the conflicting identities of most Afro-Americans and those of other hyphenated American groups, but also the perilous, conflicting perspectives of her "Bajan" father and mother—one of whom, Deighton, rejects the idea that success for immigrants is owning a Brooklyn brownstone symbolic of the white family who had owned it and of the white race's former ownership of black people; it also symbolizes the immigrant's journey from poor islander to middle-class American. Instead, he longs to return to the sweet island life he remembers from his over-indulged childhood in Barbados. Selina's mother, Silla, however, leads a tenacious, sometimes brutal fight to achieve the American Dream so central to righting the wrongs of her childhood in the same island's cane fields and her immigrant struggles in America.

Selina must eventually be exposed to the stereotyped racial identities offered by her parents, and by the West Indian community in Brooklyn, as well as by mainstream groups. She finds that despite their common African roots, even Southern blacks are combatants with the Caribbean immigrants for scarce resources and status of the 1950s. But the knottiest identity crisis Selina faces is the one she has internalized as a female adolescent straddling two cultures and as a self-perceived powerless human being. She is filled with self-loathing and loneliness because she has allowed herself to be caught in so many feelings of ambivalence: toward her parents, her race, her self-image, and her Caribbean heritage. All these aspects of her life are part of the fractured identity she must resolve to become comfortable with her hybridity and to move toward bringing together the past and the present. As one critic notes, Marshall's work always "demonstrates how personal choices are inextricably linked to the social order within which each individual character moves" (Christian 108).

Some critics have termed dilemmas like Selina's "double-consciousness," others have described the fracturing of identity by two cultures as a "crossroads identity" (Cliff 263). Critic Dorothy Denniston explains Selina's dilemma in this way: "Cultural adaptations are often in conflict with indigenous customs and beliefs and frequently lead to ambivalence and confusion about one's place in society and the larger world" (33). Selina, who had always identified with her father's perspective of the world, fiercely rebels against her mother's struggle to be both an independent woman (going against traditional gender roles) and an economic success. When her mother has Deighton deported and he accidentally dies, she finds even more reason to despise Silla.

Selina's eventual acceptance of her mother's struggle to survive and of the strength of will needed by other immigrants to carve a niche for themselves comes only after an adolescent rite of passage among the dominant white culture, which she had blithely thought would accept her, puts her in her racial place. Joining her troupe at a white friend's house after a dance performance,

Selina is bombarded with a barrage of cruel racial cliches by the friend's mother. Eugenia Collier describes the effects of this scene:

Margaret's mother smoothly and graciously cheapens Selina's triumph and lets her know that nothing she does, no accomplishment, no excelling of white people will make her part of the white world. She validates Selina's existence by comparing her with Ettie, their honest, diligent West Indian "girl" with the charming accent, who kept their house spotless and was "just like one of the family." (16)

The crisis of identity following this incident reunites Selina not only with her mother, but with the Barbadian-American community, which she had rejected for their "provincial" ways. It also helps empower Selina to accept her past with all its baggage and to begin to choose from among those conflicting values to pave a path toward self-definition. To define herself on her own terms, she must also be able to see herself in terms of the black cultural matrix of all diasporan people, not merely a conjoining of her mother's or father's self-definition nor that of the romantic adolescent brown girl she had been.

Near the end of the story, Selina's telephone call to her friend Rachel to arrange passage aboard a ship to the Caribbean to explore her past marks her departure from adolescent confusions and her journey toward becoming a part of the newly emerging women who seek to build a new role for themselves within the larger community while building links with ancestral traditions. As a character from Belizean writer Zee Edgell's *Beka Lamb* expresses it, "It is only time, experience and emotional maturity that teaches some pioneers to try and graft the best of the old onto the best of the new" (90).

Marshall's portrayals of protagonists' negotiations between communities, and thus identities, become ever more complex with each new fictional creation. Not only do these negotiations mirror the cycles of aging and maturation natural to all humans, they also reflect the author's increasing concern with wider circles of humanity and the necessity for her Afro-American women to develop bridging relationships with other diasporan cultures, classes, and their own historical determinants.

As the novels progress, her heroines in particular seek to identify themselves with a wider swath of their migratory history than that represented by their West Indian community in Brooklyn or their small village in the Caribbean. To understand and complete themselves, they must go on to understand how their African traditions and the events of Empire and slavery have led to their present feelings of unease in the modern world—their double consciousness. To merge that consciousness, they must encounter the past through a physical return to the sites of their ancestral cultures and through ceremonies that reenact important cultural affirmations of solidarity or symbolic rituals that reverse historical tragedies of slavery and colonialism.

In *The Chosen Place, the Timeless People*, Marshall sets the stage for her Afro-Caribbean female protagonist to interact with characters and rituals who represent this cultural solidarity. Barbara Christian describes the evolution from Marshall's earlier work in this way: " In it she moved from a localized context in which she focused primarily on one character or one family to a portrayal of the entire socio-cultural fabric of . . . a prototypic Caribbean island. . . . Her vision does not change dramatically; rather, her emphasis moves from the way the world affects an individual psyche to how many psyches create a world" (112).

In this scenario, we meet island-born but newly returned exile Merle Kinbona, a woman who went to London to escape the limitations of her rural island home—a migration that resulted in two failed relationships with men, one failed relationship with a white woman, and the loss of her husband, her only child, and nearly her sanity. Her need for psychic healing has brought her back to Bourne Island and motivates her as well as the American Jew, Saul, to confront the parallels in their ancestors' historical suffering and diasporan separations from home.

Though the protagonist is a former colonial subject of Bourne Island who has returned from a traumatic sojourn in London, we can easily transpose Merle Kinbona with first-generation post-World War II Caribbean immigrants to America. Having traveled to the metropolis to seek relief from the poverty and lack of educational opportunities in the Caribbean, this group found a need to reconnect with their community, not only because of their exclusion from the dominant culture, but also because of the loss of identity they experienced being half in one culture and half in another. Like many immigrants who felt this loss, Merle rejoins her people, completing the pattern of exile and return seen frequently in Caribbean literature.

Merle's return gives her the spiritual sustenance and will to recover from her traumatic sojourn. She stops being a victim and, in the spirit of the 1960s, becomes a social activist working to ameliorate the postcolonial poverty and lack of economic base for the people of Bournehills. The American characters in *The Chosen Place* represent that good old sixties slogan: "If you are not part of the solution, you are part of the problem." Saul Amron, an anthropologist who is part of a team sent by a philanthropic agency to help restore Bournehills' financial and cultural health, is a positive influence. As such, he and Merle become soul-mates and co-workers. Harriet is his upper-crust Philadelphia wife who, despite her initial empathy for the people and the cause, eventually reveals her racist attitudes and need for control over others reflective of her family's slave-owner past. The members of this team believe they have come to this island to help poor islanders enter the twentieth century with American technical know-how. Instead, they find that it is too little, too late in terms of righting the wrongs that both colonialism and neocolonialism have imposed on the people.

Merle Kinbona travels beyond the psychic space inhabited by Selina Boyce when, as an immigrant living in London, she abandons her past for a metropolitan identity. It is not a space in which she can thrive; it is only when she begins to make choices premised both on her personal and her people's history—to stay within the traditions and lifestyle of their culture rather than use Western notions of progress as a measure of success—that she is able to carve out an existence that heals her personally and joins her to her community.

The culmination of this healing is effected by joining forces to bear witness to the village's finest moment: the heroism of a slave rebellion led by Cuffee Ned that resulted in the burning of the slave-master's plantation. Merle and Saul's participation in this ritual celebrates their personal healing process as well as those of their ancestors' tragic past. For Merle, the traditions of her ancestors in Africa before slavery are remembered by the rituals of Carnival: the singing, dancing, masques, and processions. For Saul, the exile and persecution suffered by his Jewish ancestors is honored vicariously by helping the islanders. For Marshall this rite is meant to honor and awaken the consciousness of oppressed people everywhere.

Marshall transforms politics and history into ritual and myth. In this symbolic re-creation of the brutal past, the survival of the timeless people is reified by the exclusion of Harriet from their midst. This literal exiling of the white controlling woman represents the demise of the Christian West as a dominant force, one whose historical cycles of wrongdoings included enslaving, colonizing, cultural imperialism, and a blind insistence on technology as the answer to all of the problems created by domination and exploitation of the islanders. Marshall uses Harriet to embody the covert arrogance of some American or Anglo expatriates toward Third World peoples, a patronizing posture. According to one critic, Harriet feels a sense of loss at the people of Bournehills' show of racial self-assertion and celebration: "She exemplifies the upper-class person so identified with privilege that it has become his or her sole identity. Without privilege, she fears that she would cease to exist" (Welch 60). But Dorothy Denniston concludes, "Marshall portrays her [Harriet's] predicament in such a fashion as to indict not so much the woman as the Western ideology that has shaped her" (121).

In addition to confronting the historical past, Merle confronts the traumas of her childhood when her white father's lawful wife killed her mother, and her father refused to acknowledge his parentage of her but tried to "buy her" an education. Part of Merle's struggle to heal her fragmentation is to move beyond the old strictures of birth and caste—social determinants that are reflective of the dominant Western values. By refusing to accept monies proffered by Harriet to leave Bournehills to search for her husband and child in Africa, she rejects such values. She had been commodified by white people in historical and in personal time frames; now she has the courage and strength to live without the patronage of others.

In essence, this parable of the destructive tendencies of Western civilization and its relations with the underdeveloped world traces the history of the relationships between whites and blacks at various times in history. Refusing to respect the lives and cultures of poorer, less powerful peoples, Western nations have tried to impose material progress on them, which threatens to annihilate their identities and connections with their past. For the female protagonist, Merle Kinbona, this belief in her people's need for wholeness even at the expense of angering dominant cultures, teaches her the necessity to bridge the present with her past—to draw nourishment from her customs and history.

Though this novel is not a thoroughgoing portrait of immigrant experiences, it does attempt to show how the impact of Western values and technology, whether in the United States or in what it considers its backyard, can result in changes, both positive and negative, for individuals and their cultures, depending on the motives of the interventionists. In this story Marshall gives a convincing account of the successes and failures of Anglo cultures' attempts to intervene in the social and political fabric of Caribbean nations since the 1960s: Merle and Saul's success in saving the natural resources of the island, including the old sugar cane factory, from being transformed into another site of British neocolonial exploitation, a tourist facility that would exclude islanders from using their beach. The failures referred to are past projects that have increased the islanders' dependency on foreign money or political power without providing them with more cultural autonomy. In the end, partnership, not hegemony, causes Saul and Merle to heal themselves and to save the community from its dependency and erasure of identity.

Through this somewhat allegorical narrative, Marshall shows us a kind of epic portrayal of the development of colonialism and the process of political and psychological liberation. This story has resonance not only for current development projects and policies sponsored by Western nations, but also for those trying to liberate themselves from the historical aftermath of colonialism and the confusions of cross-cultural identities exacerbated by the dominance of American culture in the West.

Some might see *The Chosen Place, the Timeless People* as a 1960s essentialist novel with its heroine's renunciation of middle-class, materialistic values and life in the metropole in favor of a back-to-the-land (and back to Africa) existence, but equally it could be read as a blending of Western ideals put to the service of securing non-Western traditions and culture. I believe Marshall sees beyond the very vital need for shaping a Caribbean consciousness to the need for acceptance of the admixture, the hybrid nature of the African cultures in the Americas.

In Marshall's next novel, *Praisesong for the Widow*, the focus is on the dangers of losing cultural connections and the restorative effects of balancing American identity and values with those of ancestral ethnic communities. This story particularizes the experiences of second- and third-generation Caribbean-Americans who wrestle with the dilemma faced by many contemporary people of the diaspora. Educated, de-ghettoized, middle class, and enmeshed in urban life and pursuits, it is easy for such descendants of immigrants to lose connections to their past and their African-ness. As one critic noted, "In this respect, *Praisesong* is a novel clearly connected with the late seventies and eighties, operating as it does, within a black middle-class setting, a context that has become much more relevant for American society in the past few years than it was before, in terms of sheer numbers, politics and social status of African-Americans" (Brock 88).

Avey Johnson, Marshall's representative of this super-assimilated condition, has all but forgotten the nourishment afforded her as a child visiting her Great-Aunt Cuney in the pastoral, poor American South and how the stories Cuney told of slaves who walked back to Africa would increase her pride in self and community. It might be said that the subtext of *Praisesong for the Widow* is a rewriting of the Matthew's biblical injunction: "What does it profit a widow to gain the world if she loses her soul?" Avatar Johnson must physically and spiritually leave her world of safe, suburban possessions and become possessed by an ancient culture she had been connected to as a child.

One's first impression of this scenario might be that the plot is inherently contrived and implausible, until one realizes that this reverse migration represents a very real choice for middle-class urban Americans. It is reflective of the larger problem of keeping the past alive and finding a sense of community in the anonymity of contemporary city life. That many black Americans are choosing to return to their Southern origins (or that immigrants from nearby areas are choosing to go back and forth across cultures) lends symbolic importance to the migratory themes considered in this next stage of Marshall's increasingly wide interest in the identity crises of the diasporan society.

The widow Avatar (Avey) is called upon to represent the spiritual or social malaise of the era. She must become an immigrant, a stranger in a strange land, in order to reassess how far she has wandered from that culturally connected young married woman who immersed herself in African-American culture, who lived in Harlem, and who remembered fondly her visits to the South, where Cuney would engage her in the oral history of the Ibos who walked back to Africa when they were enslaved in the new world.

As a tourist, force of circumstance causes Avey to give up, literally and figuratively, all her superficial notions of what is valuable in life. Marshall creates in *Praisesong* not only a middle-aged female immersed in the materialistic lifestyle of her white neighbors, but also a black woman who has strayed so far from her roots and her history into the lifestyle of the American Dream that she has lost touch with everything that was once important to her: her childhood experiences in the South, her personal relationships, and the black culture of Harlem. In essence, she has lost connection with her past and her people.

Furthermore, like her fictional predecessor, the young girl from America visiting her Caribbean grandmother in Marshall's short story, "To Ta-duh, In Memoriam," Avey has developed the attitude of the newly assimilated toward so-called Third World ancestors: a sense of superiority, an arrogance mirroring the larger model of Western societies' hegemonic behavior toward the culturally different and less powerful nations of the Americas.

Both in this novel and the previous one, Marshall creates scenes in which the newly rich and/or powerful black elite haughtily separate themselves from other diasporan blacks who are comfortable with their own traditions. Avey's friend and co-traveler, Thomasina Moore, portrays this disdain when she tries to insult Avey by comparing her behavior to an Afro-American woman she remembers who danced in an uninhibited and erotic fashion during a Carnival revelry in Cartegna: "That's why if I've said it once, I've said it a thousand times: it . . . don't . . . pay . . . to . . . go . . . no . . . place . . . with . . . niggers! They'll mess up ever' time!" (27). Marshall thus makes clear her disdain for elites of any race who patronize or exploit others, particularly those whose ancestors had endured the insults and hegemony of powerful elites.

The coda of the narrative promises a reversal of that hegemony—Avey will, like the prototypic African elder, pass on the heroic and cautionary stories to the next generation, imbuing them with the sense of who they are and where they came from and shielding them from losing their sense of self amid the Western present and hegemonic histories so omnipresent in the Americas. But before she can reconnect and regain her serenity, Marshall has her undergo a ritual cleansing of her body at the hands of a Carriacou islander who is a symbolic stand-in for a midwife giving birth or rebirth to Avey's lost connections to her identity. As Rhonda Cobham explains its significance, "The healing bath and massage to which Avey submits herself . . . recalls the laying on of hands within Christian and neo-African traditions. Subsequently, Avey participates in the island rituals, purged, cleansed and anointed; a fitting vessel for the spirits of the ancestors" (58).

Mrs. Parvay and her father, Joseph Lebert, who deliver Avey from her disconnected self, are stand-ins for Great-Aunt Cuney and for the generations of black people whose function it was to provide connection to their culture both in Africa and in the diaspora. This bridge is provided through Avey's inclusion in a ritual prayer asking forgiveness from ancestors for wrongs done to them and a tribal dance of inclusion in which she is transformed from Mrs. Johnson of White Plains, New York, to Great-Aunt Cuney's Avatar, who understands her mission as mediator in the cultural connection of her people with the past. Her spiritual experience, which reverses the direction of the Middle Passage, is both personal and collective.

Individually, each of Marshall's women are able to overcome their self-defeating behaviors and regain a sense of purpose in life, no matter what their age or social status. Collectively, they are able, as was Selina Boyce to some degree, and Merle and Avey to a larger degree, to then devote themselves to the preservation of the past and the building of bridges between ancestral wisdom and the contemporary materialistic world. Like the African mothers and grandmothers, they function as conduits who provide the younger generation with an understanding of the richness of their culture so they will feel like members of a community no matter how far they wander from the source.

In this novel, Marshall celebrates the essentialism needed to reconnect assimilated ethnic Americans to their traditions. But she is equally creating a cautionary tale of the dangers of Western materialism for all people—mainstream as well as minority. Having sloughed off ancestral culture for the economic and social gains of becoming upwardly mobile, Avey and others can fill this vacuum only by finding their spiritual center through community. Marshall believes in solidarity not only for all Africans in the diaspora, but also for all people who have become culturally and spiritually stranded or separated from the context that links them to others and shapes their sense of self.

In its thematic thrust, Marshall's next novel, *Daughters*, extends the use of an ever-widening referential circle. She begins with an extended family that includes a mix of individuals with lives lived in or linked to both the United States and the Caribbean. By interweaving the fate of Africans in two diasporan settings—the

United States and an Afro-Caribbean island called Triunion—Marshall is able to show how interrelated are the racial and sociopolitical problems in postcolonial new world societies. What happens in the United States affects Triunion and vice-versa. What happened in the colonial past influences the now independent island's "native son" political leaders, even those sworn to redress past inequities.

Daughters is a continuation of *Praisesong*: here again it is the middle-class American who is the wanderer or migrant in the Caribbean. Carol Boyce Davies notes the prevalence of the theme of migratory women in Marshall's works, especially the connection between these two novels when she writes, "In a variety of Marshall's works, the sense of physical and ideological examinations of identities is always posed" (148), but she sees this trope of journey and displacement as part of a larger pattern: "Migration and the fluidity of movement which it suggests or the displacement and uprootedness which is often its result, is intrinsic to new world experience, fundamental to the meaning of the (African) diaspora. . . . And each movement demands another definition and redefinition of one's identity" (128).

Estelle is such a woman. That her Afro-Caribbean husband Primus has political and social standing in the former British colony where she emigrates with him from the United States does not make it easier for her to implement her plans for helping the island's poor. Caught on the borderland between two cultures, both she and her daughter Ursa, whom she has sent to the United States to be influenced by the 1960s style liberationist black female ideology, at first watch helplessly as Primus leaves behind his youthful ideas of social justice and drifts into a kind of neocolonial alliance with powerful monied interests from abroad, one that disregards the needs of "the people" of Triunion. Initially, because his patriarchal hold over them is so powerful, Estelle and Ursa are unable to put aside their emotional ties to Primus in order to protest against his dwindling idealism and imminent co-option by outsiders. Eventually, both women overcome their traditional gender roles as wife and daughter to confront him and devise a plan to stop him from selling out to white developers who would once again exploit the island's resources for their own gain.

The major contrast between Avey and Estelle is that Avey represents the 1980s mentality—the generation of diasporan blacks whose economic success has led them away from a life and a culture that reminded them of oppression and marginalization, whereas Estelle is a woman of the 1960s or 1970s—educated and potentially a political activist who, because of her marriage and migration to Triunion, is stymied in her attempts to do the right thing. Her personal life has prevented her from acting according to her social and political conscience, a schism that threatens to fragment her sense of self. Avey is disconnected from her past, whereas Estelle and Ursa are all too aware of how love, sex, and so-called racial solidarity can keep black females from their individual and community responsibility to rise up against oppressors, even when those oppressors are their husbands, fathers, or lovers.

A political parallel to the power relations played out between men and women is played out in two arenas—on the postcolonial island of Triunion and in the eastern United States, where Ursa, the daughter of an Afro-Caribbean father and an Afro-American mother, has been sent to learn her mother's birthright. Having come from a family of civil rights-era activists, mother Estelle determines her daughter Ursa needs to be educated in her homeland so that she will model herself after women who are independent and politically astute. Estelle fears the role models in the Caribbean include too many "stand by your man" types who are economically and emotionally dependent on the island's males, even when they become corrupt. Ursa's role as a migrant in the United States involves trying to get a grant to help a black community in New Jersey recover from its slum-ridden economic state and become a viable, thriving community. This parallels the MacKenzie's idealistic plans for Triunion. As Joyce Pettis explains, Marshall juxtaposes the Caribbean and American communities to call "attention to a perplexing phenomenon: social, political and economic liabilities in so-called Third World countries are visibly similar to those that plague black people in First World countries" (89). As happens to many well-intentioned reformers, Ursa runs up against powerful agents: the mayor who sells out the community by letting a highway further divide them and a professor who rejects her community-based master's degree proposal. These experiences prime her for the realities of the world of power brokers, both black and white, including her own father. Marshall uses Ursa to portray the evolution of women by showing how she deals with the realities of power:

Ursa Mackenzie represents Marshall's pulling together of many ideas of women and power. Through her we can see both the expression of power as potential, the ability to define one's own values and to try to achieve them; that is, to live one's life according to those values. She rejects the idea of power over others, the power hierarchy that places its values in material goods and money, and one in which your place is too often determined by race, class and gender. Power to Ursa should be used to construct rather than to destroy. (Miller 50)

Primus Mackenzie, Estelle's husband, Ursa's father, and Astral Forde's lover, becomes the kind of destructive power broker Ursa ultimately rejects. But initially, these three female characters with heavenly names are set into motion as a constellation pulled irresistibly along in the powerful orbit around Mackenzie (called PM) to illustrate diverse and problematic male-female relationships involving one human being's control over another. The personal becomes political when that control involves watching PM's political ideals become increasingly self-serving and neocolonial. His wife, Estelle, though she fights the good fight to save him from himself, cannot leave him and cannot understand how his need for status and power springs from his childhood experiences as a colonial subject. It becomes the responsibility of his much doted-upon daughter, Ursa, to find the strength to both literally and figuratively leave his orbit of influence long enough to shed her emotional dependence on him and gain the reformist zeal needed to topple PM from his irresponsible and corrupt use of power.

It is not hard to see this novel as Marshall's clarion call for solidarity for all women of the African diaspora, to use their influence to transform and democratize life for the marginalized poor of Western societies. As daughters of Africa, they must move toward an identity that knows no borders, but reject imperialism from one's father or fatherland.

In these novels, Marshall has created a series of dilemmas for her female characters that resembles those created by Alice Walker for her women. But Marshall has upped the ante to include not only the need for women to find their own identity, but also the need for them to use that identity, be it gendered, racial, or humanistic, to reject tribal solidarity when it becomes necessary, to act for the good of their total community or the global community. For her, it is not enough for people to gain a sense of self by connecting with their ancestral past; they must also use the lessons of history in order to avoid the exploitative acts of slavery and colonialism, and to keep leaders, even men from their own family, from repeating the same sins.

Like Jamaica Kincaid in *A Small Place*, Marshall protests, albeit in a less strident voice, the domination of postcolonial black leaders who have fallen prey to the same exploitive mentality as their former colonial masters and present-day absentee landlords. She also implicitly connects current Caribbean politics to black politicians in the United States such as Marion Barry, who can use their power and the loyalty of their constituents to harm rather than help those they originally set out to uplift. The point is that unchecked power in all humans, especially those with large egos and perverted senses of entitlement because of past oppressions, creates the tendency to emulate those who oppressed them. Earlier novels such as George Lamming's *In the Castle of My Skin* and Earl Lovelace's *The Wine of Astonishment* portrayed this tendency of Afro-Caribbean leaders, when freed from exploitative colonial rulers, to degenerate into the same patterns of greed and betrayal as those who oppressed them, but Marshall's twist on this cautionary tale is to link the inertia and betrayals of Caribbean reformers to those of black leaders and political activists in the post-civil-rights era United States.

It is left, some may say unfairly, to those seemingly less maimed by the past and perhaps by the need to dominate—the females in Marshall's fictional world—to realign those temporarily out-of-kilter members of the family and point the way toward a truer path. But Marshall does not let the female characters show all the strength of will while the males all signify surrender to baser motives. She also aims her barbs at the female supporters and entourage of leaders such as PM, whose passivity in the face of their friend's, lover's, or husband's folly makes them as guilty of aiding and abetting as does Primus's elitist alliance.

Estelle is not able to effectively deter Primus from his hypocrisy in joining forces with financial investors who act in the name of promoting a new kind of imperialism—one based on the needs of tourists, to the detriment and loss of the native islanders. She is impotent to act herself, so she grooms her daughter in the United States to carry on the politics of resistance that she and Primus as young people were so committed to act on. Likewise Primus's mistress, Astral Forde, who is treated as little more than a servant, cannot resist Primus's exploitation of her. It is left to Ursa to be the new Nanny Maroon, a.k.a. Congo Jane, historical icons who symbolize black female resistance to oppression since the time of slavery. She will reenact the historical rebellion of female Caribbean heroes, but this time it will be against a neocolonial, her own father.

When Ursa perpetrates the rebellious act that unseats her father from power, she exorcises not only the stifling influence of her father over her, but also, symbolically, she liberates all the female descendants of African slaves who have not played an active, and when needed, dissenting role in the black community to ensure that the same cycle of domination is not repeated by their own leaders.

This novel, then, completes Marshall's trajectory of ever-widening paths to be discovered and traveled in the journey toward self-definition. Acting for oneself as well as for others is, as Marshall's vision shows us, the only path toward a bright future for all. The recovery of the many facets of one's identity turns out to be not merely a self-healing process, but is also representative of one's connection with the past by helping to create a community that will nurture the belongingness of diasporan people, and thereby help them shape a strong identity in whatever cultural context they find themselves.

Marshall's fiction has evolved in time and space from first-generation immigrants who are closeted in a parochial neighborhood of Brooklyn and trying to mediate between cultural identities and imperatives, to second and third-generation transcultural representatives of the African diaspora who are now secure in their racial skins, reconnected with their heritage, and attempting to negotiate a transformative global identity for themselves and others. While addressing the empowerment of blacks and other marginalized people in the Americas and the hybrid culture that binds them together, this literature highlights the dilemmas and triumphs of black women in evolving identities linked to the past but able to create new frontiers as their worlds change.

PRIMARY SOURCES

Edgell, Zee. *Beka Lamb*. Portsmouth: Heinemann, 1982.

Kincaid, Jamaica. *A Small Place*. New York: Penguin, 1988.

Marshall, Paule. *Brown Girl, Brownstones*. New York: Random, 1959; Chatham: Chatham, 1971; Old Westbury: Feminist, 1981.

———. *The Chosen Place, the Timeless People* (originally titled *Ceremonies at the Guest House*). New York: Harcourt, 1969; London: Longman, 1970; New York: Avon, 1976; New York: Vintage, 1984.

———. *Daughters*. New York: Atheneum; 1991: New York: Plume, 1992.

———. *Praisesong for the Widow*. New York: Putnam's Sons, 1983; New York: Penguin, 1984.

———. "To Da-Duh: In Memoriam." *New World Magazine*, 1967. Rpt. in *Black Voices: An African Anthology of Afro-American Literature*. Ed. Abraham Chapman. New York: New American Library, 1968. Rpt. in *The Heath Anthology of American Literature* 2d ed. Paul Lauter. Lexington: D. C. Heath, 1990.

SECONDARY SOURCES

Brock, Sabine. "Transcending the 'Loophole of Retreat': Paule Marshall's Placing of Female Generations." *Callaloo* 10.1 (1987): 79–80.

Christian, Barbara. *Black Feminist Criticism: Perspectives on Black Women Writers.* New York: Pergamon Press, 1985.

Cliff, Michelle. "Clare Savage as a Crossroads Character." *Caribbean Women Writers: Essays from the First International Conference.* Ed. Selwyn R. Cudjoe. Wellesley: Calaloux, 1990.

Cobham, Rhonda. "Revisioning Our Kumblas: Transforming Feminist and Nationalist Agendas in Three Caribbean Women's Texts." *Callaloo* 16.1 (1993): 57–58.

Collier, Eugenia. "Selina's Journey Home: From Alienation to Unity in Paule Marshall's *Brown Girl, Brownstones.*" *Obsidian: Black Literature in Review* 8.2–3 (1982): 6–19

Davies, Carole Boyce. *Black Women, Writing and Identity: Migrations of the Subject.* London: Routledge, 1994. 119–20.

Denniston, Dorothy Hamer. *The Fiction of Paule Marshall.* Knoxville: U of Tennessee P, 1983.

Miller, Adam David. "Women and Power, the Confounding of Gender, Race and Class." *The Black Scholar* 22.4 (1992): 48–51.

Pettis, Joyce. "Legacies of Community and History in Paule Marshall's *Daughters.*" *Studies in the Literary Imagination* 26 (1993): 89–99.

Welch, Sharon. "Memory and Accountability." *A Feminist Ethic of Risk.* Minneapolis: Fortress, 1990. 49–64.

10

Motherland Versus Daughterland in Judith Ortiz Cofer's *The Line of the Sun*

Carmen Faymonville

For many contemporary U.S.-based Puerto Rican immigrant writers such as Judith Ortiz Cofer, Puerto Rico serves as their frame of reference for continuity with ancestral "roots."[1] Cofer's work exemplifies this referentiality through a female connection between mothers and daughters that is fraught with tension and loaded with pain. This tension is thematized in *The Line of the Sun* through the characters Ramona and Marisol, whose roots are the same but whose worlds do not meet. Unlike the father who left behind what hindered his family's social mobility, Cofer's fictional representation of the maternal force, the character Ramona, brings the island with her to "El Building" in New Jersey but refuses to live in the present or to acknowledge the hybridization of her world. Entirely focused on maintaining island culture, Ramona, unlike her daughter Marisol, is unable to negotiate double identification and therefore remains unable to bridge the growing gap between them. Marisol, the Puerto Rican daughter who grew up in a bicultural environment in the United States is, however, unable to identify wholly with the island part of her identity. She has had to construct for herself simultaneous worlds that enable her to breathe island air right where she is. Rather than claim a diasporic heritage that would connect her to Puerto Rico as the land of her ancestors, Marisol instead possesses direct access to Puerto Rican reality because the island continues to be easily reachable, and continuous migration back and forth constantly refreshes the static exile and emigrant culture.

Cofer herself shuttled between New Jersey and Puerto Rico throughout her childhood. Once or twice a year, when her navy officer father shipped out to Europe, the rest of the family went back to the island for several months at a time.[2] She currently teaches at the University of Georgia, living and working away from the large Puerto Rican enclaves farther north and south. Despite, or rather because of, her geographic isolation, she has published several novels and collections of poetry dealing with the Puerto Rican migrant experience in the United States. Her autobiography, part poetry, part personal essays, *Silent Dancing: a Partial Remembrance of a Puerto Rican Childhood* (1990), and her collections of poetry, *Peregrina* (1986), *Terms of Survival* (1987), *Reaching for the Mainland* (1987) and *The Latin Deli* (1995) thematize her migrant and ethnic experiences, which are ridden with the tension of belonging no place: "When I go to Puerto Rico," Cofer complains, " I am always reminded that I sound like a gringa." Her situation reflects the migrant's situation of "never quite belonging" territorially or linguistically: "I speak English with a Spanish accent and Spanish with an American accent. I may end up with a Southern/Puerto Rican/American accent!" (Acosta-Belen, "A *MELUS* Interview" 89). In her novels of the immigrant experience, Cofer's narrators often grieve her marginality to both cultures but insist, more constructively, that their Puerto Rican-ness can be translated even into locations such as Georgia, where Cofer lives. In several interviews, Cofer has explained this new sense of Puerto Rican transnational identity that can be maintained independently from geographical location: "The Puerto Rican experience [formerly] was the experience of the people on the island; then it became the experience of people in New York City. Now it is the experience of people like me, who started out in New Jersey, and now I am in Georgia" ("Infinite Variety" 735).

Clearly, Cofer's new, different reality of diaspora cannot be understood through traditional concepts of nationhood and literary borders. As the history of the development of the modern nation-state shows, nations were formed by drawing borders quite arbitrarily and by disregarding the hybridity created through emigration and immigration, or conquest, in almost any society on earth. The crucial difference lies in the separation of geography from identity and a subsequent renegotiation of national belonging that questions cultural roots as a literal metaphor of soil and land. Cofer's own cultural repositioning, however, opens up a whole new discussion as to how to categorize literatures by migrant authors. Should we consider Cofer a Puerto Rican, a Puerto Rican-American, a Hispanic, a Latina, or simply an American author (given that the term "America" includes the whole continent, not just the United States of America)?[3]

In "Puerto Rican Literature in Georgia?," Ocasio labels Cofer a "Hispanic author resident in the United States" who tries to balance between assimilation and the expression of a unique, individual voice (43). This double focus of the female immigrant torn between acculturation to the customs of the new country and the maintenance of cultural traits, or at least, her own personality, emerges in *The Line of the Sun* as a conflict between choosing the world of the father or the world of the mother. Each choice, however, removes the immigrant character from several communities, and thus produces isolation and distance instead of multiple belonging. The question of belonging is, of course, a deeply personal one for any immigrant writer who has to assert her right to native authenticity. Hence, Cofer repeatedly insists in response to doubts about her own right to call herself a Puerto Rican that even if she doesn't live in Puerto Rico, she considers herself Puerto Rican ("*MELUS* Interview" 90). She thus draws a clear distinction between civic citizenship and national identity. Location for her no longer defines how a migrant finds political and geographical homes. In order to be Puerto Rican, one does not have to possess Puerto Rican genes or a U.S.-Puerto Rican passport. As Cofer further argues throughout her work, citizenship need not be synonymous with national identity, and neither does national identity nor state subjecthood need to be identical with cultural identity. Citizenship can be strategic and transnational when it is not based on ethnic belonging (through descent and birth) but is defined through civic participation, especially since Cofer's own version of *puertorriqueñidad* [Puerto Rican-ness] has existed in the form of a colonial relationship with the United States for almost 150 years now.

What makes Cofer special as a Puerto Rican immigrant writer is her distance from the styles and themes developed by an earlier generation of mostly male writers settling in the New York area who developed the so-called "Nuorican" style. Positioning herself outside the traditional diaspora culture, Cofer continues to place herself in the diaspora history of her people who also straddle the culture of their parents and the new environment, which compels them to change some of their thinking and behavior. Importantly, Cofer's Puerto Rico is not simply the Puerto Rico of her parents and ancestors; it is also currently and directly Cofer's because of the accessibility of the island through modern means of transportation and the instantaneous reality of the electronic media that allows her to keep Puerto Rico a living presence, not just a memory. Cofer herself asserts that she wants her work to be considered as part of the Puerto Rican literary tradition, "even though it sounds different" ("Infinite Variety" 734). Fully aware of the dangers of nationalist identification, Cofer, however, needs to stress her Puerto Rican-ness because it is the quickest and easiest to be elided in a U.S. context in which assimilation is massively enforced. Although cognizant of the advantages of her own Americanization, Cofer also positions herself as anti-assimilationist. In an interview with Marilyn Kallet, Cofer explains that "Many people of my parents' generation felt that if we assimilated, if we learned to live within the culture, it would be easier for us. I can see that as an economic survival technique, but as an artist I discovered that assimilation is exactly what destroys the artistic" (68). Cofer's juxtaposition of the artistic against economic survival would seem to favor her mother's discourse of ethnic separatism over the father's acceptance of new cultural norms offered to the protagonist of *The Line of the Sun* as guiding models.

Cofer is thus not simply seeking to recover the culture of her parents through roots and memory. As both a Puerto Rican and U.S. citizen without the hyphen that would make her into a Puerto Rican-American, she simply transcends traditional identity dualisms in her writing by rerooting the essences of culture and customs that supposedly form Puerto Rican identity naturally on the home soil. In this sense, Cofer's technique is one of defamiliarization and rerouting. What further complicates an understanding of this defamiliarization is Cofer's awareness that Puerto Ricans, although U.S. citizens, are often wrongly classified as "Spanish origin" or "Hispanic," and thus in the dominant imagination, as "foreign." Given the colonial legacy of Puerto Rico's survival as a nation, the assertion of Puerto Rican-ness in the face of U.S. imperialism can be read as an act of postcolonial resistance that nevertheless acknowledges the special position that colonial history affords Puerto Ricans in the heart of the empire, whether in New Jersey or Georgia. On the other hand, just because Puerto Ricans are U.S. citizens, not foreigners, does not mean that they do not have to face the psychological and political effects of dislocation and deterritorialization. Puerto Rican culture, language, and religion continue to be markers of difference, even if they can be traced to hybridizations introduced centuries ago by various colonizers of the island people.

In view of the recent efforts in American Studies to rename "American Literature" the "Literature of the Americas" in order to include the whole continent of American writing in American indigenous and settler languages, Cofer's own positioning of herself as a Puerto Rican writer clearly arises out of a resistance to homogenization. Although living in America, she is not just simply an "American" writer if that means inclusion only into the national category of U.S. literature.[4] Any writer from another country moving to the United States undergoes ethnicization when she is classified as a hyphenated American writer. That ethnicization, however, is not always welcome: exile writers, for instance, have always resisted incorporation into the national literature of their new residence because it elides their own sense of national belonging and the temporariness of their sojourn. In that sense, Cofer's assertion of Puerto Rican identity has to be seen as strategic even if she does not celebrate the joys of exilic existence. She therefore asks, "How can I separate my national background from my artistic impulse? I am a Puerto Rican woman possessing knowledge of that fact in a very intimate, personal, and intrinsic way" ("Puerto Rican Literature in Georgia?" 49).

The Line of the Sun thus contextualizes both the phenomenon of national subjectivity and the complexities of cultural affiliation constructed out of the intersection of diverse cultures. The long-accepted scenario of a "politics of arrival" thematized, among others, by Oscar Handlin in his famous study of immigrants, *The Uprooted*, is thus redirected by Cofer as a politics of cultural interchange and constant back-and-forth movement that reinvigorates both the society of origin and the society of destination. Consequently, none of Cofer's female characters can claim an identity anchored solely in one cultural heritage, or one nation, and therefore, none of them can simply "go home." Although many of the migrants peopling Cofer's fictional world attempt to transplant their matria, Cofer shows the limits of that project; simultaneously, however, she also shows the limits of the assimilation paradigm. In that median position, negotiating between cultural nationalism and cultural intermixing, Cofer has developed a defiant voice. She wants her readers to understand that in her representation of the Puerto Rican immigration experience there are different realities ("Puerto Rican Literature in Georgia?" 46).

Though Cofer rejects the assimilationist position, she continues to use English as her main fictional language and thus meets the expectations of her mostly English-speaking audience. How does this linguistic choice, given the cultural imperialism that the use of English symbolizes to many native Spanish speakers, balance a representation of Cofer as a Puerto Rican writer? Has the power of English and American imperialism not manifested itself to project a powerful influence beyond its own geographical borders and begun to push to the margins the Spanish mother tongue? In response to the problematic use of English as the colonizer's language, Cofer mixes the standard American English of her education with hybrid "Spanglish" forms by rendering Spanish idioms and sentence structures into English in her fiction.[5] As a personal rhetoric of resistance, the "Spanglish" works well to signal the independence of thinking and a resistance against an ethnification process that erases the specific national identity that Cofer wishes to retain.

A further effect of this technique is that it helps Cofer to transform both of her linguistic heritages: she transforms the English language by using Spanish, and Puerto Rican Spanish by using English that reflects the reality of transnational cultural interchange. Living in the United States where English-only movements increasingly gain recognition, Cofer implicitly challenges the "English-only" rule tacitly enforced in U.S. education and U.S. literature.[6] Although the "Spanglish" is clearly a compromise, Cofer's novels and poems contribute to a growing awareness that U.S. literature and culture is not only multicultural but also multilingual. Multilinguality, however, has traditionally fared badly in the United States, and it remains to be seen how modern communications and national awareness force the dominant forces in United States culture to integrate its "minor tongues." On the part of a bi- or multicultural author, this integration process in the present cultural moment still requires an act of translation when rendering the speech of characters. Cofer has stated that when she imagines characters, they speak Spanish to her and she translates them; she hopes to create characters who think differently and have a different syntax, yet are understandable to an American audience (Ocasio, "Infinite Variety" 734).

Besides her insistence on hybridity and translation as an act of resistance against cultural homogenization, what mainly differentiates Cofer from many of the emigré and Nuyorican writers is her focus on the dilemmas that women migrants face in relocating to a different society and language. Cofer concentrates especially on the consequences of migration and transnational existence for women and recognizes that gender is often pitted against ethnicity in their daily struggles of living in a new world. As women, they may want to choose liberation from sexist and misogynistic cultural practices and thus feel compelled to give up "ethnic" customs and behavior if they suggest limitations to female self-development. As an alternative to the sexism of certain customs or particular worldviews associated with national or ethnic culture, they instead choose Euro-American forms of femininity that seem, at least at first glance, more liberating. Yet that very attempt at female liberation often brings with it intense cultural alienation and the loss of psychological and philosophical homes. Cofer's migrant women struggle to establish a transnational space where constant interaction between their cultural identities can happen precisely because their cultures of origin are as patriarchal as their cultures of settlement. Paradoxically, only within that space of displacement can the power of traditional constructions of femininity be displaced by female immigrants. Generally speaking, all of Cofer's immigrant women protagonists face gender as well as ethnic subordination, which causes them to defend their culture of origin, despite its apparent sexism, against the perceived dominance of another culture, even if that culture includes other women who face oppression through their gender identity.

One of the main projects of *The Line of the Sun* is thus an exploration of the different choices migrant women face in their complex allegiance to contradictory cultural and national identifications. On the one hand, there is Ramona, the protagonist's mother, who grew up on the island and resents her relocation to the mainland as an act of dispossession. Ramona engages in nostalgic reverie but also finds a community of other expatriates who help her in her active maintenance of Puerto Rican traditions such as the religious practice of santeria, an indigenous non-Christian religion brought over from the island. Throughout the novel, Ramona clings to her idealized view of the island as paradise and continues to feel suspicion of and resentment toward Americans. When she encounters a young, blue-eyed American, for example, she wonders, "How could anyone who had no depth in his pupils see the world the same as she did with her dark brown eyes?" (160). For Ramona, cultural differences are absolute. Even after living in New Jersey for many years, she continues to find mainstream American culture impenetrable. In part, this impenetrability can be attributed to her culturally coded responsibility as a wife and mother that limits her mobility in the United States to the point that opportunities to learn English or acquire job skills are virtually non existent.

Ramona's retention of her native cultural identity also reflects the stereotypical social conservatism of traditional immigrant parents, which her daughter Marisol finds hard to bear as she understands the problematic stasis in her mother's hope that her island life might survive unchanged when translated to New Jersey (172). Ramona and her clique of Puerto Rican-born women living in "El Building"—an ethnic enclave, housing mostly Puerto Rican migrants—are thus marginalized as a result of both their migrant status and their gender-based lack of access to economic advancement (mainly through linguistic restrictions). But Ramona's cultural and political allegiance to the island is not solely born as a reaction to oppression; it is born even more out of a deep affinity with her national culture of origin. Ramona's choice of clothing, for instance, shows that she has consciously not assimilated. Her wild, loose hair, red coat, black shawl, and spike heels signify defiance rather than ignorance of American dress codes.

Her daughter Marisol, on the other hand, possesses a strong desire to assimilate to Euro-American standards because she witnesses the negative effects of her mother's choices. Cofer initially portrays Marisol as a typical assimilationist in the tradition of Mary Antin, who does not experience her biculturality as a source of enrichment.[7] For most of Marisol's childhood, biculturality simply confuses her. Although she recognizes the pull of different cultures, she has no identity-supporting link to an island that is located mainly in her mother's stories and an oral "other-world." Although Marisol is definitely linked to Puerto Rican culture through her family and her own back-and-forth migration, she seeks her young adolescent identity in the United States, which she largely prefers to her mother's homeland.

Marisol fears, for example, that her mother's dress code does not come from active resistance to assimilation, but from the fact that Ramona simply does not know how to dress correctly, that is, American-style.

What the mother treasures as cultural continuity and as self-expression in the style of her upbringing, the daughter cannot but perceive as outlandish. Throughout the novel, Cofer thus carefully explores both Ramona's allegiance to Puerto Rican ways of life as a refusal to assimilate on the one hand, and, on the other, as nostalgia. In the same dialectical fashion, she also critiques the daughter's anti-ethnic stance while showing the young adolescent's absolute need for individuation and self-definition. In a complex web of mother-daughter struggles, Marisol's assimilationist stance represents partly rejection of parental authority and partly kinship continuity: "She was what I would have looked like if I hadn't worn my hair in a tight braid, if I had allowed myself to sway when I walked, and if I had worn loud colors and had spoken only Spanish" (220). These dynamics of the mother-daughter relationship and the processes of young female adolescent identity development through separation from the mother are forcefully explored by psychologist Nancy Chodorow, who argues in *The Reproduction of Mothering* that many daughters seek to become the opposite of their mothers in order to find their own identity but discover gradually that they remain deeply connected by the umbilical cord. This need, and the concommittant failure to separate from her mother, is why the if-clauses structure Marisol's adolescent grammar as imperatives.

In her anxiety to differentiate herself as a person from her mother, Marisol feels her mother's embodiment of Latina femininity and sexual identity is undesirable, and instead prefers the self-concept of the stereotypical WASP, white American woman, an image that most American women, even if technically "white" or European-featured, find quite hard to match. Unable to separate ideal from reality, for Marisol, the media images of American femininity limit her desire to become her own self. Moreover, as an extension of Marisol's own fragile self, her mother threatens to destroy the assimilated public self that Marisol tries to portray. Americanization thus becomes a matter of individuation since only in her public persona as an American can Marisol be the complete opposite of her exotic "un-American" mother.[8] For her, the mother's body and sexuality stands for a form of cultural retention that leads to nostalgia and false claims to the authenticity of cultures. As the "strange" daughter, on the other hand, Marisol herself stands for an equally "impossible" total Americanization at the cost of ethnic memory. For the cost of total Americanization is the connection with a "line," the line of the sun and its homophone, the genealogical line from the motherland.

The negative effects of Marisol's break with ethnic culture become dramatically apparent in a crucial scene in *The Line of the Sun* involving the religious ritual of santeria.[9] Marisol so fears the ethnic tribalism that she enters a room of santeria worshippers in "El Building," in which candles and open fires are lit, and causes the whole building to go up in flames. Finding she cannot breathe while she searches the dark room for her mother and scared that the American police are about to storm the building because they suspect a form of terrorist conspiracy, she opens a window. This opening effectively brings in the destructive outside world that the women of "El Building" have tried to keep at bay. This act of opening the window breaks through the ethnic communal experience and forces the worshippers to realize their American environment. In a very physical sense they have to acknowledge the winds of change. The reader is left uncertain as to whether Marisol realized that the opening of the window would cause massive destruction. Yet her act ultimately destroys the ethnic community: the building burns down, everybody disperses and Marisol's family moves to the WASP-American suburbs because the building now bears the taint of ethnic revolt and lawlessness.

Importantly, however, Marisol, still imagines that island life would have been better than her U.S. existence, and she finds her 100 percent American status harder to establish than she initially thought. Because of her homelessness in both locations, Marisol feels like an outsider both in the American and the ethnic world: "I was already very much aware of the fact that I fit into neither the white middle-class world of my classmates at Saint Jerome's nor the exclusive club of El Building's 'expatriates'" (177). So where does the young immigrant daughter fit? In fact, dominant society continues to define her as "other" against her desire to blend in. In school, for example, Marisol is still identified as foreign, different even from the other immigrants of European origin. So, despite her desire to blend in, others continue to address her only in terms of her ethnic identity. Marisol has to realize that racial and ethnic difference is assigned to her from the outside and is not hers to choose. Marisol's skin color, for example, is visibly different from that of her classmates and thus sets her apart. She is "the smallest, darkest member of a class full of the strapping offspring of Irish immigrants with a few upstart Italians added to the roll" (218). The visible racial difference inscribed on her body cannot be hidden or made invisible. As Marisol gradually discovers about her own position, pretending to be Anglo will not by itself lead to acceptance. As a non-white subject, she will remain a cultural icon represented precisely by her "over-visibility." Her skin color becomes, in Mary Ann Doane's words, a "locus of an alienation more acute to the extent that it is inescapable" (223).

Despite her seemingly adamant rejection of Puerto Rican diaspora culture, Marisol remains fascinated with island culture, particularly through her connection with a son of the island, her Uncle Guzman. Marisol's imaginative reconstruction of her uncle's biography in fact takes up more than one-half of the novel and reveals the immigrant's desire to connect, at least in dreams and in the imagination, to share the everyday lives of people on the island. Marisol's imaginative reconstruction of Guzman's story represents her psychological need to imagine Puerto Rican culture outside her mother's realm. In imagining and apparently narrating Guzman's experience of love, passion and destruction, Marisol scripts her family history and the history of her country into her own developing self. In the style of magical realism, Marisol imagines the sensuous landscape of Puerto Rico, her uncle's childhood as it must have been, his initiation to sexuality, and his people's reaction to his transgression of customs as a foil to her own daily struggles.

In following the genealogical line in the pattern of the line of the sun, Marisol eventually returns to her very own reality and decides that "Though I would always carry my Island heritage on my back like a snail, I belonged in the world of phones, offices, concrete buildings, and the English language" (273). The United States appears as her rational home, the home where her ego resides in contradistinction to Puerto Rico, which remains the realm of her unconscious.

The generational difference between Marisol, who came to the United States as a child, and Ramona, who left behind a life full of family connections and memories, remains unbridgeable and is never resolved in the plot of *The Line of the Sun*. For Marisol, national identity can never represent quite the same definable essence as it seems to for her mother. Contrary to Ramona, who tries to maintain her ethnic and national culture through food, style of dress, choice of neighborhood, and friends, Marisol is not willing to reify her own ethnicity as a relic from the past that needs to be preserved at all costs. Although she appreciates the island music, for example, she cannot quite understand how the adults believe they are maintaining authenticity. For Marisol, the island food and the spiritist meetings are rendered increasingly meaningless as symbols of an authentic culture that ultimately relies on the enforcement of essentialist categories. She realizes that El Building, the "ethnic beehive" in which the resident Puerto Ricans have seemingly re-created the island, cannot represent "true" Puerto Rican culture and can only appear as a parody to her (223). Contemptuous of what she experiences as emotionality and nostalgic revelry that clashes with her perception of superior rationality, Marisol can find no other stance but mockery in her own need for a separate identity: "They would become misty and lyrical in describing their illusory Eden. The poverty was romanticized and relatives attained mythical proportions in their heroic efforts to survive in an unrelenting world" (174). In a complex psychological act of separation, Marisol's analytical mind dissects the visceral ties that bind her to her mother's culture in favor of an empiricist American worldview.

Trying to exorcise the color of her life and her own coloredness, Marisol even desires a bland color-coordinated home, Sears catalog-style: "curtains, sheets, throw rugs, and cushions matched in the best middle-class American taste" (283–84). In this desire she is supported by her father who, unlike her mother, tries to promote the family's assimilation. But when he seeks housing, he realizes that he and his family have not made it into the American mainstream as they are now segregated with Italian immigrants in a more middle-class but still marginal neighborhood (282). In a culture in which racial and ethnic lines are still stringently enforced, the irony of their compatibility with Italians is solely based on their apparent comparability in appearance, name, accent, and similar ethnic customs, an assumption that erases enormous cultural and historical differences. Painfully aware of their ethnicization by mainstream Americans, Marisol and her father are trying to erase ethnic visibility by becoming colorless even in the privacy of their home.[10] Ramona, on the other hand, reacts with depression to life in a suburb, which signifies spiritual loss and the absence of cultural familiarity. In contrast to El Building, where Ramona could still define herself in the familiar terms of her childhood culture and, thus establish psychological stability, the social fabric outside the ethnic enclave fails to support her. In her mind, the suburbs are "the square homes of strangers." In a surreal act of cultural understanding, Ramona perceives the Stepford Wives atmosphere of a midcentury suburb as soul-destroying and robotic: "You could see the people moving and talking, apparently alive and real, but when you looked inside it was nothing but wires and tubes" (172–73). In this "white" world, there is no space for her or "the brilliant reds and greens and yellows" of her memory of Puerto Rico.

Marisol and her father, on the other hand, have eliminated the cultural dimension expressed in color signifying their own nonwhiteness, and thus instituted the dominant culture surrounding them even at home. Father and daughter thus collude in Ramona's isolation in a country that remains foreign to her now also in her close family circle. Ultimately, Ramona becomes the "proverbial gilded bird in the cage," who no longer leaves the house or interacts with the world that offered her a house but not a home (285).

Cofer's main contribution to the representation of Puerto Rican women's immigrant experiences in the United States in this novel is her message that ethnic and national identification involve a process of continuous invention that links past, present, and future. For her characters, identity is always a constant negotiation between their perceptions of culture, ethnic essentialism, competing national affiliations, and gender roles. In pitting mother against daughter, Cofer models a range of responses to the migration process, which are all influenced, nevertheless, by the Anglo-American intrusion into Puerto Rican lives both on the island and on the mainland. Seen from Cofer's position as an academic living in Georgia, what Ramona and her friends defend as "truly" Puerto Rican culture, is, in fact, a culture that has long interacted with United States culture and thus has many intercultural traits. Thus, despite her acknowledgment of her own roots, Cofer is not a cultural nationalist, and she challenges concepts of cultural homogeneity even in the interest of national liberation projects. In *The Line of the Sun*, Cofer makes a good case for cultural relativity, since any attempt to recreate Puerto Rico in New Jersey authentically and statically in the way Ramona seeks to do must inevitably fail, just as a frozen-in-time memory of the homeland prevents a constructive dealing with the past.

In the larger scheme of current political discussion, Cofer argues against visions of cultural purity in which Puerto Rican identity is seen as fixed and unchangeable. In contrast, she also shows the pain and confusion of the migrant characters who are forced to deal with their eroding sense of cultural self. Just as her fatherland, the nation her father chose, constricts the young immigrant's vision of herself, Marisol's motherland also negatively affects her independent development. Cofer, in fact, warns that although it is dominant society that assigns essentialized ethnic identity, ethnic communities relying on essentialism themselves can aid in their own destruction. The author instead rejects the drawing of borderlines on either side by arguing for culture flow. Thus, the immigrant's conflict, as Cofer analyzes it, is not so much ethnicity pitted against American-ness but determining what kind of a national or cultural allegiance to choose in a world that has become transnational, and where the local is global and vice versa.

As *The Line of the Sun* illustrates, ethnic identity is always in progress and cannot be defined simply by static notions of "authentic" and time-honored ways of doing things or speaking a certain way. Thus, neither of Cofer's characters can produce a stable and essentialist Puerto Rican or U.S.-American identity. Cofer shows through Marisol that assimilated American identity is an illusion, just as the homeland as pure container of culture is an illusion. Aware of the dangers of cultural domination by one group in a multicultural society, Cofer illustrates the responsibility of immigrants to maintain aspects of their selves and their cultural attributes by documenting the police reaction to the fire in El Building. The hysterical reaction of the police to the perceived threat of ethnic difference and subversion demonstrates to readers that ethnic erasure is a real threat and that states often do enforce cultural uniformity in the guise of security and order. Cultural erasure happens despite the separate space that U.S. culture affords its minorities. Where immigrants legitimately fear the death of ancestral culture, Cofer's transnationalist stance offers ways of keeping up the ancestral in the present. In Cofer's ideal immigrant world, reality is always hybrid; this hybridity affords both the individual and the community a foot in more than one culture, and in coexisting nations.

Cofer's politics of identity joins those who are geographically scattered into an imagined unity of identification: a placeless community of interests to be imagined by anyone who feels connected by heritage or history to the Puerto Rican nation. *The Line of the Sun* thus succeeds in constructing counter-narratives to traditional nation-space and in creating new literary spaces. Cofer's argument goes beyond alternative conceptions of nationhood to a re-visioning of the nature of the nation and who should be understood as representing the nation. From Cofer's perspective in Georgia, the creation of the Puerto Rican nation is ongoing and open to reinterpretations and rediscoveries.

The larger significance of Cofer's identity politics lies in her critique of ethnification and the limits she perceives in visions of multicultural societies. As the multicultural ideal is still tied to the notion of a singular nation, only identities within the nation can be contested, not the identity of the nation itself. As a Puerto Rican living in the United States, Cofer questions the long-standing rhetoric of "us" and "them," citizen and foreigner, through the lens of a transnational perspective. Although her novels are not openly didactic, Cofer's recent poetry/prose collections and novels are testimony to her critique of both United States and Puerto Rican nationalist orthodoxy, which, she feels, can draw an unnecessary tie between race, nation, and culture.

Although Cofer respects the right of the immigrant to retain cultural identity, her use of the label "Puerto Rican writer" suggests something different from both multicultural American identity as a hyphenated member of the nation and from ethnic nationalist membership in one particular diaspora group. In her claiming of the "Puerto Rican" literary-national category, she avoids hyphenation, prefix, suffix, and hybridity. Whereas other authors such as José Marti had opted for cosmopolitan universalism, Cofer insists on the power of descent to define the lives of people, and particularly writers who are in the process of creating a more diverse literature of the Americas. For Cofer, then, globalization does not represent an abstract force but the emergence of a very local transnational culture. To some degree, *The Line of the Sun* binds its creator to a larger regional Latin and Middle American context by its Garcia Marquez-style magical realism. To yet another degree, Cofer fits into a long line of American immigrant authors who write about their adjustment to a new culture. Through her double-perspective imaginative act, Cofer connects her migrant protagonists to their homeland as a special place that is more than a mere geographical area.

Echoing Werner Sollors' groundbreaking argument in *Beyond Ethnicity*, Cofer points to the difficulties of ethnic identification in today's postmodern consumer culture in which ethnicity is not a matter of descent but a matter of consent or voluntary identification. Although Cofer does not argue that one can select from the shelves of ancestors at will, her own choice of calling herself Puerto Rican despite her U.S. citizenship and residence uncovers the way identities are chosen, not assigned. In other words, as Sollors describes the complex psychology of national and ethnic affiliation, "ethnicity . . . is a matter not of content, but of the importance that individuals ascribe to it" (35). With historian Benedict Anderson, Cofer shares a belief in the construction of national communities through the imagination. Thus, her own representation of Puerto Rico as an imagined community addresses the specific history of emigrants in that imagined community. Having relocated to the United States, for Cofer, the imagining of her country involves the imagining of a home beyond the immediate experience of place. This separation of soil from political and psychological space, according to Anderson, is necessary because community always has to be imagined. It has to be imagined mainly because community must go beyond immediate experience and location if it is to embrace inclusiveness rather than exclusiveness.

Importantly, the strength of Cofer's identity politics in *The Line of the Sun* is that she is breaking with the modernist nationalist imagination in which separate nations stand completely apart from each other and in which borders that distinguish between citizens and noncitizens are being tightly controlled. In this modernist conception of nation, one national territory can never overlap with another as nations supposedly stop and start at borders, however arbitrarily drawn. What we now consider modernist theories of nationhood stipulate that a people, a place, and a state should be bound in unity, yet for Cofer the emigré writer is compelled to create a new construction that questions a quasi-mystic bond between people and place. The special quality of identity shared by Puerto Rican islanders and emigrants does not stop at the border and the water separating the island from the mainland. Even the border of an ocean cannot stop the sense of national belonging that many of the island's migrants feel. In looking both at totality and particularity, *The Line of the Sun* effectively looks beyond boundaries and a universalist homeland to a new concept of national identity where "we" and "them" are no longer reproduced. Cofer instead recognizes that the consciousness of national identity assumes an international context and that any nation must be imagined as a nation among other nations. It is Cofer's achievement to conceptualize Puerto Rican-ness simultaneously as the universalization of particularism and the particularization of universalism.

Although the preservation of different ways of being in the world is of special importance to Puerto Rican migrant authors such as Cofer in their attempt to maintain affiliation with island culture, *The Line of the Sun* illustrates in the end that migrant women cannot easily recover a culture of origin even if they follow the lines of the sun back to ancestral spaces. Yet for those immigrants who have never lived in the actual world of island culture, re-creation and imagined communities can provide a lifeline that can sustain them through times of discrimination in their place of residence.

NOTES

1. Though back-and-forth migration intensity varies with changes in the U.S. economy, the fact that Puerto Ricans are U.S. citizens has aided their back-and-forth migration patterns and continues to bring new migrants to the United States.

2. Born in Hormigueros in 1952, Cofer translocated to Paterson, New Jersey, with her family at age two. After the 1968 riots in the Puerto Rican neighborhood in Paterson, the family moved to Georgia.

3. Each of these choices signifies different identity markers and historical constellations with wide-ranging political effects. Increasingly, Latina/o, Chicana/o, Mexican, Canadian, and Caribbean scholars see the entire literature of the continent as interconnected. See, for instance, Lauro Flores, *The Americas Review*, 23.3–4 (Fall/Winter 1995); 9–15; Silvia Spitta, *Between Two Waters: Narratives of Transculturation in Latin America*, (Tulsa: U of Oklahoma P, 1996); Ileana Rodriguez, *House/Garden/Nation: Space, Gender, and Ethnicity in Post-colonial Latin American Literature by Women* (Durham: Duke UP, 1994); and Gordon Brotherston, *Book of the Fourth World: Reading the Native Americas through Their Literature* (Cambridge: Cambridge UP, 1993). As an example of this new concept of the Literature of the Americas, Cofer's transgression of the traditional separations of nationality, race, and gender helps readers to see how the boundaries between the American hemispheres can be overcome on the basis of shared cultural, social, and economic relationships.

4. For information on the concept of the "Literature of the Americas," and the changed perception it allows of national literatures and writers' identification within literary national borders, see, among others, Judith E. Petersen, "Golden Discoveries: Literature of the Americas," pp. 39–45.

5. Even in Puerto Rico, she went to American, mostly Catholic schools. Spanish is her second language, though it was spoken at home. Cofer calls Spanish her "subconscious language, [her] cultural language, [her] birth language" ("*MELUS* Interview" 90).

6. In Puerto Rico, and among the emigrant and transnational communities, a sometimes bitter debate is being waged over the use and "abuse" of Spanish and its political functions in a country that actively discourages foreign and indigenous language use. American cultural imperialism on the island is so strong that ethnic nationalists advocate Spanish use only. As writer Rosario Ferre states in an interview with Marie-Lise Gazarian Gautier, "What's sad is that we've forgotten Spanish and never learned to speak English. We have no

language of our own" (83). In addition, some island residents seem to resent the current popularity of U.S.-based, Puerto Rican-identifying writers who choose English as their language, and who disregard a community of readers speaking only Spanish on the island. Cofer, however, translates her own work into Spanish and makes it accessible to both linguistic communities she embraces.

7. In *The Promised Land*, Mary Antin describes her own experience as an immigrant at the beginning of the twentieth century. Antin represents life in the United States as paradise and advocates complete assimilation and the revocation of ethnic ways of life through describing her "re-birth" as an American sister of hero George Washington.

8. Nancy Friday's *My Mother, My Self* is also helpful in understanding the paradoxical dynamics of mother-daughter relationships in which the close bond mothers and daughters share produce both a feeling of interconnectedness and a sense of stress that can hinder the psychological development of self.

9. Cultural identity is often expressed as practical and conceptual difference from dominant modes of religious practice. To be ethnic in America has historically been associated with spiritual otherness: the Irish, the Germans, and the Italians, for instance, had been branded as unassimilable not only because they spoke differently, but also because their Catholicism flew in the face of American Protestantism. Yet for Marisol, religious differences appear to be coded as inferiority and "primitivism" (246).

10. Even before Marisol was born, Rafael had wanted to choose a name for the daughter that could easily be pronounced in English (167). Another sign of the family's pre-emigration assimilation to Euro-American practices is that they no longer celebrate Christmas on Three Kings' Day, as the Puerto Ricans do, but American-style on December 25 (186–87).

WORKS CONSULTED

Acosta-Belen, Edna. "The Hispanic Legacy." *The Hispanic Experience in the United States: Contemporary Issues and Perspectives*. Ed. Edna Acosta-Belen and Barbara Sjostrom. New York: Praeger, 1988.

Anderson, Benedict. *Imagined Communities: Reflections on the Origin and Spread of Nationalism*. London: Verso, 1983.

Antin, Mary. *The Promised Land*. Boston: Houghton, 1912.

————. "A MELUS Interview: Judith Ortiz Cofer." *MELUS* 18.3 (1993): 83–98.

Brotherston, Gordon. *Book of the Fourth World: Reading the Native Americas through Their Literature*. Cambridge: Cambridge UP, 1993.

Chodorow, Nancy. *The Reproduction of Mothering: Psychoanalysis and the Sociology of Gender*. Berkeley: U of California P, 1978.

Cofer, Judith Ortiz. *The Line of the Sun*. Athens: U of Georgia P, 1989.

————. *Silent Dancing: a Partial Remembrance of a Puerto Rican Childhood*. Houston: Arte Publico, 1990.

————. *Peregrina*. Chicago: Riverstone, 1986.

————. *Terms of Survival*. Houston: Arte Publico, 1987.

————. *Reaching for the Mainland*. Houston: Arte Publico, 1987.

————. *The Latin Deli: Telling the Lives of Barrio Women*. New York: Norton, 1995.

Doane, Mary Ann. *Femmes Fatales; Feminism, Film Theory, Psychoanalysis*. New York: Routledge, 1992.

Ferre, Rosario. Interview with Marie-Lise Gazarian Gautier. *Interviews with Latin American Writers*. Normal: Dalkey Archive P, 1989.

Flores, Lauro. *The Americas Review: Review of Hispanic Literature and Art of the USA* 23.3–4 (1995): 9–15.

Friday, Nancy. *My Mother, My Self: The Daughter's Search for Identity.* New York: Delacorte, 1977.

Handlin, Oscar. *The Uprooted.* 1955. 2nd ed. Boston: Little, 1973.

Kallet, Marilyn. *Worlds in Our Worlds: Contemporary American Women Writers.* Upper Saddle River: Prentice Hall, 1997.

Ocasio, Rafael. "Puerto Rican Literature in Georgia?: Interview With Judith Ortiz Cofer." *The Kenyon Review* 14.4 (1992): 43–50.

———. "The Infinite Variety of the Puerto Rican Reality: An Interview with Judith Ortiz Cofer." Special Issue: Puerto Rican Women Writers. *Callaloo* 17.3 (1994): 730–743.

Petersen, Judith E. "Golden Discoveries: Literature of the Americas." *English Journal* 81.5 (1992): 39–45.

Rodriguez, Ileana. *House/Garden/Nation: Space, Gender, and Ethnicity in Post-Colonial Latin American Literature by Women.* Durham: Duke UP, 1994.

Sollors, Werner. *Beyond Ethnicity: Consent and Descent in American Culture.* Oxford: Oxford UP, 1986.

Spitta, Silvia. *Between Two Waters: Narratives of Transculturation in Latin America.* Tulsa: U of Oklahoma P, 1996.

11

Obasan and Hybridity: Necessary Cultural Strategies

Matthew Beedham

Sometimes based on artifacts, sometimes on dreams, on recollections, newspaper clippings, a letter and an undelivered letter-turned-journal, Joy Kogawa's novel *Obasan* displays many different types of discourse working together to relate a particularly brutal chapter in Canadian history. In the midst of this *bricolage*, perhaps it is not a surprise to find numerous instances of juxtaposition: a brother with "peanut-buner sandwiches," and his sister with "two moist and sticky rice balls" (153) should not seem too out of place; nor should a child pondering an Old Testament story of a Buddhist cremation (131). However, the stakes involved in these contrasts surpass narrative play; *Obasan* portrays a Canada laden with stagnant racial thinking that forces the immigrant community to confront the fracture in their cultural identity. By tracing the dual identities pressed upon Japanese Canadians, and the progress of one member of this group from detachment to involvement, Kogawa discloses the terms for cultural survival. Although we cannot plot cultural integration with pins and ribbons on a large map, we do need to be aware of the need for constant renegotiation of what constitutes our society as we attempt to live up to our self-proclamation of "multicultural." Although it is a start, calling ourselves multicultural does not make us so.

A crucial interstice for both the colonized and the immigrant is the issue of hybridity. Hybridity is an oft-debated issue in postcolonial studies, and as the plurality inscribed in its name suggests, it exists in a heterogeneous and often fragile state. Bill Ashcroft, Gareth Griffiths, and Helen Tiffin's attempted definition captures this diversity; they write, "Hybridity occurs in post-colonial societies both as a result of conscious moments of cultural suppression, as when the colonial power invades to consolidate political and economic control, or when settler-invaders dispossess indigenous peoples and force them to 'assimilate' to new social patterns" (183). By documenting the experience of Japanese Canadians shortly before, during, and in the years following the Second World War, Kogawa provides a contemporary and important example of this process.

The unconventional twist in the case of the Japanese Canadians is that they were invaded, dispossessed and interned by the country to which many of them belonged. Through Kogawa's principal character Naomi, we are able to read of the extent to which Japanese Canadians had established themselves in Vancouver before the war, and we see the internment camps into which the Japanese Canadians were ordered. Further, we watch the disintegration of Naomi's family, including her brother Stephen's detachment, which was initiated by the internment, and the "new social patterns" to which they were encouraged to conform. In this last phrase, as Naomi goes through the process of recounting, we are able to see the effect of her remembering: the extent to which Naomi is able to join the challenge to an oppressive hegemony and how the challenge helps her resolve her hyphenated existence as a Japanese Canadian.

Very early in the novel, on the second page to be precise, the stakes in studying hybridity are adumbrated by the connection Kogawa asserts between Japanese Canadians and First Nations people. Naomi observes that her uncle resembles Chief Sitting Bull, with similar coloured skin and wrinkles. True, he is missing a war bonnet, but with that he could appear on a souvenir postcard from Alberta, labeled "Indian chief from Canadian Prairie . . . made in Japan" (2). This imaginary postcard gathers together three important political distinctions: the Indian chief reminds us of the identity of the indigenous population of Canada. This recollection leads to the present state of the Indian chief; his value has been re-inscribed in the reduced and framed representation of a souvenir: a cardboard reminder of that *exotic* group who first occupied the land. It is a souvenir of "Alberta" because of the lines drawn on a map by the colonizing government, but surely the Indian chief does not consider himself an "Albertan." Third, the final clause tells us the deceit of the representation; despite the stated authenticity of the souvenir, it is really made in Japan. Having noted these considerations, we are asked to question what this postcard says about Canadian society: what value do our signifiers hold, and what deceit interrupts their connection to the signified?

This line of questioning is justified as Naomi elaborates that many of her Native students appear Japanese both in their physical appearance and shy behavior (2). This intertwining posited at the outset of the novel establishes a line of thinking that Kogawa returns to sporadically, such as when Naomi outlines her membership in a youth club. The name of the club, the Tillicum Club, their badge, a totem-pole pin, and their slogan (174), all connect the Japanese Canadian children to First Nations people. Rough Lock Bill, who offers to tell Naomi a story, says that kids of all coloured skins like to hear stories; he sees that concern for skin colour makes little sense (145). However, despite Rough Lock Bill's sensibility, skin colour is important for the Japanese Canadians as it has been for First Nations people. They have been legislated as "other" based in part on this factor. However, in these earlier instances, the borders that mark the "authentic" are subtracted, establishing an equation where different coloured skins produce a result of "any skin." And in this re-negotiation, the sign that invests a group with power, skin colour, returns as a nondifferential factor.

The final connection of Japanese Canadians and First Nations people demonstrates the calculation without this re-negotiation and the false right of ownership it entrusts. Mr. Barker has haplessly noted, "It was a terrible business what we did to *our* Japanese" (225, emphasis mine). Naomi recognizes in his choice of words a kind of unintentional patronization. The nonwhite Canadians do not belong to the whites. Questions such as, "How long have you been in this country?" reveal a deep lack of understanding of Japanese Canadian history (225). The collective "our," modifying "Indians" and "Japanese," creates a relationship of authority and subordinate; thus Naomi feels she is being offered "crutches" in midstride, for this authority marks a limit to her sense of belonging. These descriptors restrict the subject group to a lesser whole within the nation; in this paradigm they are the Indians and Japanese of the Canadians, Canadians such as Mr. Barker. With this perspective, arguments of racism are displaced, and the stakes are reduced to those of a parent who has made a bad decision. The questions that follow are less subtle examples of the difference that can be constructed when a person, or group, does not fit the perception of the possessing Canadians. We are asked, consequently, to consider who is part of this "our" and what it means to be one of the subordinates. The structure of this dialogue reminds us of Naomi's duality; she is able to reiterate the comments of those who see her only as Japanese, and she is able to voice her indignation at the attempt to discount her citizenship.

Naomi experiences what Bennett has described as "the postcolonial condition of belonging to two cultures within the same country—that is, on what it means to identify oneself both as Canadian and as a person from a culture that exists as a de facto colony, a marginal group that is no longer as closely related to the mother country as it would appear to be to outsiders, or even as it might claim" (191). This duality is in evidence throughout the novel, but one of the most fitting examples is from Stephen's elementary school experience: Naomi recounts an incident in school when Stephen is called a "Jap" by a classmate. When Naomi questions her father, he patiently explains that they are Canadian. Stephen tells Naomi that because they are "both the enemy and not the enemy," the situation is a riddle (70). One page later we read that Naomi and her aunt and uncle cannot understand Stephen's riddles (71). But Stephen's solution to the riddle of his being both enemy and not enemy is to deny his family and community.

In fact, the dangerous ability of hybridity to fracture a community is clearly exemplified by Stephen. During the intense emotional strain of the internment, Stephen, with his leg in a cast, scowls and rejects Japanese rice balls offered by Obasan. Naomi compares Stephen to Humpty Dumpty—grouchy, broken, and immobilized (115). In this last description, Kogawa establishes the connection between Stephen's temporary physical disability, and the larger psychic illness caused by his being both the enemy and not the enemy. Stephen's nightmare illustrates the depth to which he feels trapped by this condition: he dreams of being trapped by a huge metal insect imprisoning him with a web of bars, which he later escapes through his music "by turning the bars into a xylophone" (220). Confronted with this paradigm, Homi Bhabha, building on Jacques Lacan, finds difficulty agreeing with Frantz Fanon that "the psychic choice is to 'turn white or disappear.' There is the more ambivalent, third choice: camouflage, mimicry, black skins/white masks" (120). And this is exactly how Stephen does escape Granton— ostensibly through his pursuit of a music career, first in Toronto, and later throughout Europe, but also by his complete repudiation of Japanese culture, his mimicry of white Canada.

By denying his community, Stephen attempts to mimic the non-Japanese part of Canada. Similar to his rejection of Japanese food, Stephen rejects the line of thinking that the older generation proposes. Obasan tells him "that the best samurai swords are tempered . . . in the hottest flames and people too are made strong and excellent when they go through life's difficulties" (131). And despite the hardships of the internment, Stephen remains focused on his musical career, suggesting he has adopted Obasan's words of perseverance. He does, in fact, become an excellent musician. At the same time, however, he finds fault in the Japanese origins of Obasan's expression, and Naomi goes on to note that Stephen dislikes hearing Obasan saying such things (131). As time progresses, Stephen worsens. When he returns to Alberta after a long absence, Naomi notices that Stephen is very displeased when anything is "too Japanese" (217), and finally that Stephen has deliberately lost his ability to speak the Japanese language (231). Stephen is entangled in his mimicry.

The novel's symbolism illustrates Stephen's sense of displacement. When he begins to recover from his leg injury, Naomi notes Stephen's awkward gait, walking with a step and a hop, like a sailor with a wooden leg. Prophetically, Nomura-Obasan adds, "Together, with strength, with energy, let us walk" (137). As events unfold, we find that the family does gain strength from its members, but Stephen, who has much more in common with the image of the unsteady sailor than the image of walking together with his family, plays a greatly limited role in this relationship. Pressured by abhorrent circumstances, the failure to negotiate the complexities of hybridity pushes this family apart, and Stephen is not part of their walk.

The psychological conflict that exiles Stephen from his family and community is amplified by the government's policy toward dispersal. Aunt Emily denotes this desire for dispersal as she describes the difference between the American and Canadian internment policies; the American Japanese did not lose their property forever and were allowed to move back quickly to their original locations. As a result, the Japanese Canadians were more severely damaged. Of course, says Aunt Emily, that was the idea—to make them disappear (33–34). However, rather than turning white or disappearing, Emily speaks out loudly to ensure her visibility. Naomi describes her as a warrior with words and "General Practitioner of Just Causes" (32). In short, Aunt Emily is the foundation of the community's resistance.

Naomi, who experienced the internment as a child, expresses her memories through the imagery she employs to express spatial relationships. She describes the trip from Vancouver into the interior of British Columbia in language that equates the trip with a descent into hell: "We are going down to the middle of the earth with pick-axes, . . . carried along by the momentum of the expulsion into the waiting wilderness" (111). Equally bleak is her perception of the prairies and her imagined expulsion into the emptiness of outer space, which makes her feel as if she is disappearing like a speck of dust, or a rocket ship shooting off into the vastness of space (186). Continuing in outer space, although she is from Lethbridge, Alberta, Naomi compares the prairie, a place where nature itself is inhospitable, even hostile, to the moon (191). Naomi senses hostility all around her and uses the language of space to articulate emotional severings and her other apprehensions.

Language is an important factor in this reading. As in many homes within a multicultural society, the language of the dominant social group, the national language, is not the only one spoken in Naomi's home. Consequently, *Obasan* is filled with crossing from one language to another—in most cases, a mix of Japanese and English. This phenomenon is best exemplified when Stephen mutters, "sakana fish." Naomi explains that their pidgin phrases are a combination of English, Japanese, and Sasquatch. Since in Japanese the word for "fish" is "sakana," "'sonuva bitch' becomes 'sakana fish'" (218). These crossings vocalize the presence of hybridity in the novel.

An inevitable result of this mixing of languages is that a gap will open between the speakers who speak Japanese as a first language and those who speak English as a first language. Communications become difficult. In *Obasan* we find the older generation, with their reliance on Japanese, will be susceptible to the difficulties that Naomi and her grandparents find with riddles: the Issei can only pretend to understand Stephen's jokes, which increases their sense of difference and lack of confidence.

A severance between generations, Issei, Nisei, and Sansei, is prescribed by the necessary near-bilingualism of the children. When Naomi first receives the letter her mother had sent several years earlier, it is in a Japanese script that Naomi cannot read. Later, when Nakayama-sensei finally reads it to her, she finds the Japanese language strange and overly formal (233). Earlier, at a funeral, Naomi cannot understand the prayer (128–29). Language is clearly a barrier between generations in these instances, but it also becomes a location of conflict as the Nisei find themselves both unable to politicize the Issei and exiled from the outside world.

Naomi's dearth of language, or silence, has received much critical attention. However, when we consider the hybridized nature of her language, we can open up other lines of questioning and see how it stems from this discontinuity between generations. As a Sansei, she should have benefited from the progressive Nisei that surrounded her; however as Mason Harris writes, "While Naomi adapts externally to her life in exile, she, like the Issei, does not really trust the outer world or believe that it belongs to her. The political discourse which Emily brings from afar seems an alien language" (46). This coincides with Dennis Lee's appraisal of his position as a Canadian under the neocolonialist rule of the United States:

To speak unreflectingly in a colony . . . is to use words that speak only alien space. To reflect is to fall silent, discovering that your authentic space does not have words. And to reflect further is to recognize that you and your people do not in fact have privileged authentic space just waiting for words; you are, among other things, the people who have made an alien inauthenticity their own. You are left chafing at the inarticulacy of a native space which may not exist. So you shut up. (47)

But part of Naomi's growth in this novel is her reaction against her silence: "I am tired of living . . . weighed with decorum, unable to shout or sing or dance, unable to scream or swear, unable to laugh, unable to breathe out loud" (183).

Once articulate, the attempted movement out of the margins by the colonized is problematized by cultural difference. In Naomi's perception of language, it becomes more than words; she discerns the difference in the way the members of her family have equipped themselves with different strategies, and she asks where she has learned that to stare or look someone in the eyes is invasive and rude. She realizes that it was probably the Issei, born in Japan, who taught such lessons, whereas she, Emily, and her father, the Nisei, are bilingual, and have dual language skills (47). This overlapping of languages proposes a dilemma for the immigrant trying to reconcile a sense of identity, for the issue of cultural difference, Bhabha notes, "emerges at points of social crises, and the questions of identity that it raises are agonistic; identity is claimed either from a position of marginality or in an attempt at gaining the center: in both cases eccentric" (177). Naomi is thereby caught and pushed toward reconciling her linguistic doubleness with all its attendant weight. In her realization of the connection of nationality, or culture, and language, we can see the beginnings of change; to learn a second language is the beginning of living in a separate space. In making this demand on hybridity, Bhabha notes that the colonized "are both challenging the boundaries of discourse and subtly changing its terms by setting up another specifically colonial space of the negotiations of cultural authority. And they do this under the eye of power, through the production of 'partial' knowledges and positionalities" (119). In this enigmatic reversal, hybridity becomes a powerful force working for those previously oppressed. Naomi's story gives these concepts life.

The novel is optimistic, then, in demonstrating Naomi's growth. We get a glimpse of this change by first noting her timid acquiescence in the classroom. Once Naomi realizes the children know she can't control them, she gives up any attempt at classroom discipline and allows them to question her (6, 8). This detachment is in direct contradiction to when she alludes, in reply to Aunt Emily's quest for facts, to the fracturing inherent in hybridity: "families already fractured and separated were permanently destroyed" (183). When given the choice to go east of the Rockies or to Japan, separated relatives were not given time to consult with each other. In this recollection, Naomi's language shifts toward the political, illustrating the element of danger that hybridity poses for a community.

Looking back to Confucian ideals, the danger of hybridity is especially volatile for the Japanese Canadians. As Aunt Emily points out, "To a people for whom community was the essence of life, destruction of community was the destruction of life" (186). Emily describes Pastor Nakayama-sensei as a "wounded shepherd" trying to care for a "shorn and tattered flock," harmed by prejudice (186). Again, the Confucian element in Japanese Canadian society is influenced by the Christian as shown in the shepherd imagery. More importantly, in this instance, is the fracturing between generations. Harris sums up the political, social, and psychological stakes involved in this process:

The internment and dispersal which destroyed the progressive Nisei movement developing in Vancouver in the 1930s left Emily an activist without a political community and Naomi a deracinated, depressed, and apolitical Sansei with the psychological conflicts of the Nisei and no ethnic community to mediate between her sense of alienness and the WASP world of rural Alberta. (43)

Degrees of cultural difference are reflected through the various generations and serve as a catalyst toward further conflict in the community. As noted, however, in spite of these circumstances, Naomi continues to grow.

Perhaps then, there is a countermeasure to the crushing fracturing of community prescribed by hybridity. Kogawa herself denies that Japanese Canadians are a divided community, although in an interview with Magdalene Redekop, she speaks of the mandated division leveled against them, of how they were isolated from one another: "we had to be 'the only Jap in town.' We had to be proud of not knowing each other. We were ordered to become betrayers; we were ordered to betray our own. It would have been the most natural thing for us to have been splattered and squished" (Hutcheon and Richmond 98). One of the strategies that *Obasan* helps elucidate is the blueprint for this resistance to adversity.

Confronted with difficulties, one of the most urgent projects that the Japanese Canadians face in the novel is to establish an identity. It is a difficult balance based not only on "Who are we?" but also, "What does it mean to be Canadian?" As early as the novel's second chapter, Kogawa lays out the difficulty plainly; a date with the widowed father of a student turns into a statement of Naomi's perceived lack of Canadian identity. The man asks Naomi, "Where do you come from?" and then continues, asking how long she has been in Canada. When she says she was born in Canada, he inquires about her parents' birthplace (7). Naomi does not fit his idea of what a Canadian should look like, nor does he readily comprehend her claim to a Canadian identity. One might assume she is deemed a foreigner because she is not white; such an assumption is later supported when the new Mrs. Barker suggests a local retirement home for Obasan; Naomi wryly muses that Mrs. Barker is quite naive to think that Obasan could live at Sunnydale Lodge: "Obasan would be as welcome there as a Zulu warrior. It's a white-walled and totally white old folks' home" (224). For the retirement home, "whiteness" inscribes belonging. However, inferring national identity from race is part of a misreading. As Emily points out, all of the Japanese were identified by their appearance (118). Thus, Aunt Emily writes in her journal to Nesan that she feels horrible when she hears "Japs" on the radio or sees the word in a headline. She doesn't mind if the Japanese are called that, but to Canadians "their" Japanese are also "Japs" and thus the enemy (83). Declared the enemy, the Japanese Canadians have a large project at hand: to reinscribe their identity on friendlier terms.

In examining this confusion of identity more deeply, one finds that it is not a one-sided conception. Both Naomi's uncle and Naomi subscribe to the Anglo-Saxon perception of Canada. With a fracturing of English, Naomi's uncle declares, "Nisei, not very Japanese-like" (40). This focus on the specificity of the community is an attractive one to a marginalized group, but also a dangerous approach, for the community's narrative, as Bhabha posits, "substantiates cultural difference, and constitutes a 'split-and-double' form of group identification. . . . The colonized refuse to accept membership in the civil society of subjects; consequently they create a cultural domain 'marked by the distinctions of the material and the spiritual, the outer and the inner'" (230–31). Aunt Emily, however, refuses to accept group identification and quickly counters the uncle's comment with, "Why should we be? We're . . . Canadian" (40). A few pages later, Naomi makes a similar mistake, thereby establishing her earlier connection to the Issei rather than the Sansei. Aunt Emily points out that Naomi was an unsmiling, silent child "fed on milk and Momotaro." When Naomi asks if mild and Momotaro represent a "culture clash," Emily replies that there is no reason why they can't both be Canadian. What Canadians citizens do is Canadian (57)! In contrast to Naomi and her uncle, Emily seizes her identity in citizenship. In her conference notes she had struck out "Japanese race" and substituted "Canadian citizen." She goes on to conclude that in harming the Japanese Canadians, Canada harmed itself (33).

The extremes that need to be resolved here are outlined by nomenclature. Genealogically, Obasan and Aunt Emily are both aunts, or both "Obasan" in Japanese; this split marks their mental outlook: one is enmeshed in both Japanese culture and language, whereas the other identifies with English language culture. Between these two aunts, Naomi is influenced by the quiet resignation of the Issei, Obasan and her uncle, and the bustling Aunt Emily, who encourages Naomi toward action, telling her that if she denies her history she becomes "an amputee." She needs to acknowledge the past even to the point of being angry and bitter; otherwise, her bitterness will fester (49–50). Part of Naomi's job, then, is to resolve this difference in order to find her identity amidst the Japan-Canada extreme.

That hybridity is dangerous and can create problems has been established beyond the putative. However, there is an ameliorative phase, for despite the difficulties involved in this act of living on borderlines, in Bhabha's reading of Rushdie, he perceives the "migrant's dream of survival" in this juncture, an interstice where hybridity is empowering, "for the migrant's survival depends . . . on discovering 'how newness enters the world'" (226–27). The opening to a resolution can be discerned as the events of *Obasan* document Naomi's move away from "a silence that cannot speak" in the proem toward the novel's final three pages: a portion of a 1946 memorandum written by a committee commissioned by the government to investigate the treatment of the Japanese Canadians (248), which Frank Davey suggests comes from Emily's archive (111).

It is while on this trajectory that Naomi returns to the earlier connection with the First Nations people to ask where any Canadians come from: indigenous people, immigrants, minorities. Her trenchant answer begins by repeating the opening line of the Canadian national anthem: "Oh Canada, whether it is admitted or not, we come from you. . . . From the same soil, the slugs and slime. . . . We come from the country that plucks its people out like weeds and flings them [away]. . . . We come from Canada, this land that is like every land, filled with the wise, the fearful, the compassionate, the corrupt" (226). In this ending, there is a beginning; Naomi can be seen writing an alternate anthem, an anthem of those overridden by the dominant culture. The anaphoric "We" serves to entrench the belongingness of the marginalized group. Although it is not in her long-lost home in Vancouver, Naomi is freed from her memories of dislocation, and she can now begin to search for her place.

As long-term patterns of immigration change, different communities will continue to inhabit the margins of society. There has been no repeat of the internment of the Japanese Canadians. However, what stories like *Obasan* exist on smaller scales? A collection such as *Other Solitudes: Canadian Multicultural Fictions* demonstrates not only the existence of ethnic diversity, but also the attempt to moderate that difference. As noted earlier by Bennett, postcolonial studies can help illuminate problems with the economy of immigration. The connection that Kogawa has established between Japanese Canadians and First Nations people does not seek to equate the two different abuses, but does help close the distance between the critical strategies used to address the dearth of power held by the colonized, minorities, and immigrant populations. By making this connection, we can begin to discern that *Obasan* is not simply a chapter of history.

On one level, *Obasan* is a highly political novel. During the Canadian government's apology and awarding of redress to Japanese Canadians in 1988, excerpts from *Obasan* were read in the Canadian House of Commons (Goelnicht 306 n.28). Politically, however, of what does *Obasan* inform us? Davey rightly perceives conflicts "about how that story might best be told, how best to explain the oppression that Japanese Canadians have suffered, what cultural strategies might best suit them, and what kind of Canada they should work towards" (101). The necessary cultural strategy is inherent in these conflicts.

Reading *Obasan* with a sensitivity to the postcolonial concept of hybridity provides an important entry point to the novel, because such a critical approach illustrates the breach between the outer and inner points of a society both on the personal level, Naomi and Stephen, and for the entire Japanese Canadian community. Further, though, if we also consider the novel's postmodern construction, there is proof here for Bhabha's thesis that social marginalization requires us to examine cultural concepts apart from artistic objects and aesthetics. We should "engage with culture as an uneven, incomplete production of meaning and value, often composed of incommensurable demands and practices, produced in the act of social survival" (172). We find such a process at work in this novel; utilizing different aesthetic standards, it incorporates into Canadian culture that which previously was not considered Canadian. In *Obasan*, Kogawa demonstrates not only fracture but also the ability to resolve difference.

That we can neither prescribe nor plot cultural integration is well illustrated in *Obasan* when Mr. Barker drops by to see Obasan following the death of her husband. The ineffectual Mr. Barker appears truly sorry for Obasan; his wife's gestures are harder to interpret (222). The Barkers visit Obasan to express their sympathy, but there is little understanding between the four; Naomi "cannot tell" what the position of Mrs. Barker's hands propose. The Barkers, of course, do not feel at "home" there; there is no point-to-point relationship, no common denominator except their loss.

It is often difficult to get along with other people; we do not always understand others, and we often have to work at communication. Cross-cultural communication both amplifies and further aggravates this paradigm. What is needed then is a third space: not the legislated "otherness" of multiculturalism, or simply another margin, but a place where the preconceptions of "Canadian" can be reevaluated. Bhabha points to the existence of this space in the theoretical recognition of the split-space of enunciation and writes optimistically about the potential of hybridity for making possible an "international culture" that would go beyond concepts of multiculturalism or diversity to "the inscription and articulation of culture's hybridity." And this is what Kogawa's novels does with her *bricolage*, mixture of skins, and the reconciling of milk and Momotaro. Kogawa's writing puts a human face on Bhabha's call to remember, or realize, "that it is the 'inter'—the cutting edge of translation and negotiation, the inbetween space—that carries the burden of the meaning of culture." An international culture is in constant renewal, expanding its history in revisions of old histories and additions necessitated by the changing culture. In moving from nationalist to internationalist, we can avoid confrontational politics and realize multiple aspects of our identities (38–39).

The redress awarded Japanese Canadians in 1988 does not make everything "OK" full stop. *Obasan* is not only about history because it points out our need to keep the discussion of these issues active and rigorous. If multiculturalism is to become more than a static catch phrase, a poetic and liberal gesture by Pierre Eliot Trudeau in 1971, the resolution of the conflicts portrayed in *Obasan* needs to be repeated as a constant renegotiation: not just a negotiation aligned and biased by the past, but renegotiation based on the most recent terms allowing for a new approach and a new site of discussion. The oft-asked question, "What does it mean to be Canadian?" has to be seen as having a plethora of answers, and our inability to answer should not be seen as a problem. Our identity must mean more than what was proposed during a recent propaganda campaign, sponsored by the Heritage Ministry of the federal government, featuring Canada geese flying over a northern wilderness, eh?

Although often used to define a one-way relationship in which an oppressor is able to efface the oppressed, *Obasan* demonstrates that hybridity can also turn into cultural resolution, if resolution does not become a constant. Hybridity and the renegotiation it prescribes allows a means of evading the false dichotomies of "indigenous" and "immigrant" defined in the past. Building on this progression, realizing the terms involved in a hybridized society allows us to develop a new perspective of who we are and who we will become.

WORKS CITED

Ashcroft, Bill, Gareth Griffiths, and Helen Tiffin, eds. *The Post-Colonial Studies Reader*. London: Routledge, 1995.

Bennett, Donna. "English Canada's Postcolonial Complexities." *Essays on Canadian Writing*. Ed. Jack David and Robert Lecker. Numbers 51–52 (Winter 1993–Spring 1994): 164–210.

Bhabha, Homi K. *The Location of Culture*. London: Routledge, 1994.

Davey, Frank. *Post-National Arguments: the Politics of the Anglophone-Canadian Novel Since 1967*. Toronto: U of Toronto P, 1993.

Goelnicht, Donald C. "Minority History as Metafiction: Joy Kogawa's *Obasan*." *Tulsa Studies in Women's Literature* 8 (1989): 287–306.

Harris, Mason. "Broken Generations in *Obasan*: Inner Conflict and the Destruction of Community." *Canadian Literature* 127 (1990): 41–47.

Hutcheon, Linda, and Marion Richmond. *Other Solitudes: Canadian Multicultural Fictions*. Toronto: Oxford UP, 1990.

Kogawa, Joy. *Obasan*. Lester & Orpen Dennys, 1981. Toronto: Penguin, 1983.

Kogawa, Joy. Interview. *Other Solitudes: Canadian Multicultural Fictions*. By Magdalene Redecop. Ed. Linda Hutcheon and Marion Richmond. Toronto: Oxford UP, 1990.

Lee, Dennis. "Cadence, Country, Silence: Writing in Colonial Space." *Open Letter* 2.6 (1973): 34–53.

12

Becoming Americans: Gish Jen's *Typical American*

Zhou Xiaojing

In a 1991 conversation with Martha Satz, the year *Typical American* was published, Gish Jen said that the novel "is about coming to America and what that means in reality." She added, "For the characters in my book, it takes a while to become American and it's not so much becoming a citizen that makes them feel American, it's something like buying a house" (133). For the Chinese immigrants in Jen's book, what coming to America means in reality, and how they become and feel American are very different matters than they are for the Chinese immigrants and their children in the works of Maxine Hong Kingston, Amy Tan, and Frank Chin. This difference marks some significant changes in the Asian American experience.

The thematic concerns and narrative strategies in fiction written by Chinese Americans are shaped by the American immigration laws regarding Asians and by Chinese Americans' social status in the United States. Since the 1940s, a relaxation in the U.S. immigration laws toward Asians, which had been characterized by exclusion and containment, has led to significant transformations in the demographics of Chinese Americans. When China became an ally with the United States during World War II, the Chinese Exclusion Act, which had been adopted in 1882, renewed in 1892 for another ten-year period, then made indefinite in 1902, was repealed in 1943. This repeal was followed by a legislative process that eventually removed race, ethnicity, and nationality as criteria which, among other things, prevented the Chinese and other Asian immigrants from becoming naturalized citizens. The resulting large number of middle-class and well educated immigrants have helped diversify the Chinese American community, which used to be predominantly working class.

These social and demographic changes have also led to shifts in thematic concerns and generated new voices and narrative strategies in the fiction written by Chinese Americans. Gish Jen's *Typical American* is indicative of both the demographic and literary changes. The locations of her stories are far removed from Chinatown, and her characters are not indentured laborers, or illegal immigrants, or displaced scholars and professionals who become "illiterate" and are forced to work at nonprofessional jobs. Jen's immigrant characters, both male and female, come to the United States to obtain higher education and become professionals and entrepreneurs, who struggle with the process of acculturation and identity transformation outside the borders of Chinatown communities. In her essay "Immigration and Diaspora," Shirley Geok-lin Lim contends that *Typical American* and Amy Tan's *The Joy Luck Club* and *The Kitchen God's Wife* "share a common set of assimilartionary themes" and "plot the acculturation of their Asian protagonists into a U.S. society represented as desirable, fetishistically possessable, and offering utopianist possibilities" (299). Lim's generalized reading of *Typical American* is reductive of the word's complexity and its critique of the myth about unlimited possibilities and freedom in the United States. It also eliminates thematic and technical differences between Jen's and Tan's works. Nevertheless, Lim's essay offers a provocative criticism of "assimilationary position" (303) in Asian-American immigrant discourse—a position that Jen explores and complicates in *Typical American.*

The American experience of Jen's characters is at once more individualized and generalized than that of the immigrant characters in the works by Maxine Hong Kingston, Amy Tan, and Frank Chin. For instance, the Chinese immigrants in Kingston's *The Woman Warrior* (1976), Tan's *Joy Luck Club* (1989) and Chin's *Donald Duk* (1991) are portrayed more as ethnic cultural signs than as individuals. Insisting on their Chinese values and customs, the mothers in the works of Kingston and Tan function like custodians of Chinese culture, and remain "unassimilated" foreigners in their adopted country, either by resistance or as a result of circumstances. Likewise, the father in Chin's *Donald Duk* seizes every opportunity to give his son (and also the American reader) lectures on Chinese culture, including Chinese local opera and customs. As Sau-ling Cynthia Wong has noted, in some works of Chinese American fiction, immigrant parents are portrayed "as symbols of either hopeless cultural stagnation or unrelentingly purposeful cultural transmission" ("Ethnic Subject" 261). Being thus portrayed as representatives of the old world and another culture, the immigrant mothers in the works of Kingston and Tan serve the double function of at once passing on the Chinese cultural heritage to their children and contributing to the difficulties of their children's identity crisis. The mother-daughter relationships are basically a narrative strategy for revealing the daughters' sense of being split between two worlds and cultures.

Although Kingston's *China Men* (1980) is devoted to the Chinese immigrants' process of becoming Americans, its focus is on the historical process of collective experience. There is no character development; the multiple characters and their stories are devoted to the construction of a Chinese American collective history, which records Chinese immigrants' contributions to the building of America through their work in farming, fishing, mining, and railroad building, and their victories in fighting against racist American laws. When stories focus on individual experiences of the immigrant mothers in Kingston's *The Woman Warrior* and Tan's *The Joy Luck Club*, they take place more often than not in China, rather than in America. The individualized process of becoming Americans is reserved only for the American-born generations.

Jen's *Typical American* has broken away from this narrative paradigm. The Chinese immigrants in her book are depicted as developed characters. With its narrative focus on the development of the major characters, Jen explores the inner world of each character as it is being reshaped and transformed by the new social environments of the United States. In order to portray characters as real human beings, Mikhail Bakhtin has pointed out, the author must establish a "fundamental, aesthetically productive relationship" to the characters. He explains, "It is a relationship in which the author occupies an intently maintained position *outside* the hero with respect to every constituent feature of the hero—a position *outside* the hero with respect to space, time, value, and meaning" (14). Jen establishes and maintains this "aesthetically productive relationship" to her characters throughout the book by telling their stories from an omniscient-narrator point of view. Her use of a humorous and ironic tone in her narrative voice also helps maintain her position *"outside"* of her characters. In fact, Jen's narrative voice and sometimes comic portrayal of characters with distinct personalities remind one of Jane Austen's novels, particularly *Pride and Prejudice*, whose influence Jen acknowledges in an interview with Yuko Matsukawa published in 1993 (113).

In her treatment of the immigrants' assimilation process, Jen shows not so much the characters' resistance to the mainstream American cultural hegemony as the changes taking place within each main character. While presenting the characters' actions and their changed lifestyle, Jen obliquely raises questions about values and morality in the characters' transition from one value system to another. With these thematic concerns, the narrative structure of *Typical American* also differs greatly from those of *The Woman Warrior* and *The Joy Luck Club*. Whereas Kingston and Tan organize their nonlinear narratives into several separate stories told in multiple voices, Jen employs a linear narrative structure and a single authorial voice in the traditional mode of nineteenth-century novels. The fragmented narratives in Kingston's and Tan's works allow them to tell disconnected stories about the immigrant mothers and aunts in China and America, and stories of the daughters' sense of fragmented identities. In other words, Kingston's and Tan's narrative structures reflect their thematic concerns of Chinese immigrants' and Chinese Americans' cultural dislocations and psychological disconnections. Jen's different narrative structure is determined by her thematic concerns of character development and the plot of her novel.

In addition, the Chinese immigrants' social and educational backgrounds in Jen's novel are very different from those of the characters in Kingston's and Tan's books. The three main characters—Ralph Chang, his older sister Theresa, and his wife, Helen—are all from elite families in China and are sent by their parents to study in the United States during the 1940s turmoil following the Japanese invasion of China and the Chinese civil war. Ralph is earning his Ph.D. in engineering,

Theresa is getting her degree in medicine, and Helen stops going to college, marries Ralph, and becomes a housewife.

Jen centers their changes on their conceptions of morals and proper conduct, which form the core of their Chinese identity. At first, they are critical of everything American. To them, "typical" Americans are "no-good"—they don't know how to get along, and they are too self-centered. When they are shortchanged by a clerk, they shake their heads and mutter, "typical American no-morals!" They are sure that they will not become "wild" in this country where they have the freedom to do whatever they want (67). Nevertheless, as the narrative of their lives in America unfolds, they all have become typical Americans. Jen uses humor and irony throughout the novel to unmask the characters and debunk their superficial criticisms.

She also employs humor and irony to show situations of cultural clash, in which the characters are caught without being aware of it. In juxtaposition to the easy conclusion about Americans' lack of morals by Ralph, Helen, and Theresa, Jen shows Professor Pinkus's accusation of Ralph's immoral conduct in contrast to American morals. When Ralph runs into trouble with his student visa, he asks Professor Pinkus, the new department chairman, for help. Pinkus promises to talk to the Foreign Student Office to straighten things out, but Ralph never hears from him. Not knowing how to approach Pinkus with his problems again, and discouraged by Pinkus's overbearing and critical manner, Ralph decides to talk to one of his children, who seems "less intimidating," especially the youngest girl, who is "plain" with "bedsprings of bright orange hair" (39). But though he follows the child home a few times, he never musters the nerve to say anything to her, thinking that as a stranger, he could be arrested for talking to a young girl, and eventually his status as an alien without a visa will be discovered. Then his deportation is inevitable.

Ralph realizes that he has to talk to Pinkus directly and starts following him around, hoping that chance will bring them face to face. One day he unexpectedly runs into Pinkus outside a bar. But no sooner does Ralph introduce himself, assuming Pinkus may have forgotten who he is, than he is overwhelmed by Pinkus's response. "Not only do I know who you are, I know what you are," says Pinkus. He then calls Ralph a "liar" and a "sneak," and threatens to have him arrested for hanging around his house. Before Ralph can reply, Pinkus presses on with his warning: "If you want to lie, you want to sneak around, you should go back to China. Here in America, what we have is morals." Ralph is dumbfounded. Jen's earlier description of Pinkus's youngest girl as "plain" and with strange, unappealing hair through Ralph's eyes, suggests that Ralph does not have the slightest interest in her as Pinkus assumes, thus rendering Pinkus's reaction even more shocking to Ralph. While Ralph is lost for words, Pinkus's threat becomes more intense. "We have morals! You keep hanging around my daughter, I'll shoot you!" (40)

This comic scene of cultural misunderstanding, though undermining the Changs' assumptions of their moral superiority over "typical" Americans, is reminiscent of the representations of the morally decrepit stereotypes of Chinese, epitomized in Fu Man Chu, a personification of the "yellow peril." This stereotype has been used to justify the exclusion of Chinese immigrants and help perpetuate their alienation in American culture. Jen's comic portrayal exaggerates the characters' speeches and behavior so as to reveal Ralph's ignorance and Pinkus's biases in their cross-cultural encounters. Pinkus's assertion of American morals, and his threats directed at what he perceives as a violation of them, are unmasked as a superior and violent American attitude toward the "other." What seems to be a typical case of cultural misunderstanding is in fact a result of the difference between a privileged American and a dislocated minority immigrant.

Jen's humorous narrative voice also allows her to expose the irony in the changes of the main characters' lives. At the beginning, Ralph's goal in life is to get his Ph.D. in engineering, then tenure as a college professor. But he is lured into business by the financial success of an American-born Chinese American, Grover Ding. He becomes acquainted with Ding at a dinner party in the home of Old Chao, Ralph's university colleague, sent over to study by the Chinese government, who eventually becomes the acting chairman of Ralph's department. When Ralph finally gets tenure, he decides to take a leave from the academic position and opens a fried-chicken diner with Grover's help, determined to become a "self-made man," that is, a self-made millionaire. He covers an entire wall of his office with inspirational quotations such as:

ALL RICHES BEGIN IN AN IDEA.

WHAT YOU CAN CONCEIVE, YOU CAN ACHIEVE.

YOU CAN NEVER HAVE RICHES IN GREAT QUANTITY UNLESS YOU WORK YOURSELF INTO A WHITE HEAT OF DESIRE FOR MONEY. (198–99)

He reads books entitled *Making Money, Be Your Own Boss!* and *Ninety Days to Power and Success* for tips on how to get rich fast. He teaches his daughters that the important thing in the United States is money: "In this country, you have money, you can do anything. You have no money, you are nobody" (199).

Inarguably, having money does make a great difference in people's lives, especially in the lives of people of color in the United States, Jen interweaves issues of class and race through Theresa's observations. Theresa is horrified by Ralph's lectures on money worship to his daughters. But as time goes by, she feels ambivalent about his lectures, which remind her of how poor people are treated in the hospital where she works as an intern in residence. "And to be nonwhite in this society was indeed to need education, accomplishment—some source of dignity," Theresa concludes. "A white person was by definition somebody." Besides, she sees that commerce is like a "brand of alchemy that turned" chickens "into a happy household" (200). With the money made from fried chicken, Ralph and Helen are able to add new appliances to their house in the suburbs of New York City. The new love seat and bridge table make Helen happy and content; Ralph earns respect from his suburban neighbors, especially when he takes his well-trained dog for a walk.

Nevertheless, this happiness and respectability are not obtained without costs.

The peaceful, harmonious relationships between Ralph, Helen, and Theresa are replaced by chaos, estrangement, and resentment. All of them have transgressed the moral codes of behavior that once gave them a proud sense of who they were. Ralph begins to experience constant anxiety and fear not only over the risks of his business, but also for cheating on their income tax. The narrator's ironic comment on Ralph's moral lapse is indirectly critical of the American worship of materialist gains. Underreporting income makes all the difference in the Changs' life; although they are not rich, they become "respectable" (202).

Ralph's obsession with becoming a self-made millionaire also contributes to the deterioration of his marriage. Every day after dinner, Ralph locks himself up in a room and plays with the cash register. His devoted wife, Helen, once an innocent and modest Chinese girl, is seduced by Grover, now a frequent houseguest and indispensable facilitator and adviser in Ralph's business dealings. When Helen first hears from Ralph that Old Chao, a married man, is having an affair with another Chinese woman, she refuses to believe it. "*Impossible*," she said. "*Chinese people don't do such things*" (168). Helen's seduction by Grover parallels her seduction by the American way of life represented in magazines. As she begins to desire a house in the suburbs with a yard and new furniture with matching curtains, her affection for Ralph transforms into fondness for Grover, who turns out to be a ruthless swindler. Helen's love affair with Grover and her attainment of the American way of life are short-lived. Ralph's business fails because of Grover's self-serving schemes. Their happiness based on material possessions proves to be as precarious as their Chicken Palace built on shaky ground.

Jen, however, assumes no simple right-or-wrong judgment of her characters. Helen has undergone some positive changes. Being the spoiled child of her privileged family with servants in China, she used to let others do things for her, including the arrangement of her marriage to Ralph by her friend Theresa. By the end of the novel, Helen has become a resourceful individual who finds pleasure in work and is capable of taking initiative in the face of hardship and disasters.

Like Ralph and Helen, Theresa has done the previously unthinkable thing—she has maintained her love affair with Old Chao, whose wife, Jannis, is a family friend of the Changs. Jen's humorous and ironic tone in describing Theresa's sense of morals and modesty enhances the changes taking place in her later: "She had always been nice about her morals; she grew nicer still. How dangerous a place, this country! A wilderness of freedoms. She shuddered, kept scrupulously to paths. Once she had allowed other residents to wink at her, and had sometimes even winked back. Now she stiffened and turned away" (142–43). The hardest thing for Theresa is not these open invitations to flirt, nor even the horrors of the emergency room. It is having to sleep in that little room which all interns shared, with men. The men disturb her because they force her to feel "how pointed her needs were . . ." (147). Theresa begins to be aware of her sexuality and allows herself to experience love and desire in ways that had been socially condemned in China. She finds satisfaction and happiness in her relationship with Old Chao, who decides to divorce Jannis. Theresa and Old Chao, both single-minded and career driven, have learned to relax and enjoy life.

Even though Theresa's love affair with Old Chao is different from Helen's with Grover, it is completely unacceptable to Ralph. She loses Ralph's respect for her, and her authority over him. Having lost her moral rectitude according to traditional Chinese ethical standards, Theresa's words lose credibility. Ralph turns a deaf ear to whatever she says. She has to compromise in her position on Ralph's materialistic attitude and teachings to his two daughters even though she does not approve of her brother's obsession with money or his relationship with Grover. Once adored and indispensable in Ralph and Helen's household, Theresa becomes alienated, her existence and needs forgotten. Eventually, Theresa has to move out of her brother's house after being humiliated by him. The destruction of the Changs' family relationships is followed by each of the three characters' transformation in pursuing his or her version of the American Dream of freedom, happiness, and self-fulfillment. The choices they have made, and what they themselves have become, run contrary to their notions of who they were as opposed to "typical" Americans. At the beginning of the novel, they were sure that "they wouldn't 'become wild' here in America, where there was 'no one to control them'" (67).

Once being removed from the strictly social structure in China, and having the unfamiliar American freedom thrust upon them, the main characters undergo not only moral crises, but also identity changes. Helen has become capable of things that were once utterly inconceivable to her. Theresa is surprised to realize that she is "another person" (200). Ralph begins to wonder who he is. It never occurred to him before that he should question his own identity, and he is surprised to find that a lot of Americans wonder quite seriously who they are. In China, individual identities are hard facts based on who your parents are and, what tier of the social hierarchy you and your family belong to in terms of inheritance and achievements. What people worry about is being recognized. Knowing who you are provides "useful information in a terraced society," which regulates how people should treat one another, and tells you what to expect from other people (177).

The social conditions that formed the Changs' individual identities and shaped their expectations have disappeared in America. In this "loose-knit country, where one could do as one pleased, a person had need of a different understanding" (178). Ralph needs to know what his limits are, and what he is capable of in terms of good and evil, but is baffled by his impulses and actions. He does not understand why he found his attraction to Grover irresistible; he does not know why he can no longer be satisfied by simple indulgences in life like plum juice, a fish pond, or a crabgrass-free lawn. He is surprised by his own reckless gamble in his business dealings, and puzzled by his alienation from his wife and sister. At the end of the novel, Ralph "was not what he made up his mind to be"—a "self-made" millionaire. "A man was the sum of his limits; freedom only made him see how much so" (296).

The paradox of freedom and limits is a major theme of Jen's novel, a lesson Ralph, Helen, and Theresa all have learned. In showing the limits of individual will and knowledge from the immigrant's perspective, Jen means also to point to the limits of the American Dream personified by the protagonists of Horatio Alger's novels. "America holds out this promise that a person can do anything," Jen notes. She hopes that *"Typical American* will be viewed not only as an immigrant story but as a story for all Americans, to make us think about what our myths and realities are. We are not a country that likes to think in terms of limits" (qtd. in Satz 134). Bonnie TuSmith, in her perceptive essay ironically titled "Success Chinese American Style: Gish Jen's *Typical American*," notes that "Understanding one's limitations is one theme of the novel," and "Jen's overall narrative strategy is to use an ancient culture to anchor a newer one—with reciprocal learning the desired outcome" (24). Kingston and Chin have employed intercultural strategies with similar outcomes. Their American-born Chinese American characters such as Wittman Ah Sing (in *Tripmaster Monkey*) and Donald Duk have learned how to be Chinese American with an integrated, hybrid cultural heritage.

Jen, however, is less concerned with the characters' integration of bicultural heritage than with the development of the characters as individuals in the process of becoming Americans. In the American "wilderness of freedoms," the Chinese immigrants have had the opportunity to do the previously unthinkable and learn about the limitations of social reality and individual knowledge. "If you have grown up in a place where you have one reality and everyone else has the same reality, you begin to believe that is reality," Jen remarks. "You are unaware of the degree to which it is artifice. Whereas if you can see the terms in which other people think you begin to realize that your reality is not so absolute" (Satz 135). In *Typical American*, Jen portrays the characters' changes in part through their perception of the differences between Chinese and American societies. In so doing, she exposes the American reader to another reality through another cultural viewpoint.

Jen shows how cultural differences are embedded in linguistic expressions. Jen contrasts the "loose-knit" American social structure with the "terraced society" of China by referring to a phrase in Chinese. In China, connections and relationships are so important that they have become part of a standard phrase—*mei guanxi*, meaning "it does not matter," literally, "it has no relationship/connection." More often than not, to say something *"mei guanxi,"* Jen points out, actually indicates how much something matters (177–178). These social and linguistic differences also shed light on Helen's perception of the difference between China and the United States In China, Helen perceived the world to be enormous, but a walled-in, finite space. Here, the enormous world for her becomes infinite with endless horizons. The contrasting metaphor of space runs throughout the novel, reflecting the character's transitional experience of acculturation. The endless horizons of America for the Changs at once represents the lack of social enforcement of moral codes, and the infinite possibilities Ralph believed in as he used to marvel at Grover, the self-made millionaire: "In America, anything is possible" (106). "A man is what he makes up his mind to be" (186). The promise this legendary America holds contrasts with the confinement Chinese culture imposes on individuals.

However, Ralph was to find out that America's possibilities and China's limits are not the absolute polar opposites they seem to be. At the beginning of the novel,

Jen reveals how in Chinese culture people are keenly aware of the limits of personal capability and circumstances, by explaining the linguistic difference between English and Mandarin Chinese. In English, the verb "listen" does not carry the connotation of not being able to hear, whereas the Chinese verb "listen" is used as a compound to indicate the results of the action of listening. *Ting de jian* in Mandarin means, one listens and hears. *Ting bu jian* means, one listens but fails to hear. Jen uses this linguistic difference as an indication of people's understanding of the personal and social limits of their abilities and accomplishments, which seem to be the opposite of Americans' confidence in their limitless capabilities. At the end of the novel, Ralph becomes disillusioned about the seemingly infinite possibilities for both himself and America. He feels trapped in himself, from which no escape is possible. He realizes that freedom in America is not as promising and limitless as he thought. His capacity is just as limited here as in China. He fails to be what he made up his mind to be. Freedom only makes him realize that he is only "the sum of his limits." America is not the America he once thought it to be.

Jen remarked in the 1991 conversation with Satz that "we [Americans] believe in endless expansion and endless expression of our will. The grandiose self." The disillusioned, humbled, and reflective Ralph, Jen noted, might suggest a parallel to a maturing stage in the American national identity. "Ralph is at a point much like the one we are at as a country," said Jen. "Our adolescence is over—I hope. We're sobered. People are starting to think about the environment, about war, about our place in the world" (qtd. in Satz 134). In portraying her Chinese characters as Americans and emphasizing their "typical American" experience, Jen directly challenges exclusionary notions of American identity. Speaking of *Typical American*, Jen said that she wants to "challenge ideas of what a 'typical American' looks like, to put forward the idea that the Changs are not any less American than anyone else." She also pointed out that "There are people who, when they choose to read ethnic writing, want comfortably exotic stuff that makes them feel like they're traveling in some foreign country" (qtd. in Matsukawa 115).

Jen shares much with other Chinese American writers in her claim of the American identity for her characters and in her resistance to the exoticized readings of works by Chinese Americans. In her essay "Cultural Mis-readings by American Reviewers," Kingston has pointed out the connection between cultural "othering" and the historical exclusion and political disempowerment of Chinese Americans: "To call a people exotic freezes us into the position of being always alien—politically a most sensitive point with us because of the long history in America of the Chinese Exclusion Acts, the deportations, the law denying us citizenship when we have been part of America since its beginning" (57). The history of Chinese immigrants' experience and the perpetuation of "otherness" of Chinese Americans in the American culture have determined both the content and narrative strategies in the fictions written by Chinese American writers. Despite their differences, both Kingston and Chin have retold and reinscribed Chinese American history in opposition to the misrepresentation of Chinese Americans in American popular culture and literature.

In their representations of their characters' American experience, Kingston and Chin seem to be more concerned about intervention in the misrepresentations of Chinese Americans than about characterization as Jen is. Their works, as protests and resistance, are directed more at social injustice than at the interiority of the characters. The inner conflicts of their characters are more often than not the results of racial stereotypes. For instance, in *China Men*, even though the narrator's brother, a fourth-generation Chinese American, was enlisted in the U.S. army, after the government certified that his family "was really American, not precariously American but super-American, extraordinarily secure—Q Clearance Americans" (299), the Chinese American pilot in the comic book *Blackhawk* was still portrayed as an unassimilated inferior "other":

Chop Chop was the only Blackhawk who did not wear a blue-black pilot's uniform with yellow and black insignia. He wore slippers instead of boots, pyjamas with his undershirt showing at the tails, white socks, an apron; he carried a cleaver and wore a pigtail, which Chinese stopped wearing in 1911. He had buck teeth and slanted lines for eyes, and his skin was a muddy orange. Fat and half as tall as the other Blackhawks, who were drawn like regular human beings, Chop Chop looked like a cartoon. (274)

A similar Chinese American stereotype is also to be found in Hollywood movies. Wittman Ah Sing, the protagonist in Kingston's third book, *Tripmaster Monkey: His Fake Book* (1987), notes that "John Wayne has a Hop Sing, and the Cartwrights have a Hop Sing. They name him Hop Sing on purpose, the name of the powerful tong, to put us down. [. . .] The way Hop Sing shuffles, I want to hit him. Sock him an uppercut to straighten him up—stand up like a man." Even when Hollywood attempted such a supposedly positive figure of Chinese America as Charlie Chan, they could not but make him effeminized and submissive, as Wittman asserts: "I want to punch Charlie Chan too in his pregnant stomach that bellies out his white linen maternity suit. And he's got a widow's hump from bowing with humbleness. He has never caught a criminal by fistfighting him" (320).

Similarly, in Frank Chin's *Gunga Din Highway* (1994), a character, parodying Charlie Chan's Number Four Son, responds to the Chinese stereotypes in the American movies with irony: "Gee, Pop! Even the apes are doing better in the movies than the Chinese. Apes have gone from *King Kong* to *Planet of the Apes*! And we have gone from Charlie Chan to *Susie Wong*, ping-pong, ping-pong" (199). In *Donald Duk*, Chin exposes the rationale underlying the stereotypes of Chinese Americans through Donald Duk's teacher of California history, a white American, who reads to his class a passage from a history book:

The Chinese in America were made passive and nonassertive by centuries of Confucian thought and Zen mysticism. They were totally unprepared for the violently individualistic and democratic Americans. From their first step on American soil to the middle of the twentieth century, the timid, introverted Chinese have been helpless against the relentless victimization by aggressive, highly competitive Americans. (2)

To counter these misrepresentations, Chin resorts to the Chinese warrior tradition and history by introducing iconistic figures such as Kwan Kung, a legendary general of courage and loyalty in Chinese history, into the book through Donald's father, who plays the most powerful role of Kwan Kung in the Chinatown Cantonese opera.

Likewise, Kingston appropriates and revises Chinese literature, history, legends, myths, and ethnic customs in *The Woman Warrior, China Men,* and *Tripmaster Monkey,* to protest against racism and sexism, to resist Eurocentric cultural hegemony, and to reinscribe the Chinese American identity in opposition to the dehumanizing stereotypes in the American media. These strategies for asserting a self-determined identity in direct opposition to stereotyped misrepresentations have led to a mode of narrative characterized by intertextual incorporations and intertextual dialogues, which raise questions about race, gender, ethnicity, class, and culture in connection to power relations. The statements made by characters in Kingston's *Tripmaster Monkey,* and Chin's *Donald Duk* and *Gunga Din Highway,* sometimes seem to echo the authors' own ideas and attitudes articulated in their nonfictional writings. The boundary between the character and the author is blurred, or rather in their author-character relationship, the author's position is not "outside" of the character.

Gish Jen's *Typical American* has also departed from this mode of narrative even as it continues to redefine the once Eurocentric and white American identity by portraying Chinese immigrants' process of becoming Americans, as do the works of Kingston and Chin. There is no mention of classical Chinese literature or myths, though there are a few Chinese sayings in her book. Her characters remain distinct individuals, whose consciousness and perceptions are clearly not shared by the author. The Changs' American experience is more pertinent to those contemporary Chinese immigrants in the United States, who are academics and entrepreneurs. However, to really understand what becoming American means for the Changs in Jen's book in a larger context of the American reality, one must be informed of what it meant for earlier Chinese immigrants to become Americans, and how it feels for the American-born children of Chinese immigrants to be Americans, as dealt with in the works of Maxine Hong Kingston, Amy Tan, and Frank Chin. In her book, *Between Worlds: Women Writers of Chinese Ancestry,* Amy Ling traces the in-between-worlds experience of Chinese Americans in Kingston and Tan to the works of an earlier generation of Chinese American women writers.

When *The Woman Warrior* appeared in 1976, Kingston realized that many readers misunderstood her book because they were ignorant of Asian American history (Kim xvi). "Chinese American history has been a battle for recognition as Americans," Kingston writes; "we have fought hard for the right to legal American citizenship" ("Cultural Mis-readings" 59). In response to the general reading public's lack of knowledge about Asian Americans' collective experience in the United States, she deliberately filled her second book, *China Men,* with historical facts. By doing so, Kingston hopes that a younger generation of Chinese American writers will be freed from the necessity of providing historical information so as to deal with other issues and explore new ways of writing fiction: "[M]aybe it [*China*

Men] will affect the shape of the novel in the future. Now maybe another Chinese-American writer won't have to write that history" (qtd. in Kim xvii–xviii).

Typical American is at once a continuation and departure from the works of Kingston and other Chinese American writers. In her recent essay "A Person Is More Than the Sum of Her Social Facts," Jen discusses the effects of multiculturalism on minority writers like herself, arguing for minority writers' freedom to explore "the very inner life that identity politics denies" (B11). She says elsewhere that "multi-culturalism has made more boxes for people" (Satz 136). Frank Chin has expressed similar feelings through his character Benedict Mo in *Gunga Din Highway*:

In Santa Barbara people ask me why I do not just write about people instead of the Chinese, whereas in San Francisco and Los Angeles, people ask me why the Chinese characters I write are not more Chinese.

Were Ralph Ellison, Richard Wright, James Baldwin, and Lorraine Hansberry capable of writing of themes and emotions and truths of characters beyond the confines of their particular, unique Black Afro-American experience? Did writers Louis Chu or John Okada have any other color inside of them besides yellow? Real writers are rainbows. That is what I'm trying to say with my play. (253)

Jen's insistence on the importance of exploring her characters' "inner life" must be considered within the contexts of Asian Americans' collective experience in American history and culture. As Kingston's and Chin's works illustrate, individuality and interiority are precisely those human qualities that are erased by racial stereotypes. In making these two aspects the center of her characterization, Jen opens up new creative possibilities for writing about what becoming American means in reality for some recent Chinese immigrants. The difference of her thematic concerns and narrative strategies from those of other Chinese American writers such as Maxine Hong Kingston, Amy Tan, and Frank Chin, is more than a matter of personal choice. In exploring the Chinese immigrants' moral ambivalence and crisis, and in confronting their questions about identity and the meaning of life in America, Gish Jen's *Typical American* marks a new departure in Asian American literature and adds a new voice to American fiction.

PRIMARY SOURCES

Jen, Gish. *Typical American*. New York: Plume, 1992.
Chin, Frank. *Donald Duk*. Minneapolis: Coffee House, 1991.
———. *Gunga Din Highway*. Minneapolis: Coffee House, 1994.
Kingston. *The Woman Warrior: Memoirs of A Girlhood Among Ghosts*. New York: Knopf, 1976.
———.*China Men*. New York: Knopf, 1980.
———.*Tripmaster Monkey: His Fake Book*. New York: Vintage, 1990.
Tan, Amy. *The Joy Luck Club*. New York: Ballantine, 1989.

SECONDARY SOURCES

Bakhtin, Mikhail. *Art and Answerability: Early Philosophical Essays*. Ed. Michael Holquist and Vadim Liapunov. Trans. Vadim Liapunov. Austin: U of Texas P, 1990.
———."A Person Is More Than the Sum of Her Social Facts." *The Chronicle of Higher Education* 23 May 1997: B11.
Kim, Elaine. *Asian American Literature: An Introduction to the Writings and Their Social Context*. Philadelphia: Temple UP, 1982.
Kingston, Maxine Hong. "Cultural Mis-readings by American Reviewers." *Asian and Western Writers in Dialogue: New Cultural Identities*. Ed. Guy Amirthanayagam. London: Macmillan, 1982. 55–65.
Lim, Shirley Geok-lin. "Immigration and Diapora." *An Interethnic Companion to Asian American Literature*. Ed. King-Kok Cheung. New York: Cambridge UP, 1997. 289–311.
Ling, Amy. *Between Worlds: Women Writers of Chinese Ancestry*. New York: Pergamon, 1990.
Matsukawa, Yuko. "MELUS Interview: Gish Jen." *MELUS* 18.4 (1993): 111–120.
Satz, Martha. "Writing About the Things That Are Dangerous: A Conversation with Gish Jen." *Southwest Review* 78.1 (1993): 132–40.
TuSmith, Bonnie. "Success Chinese American Style: Gish Jen's *Typical American*." *Proteus* 11.2 (1994): 21–26.
Wong, Sau-ling Cynthia. "Ethnic Subject, Ethnic Sign, and the Difficulty of Rehabilitative Representation: Chinatown in Some Works of Chinese American Fiction." *The Yearbook of English Studies* 24 (1994): 251–262.

Epilogue

Toby Rose

The demand by recent ethnic writers and critics to recognize the presence of the "other" in American literary history has created controversies as to how to assess, categorize, and evaluate the literature produced by various ethnic groups. Newly arrived, newly American, or newly empowered to embody their "tribe's" experiences in North American literature, these writers have added to the older traditions of stories of pioneering in a new land, leaving home, coming of age, intergenerational conflict, and the more postmodern tropes of seeking and finding one's identity in terms of race, class, gender, and lifestyle. What are the differences in the way the immigrant experience was portrayed by writers of the earlier literature and its treatment by more recent writers, in a genre which is now often labeled multicultural or transcultural as opposed to ethnic or immigrant? And how have these works been received by the reading public, critics, and scholars?

These essays have taken us on a journey across a great deal of American terrain covering many of these literary and nonliterary issues and have given us some answers to these questions. Except for Qun Wang's essay, which explores the controversies among Asian American writers and critics, the critics/scholars of these essays, several of whom are, themselves, first-, second-, or third-generation Americans, have each focused on the ideas and perspectives of a specific ethnic group featured in novels or autobiographical stories of the immigrant experience. To take a closer look at the interrelationships between the subjects of these essayists, let us first embark on a historical consideration of the life and times under which these immigrant writers worked.

In the early part of the century, many authors wrote their stories, in part to allay prejudices against the waves of immigrants who arrived in the early twentieth century and to challenge the stereotypes of ethnic groups created by historical legend or by majority-group authors such as F. Scott Fitzgerald in *The Great Gatsby,* who described certain ethnic groups in a socially realistic style, but not necessarily in ethnographically valid terms. However, even early immigrant writers tried to convey in their novels impressions of their communities that pandered to public expectations to guarantee a readership. For example, Si Sui Far (Edith Eaton), an early twentieth century Chinese-American writer, attempted to gain a readership by making her protagonists good citizens who followed the American road to assimilation.

This trend continued well past the time when anti-immigrant sentiment was at its peak. Novels such as Mario Puzo's *The Godfather* (1969), which portrayed Italian immigrant men as stereotypic gangsters, found a readership much more easily than his earlier novel *The Fortunate Pilgrim* (1964) involving a more typical Italian family who escapes the ghetto and becomes middle-class in New York City through hard work. Although the reading public was used to stories of the Horatio Alger rags-to-riches variety, success stories that were consistent with American (read Eurocentric and Puritan) literary paradigms, the association of this ethnic group with crime was even more attractive to this audience.

The events of the civil rights and women's liberation movements of the 1960s and 1970s changed both the paradigm and the readership, and thus newer immigrant writers' styles. Whereas many older ethnic writers, especially women such as Yezierska, Antin, and Stern, had been anxious to throw off the yoke of old world traditions in order to find their place in American society, post-1960s writers such as Maxine Hong Kingston, Paule Marshall, and Bharati Mukherjee proudly displayed their cultural heritage in immigrant stories to explain the part it played in the formation of their identities and the resolution of their conflicts, which were often the subjects of their stories of the acculturation process.

The social and political revolutions of the 1960s saw the rise of both ethnic and female writers of literature, because writers and publishers were attuned to the growth of a readership with different politics and with an ability to empathize with conflicts grounded in race, class, and gender, as well as cultural difference. Women, in particular, wished to read about the emancipatory feelings of their "sisters" of whatever ethnicity. It was exactly the right moment for the burgeoning of a group of second- and third-generation ethnic writers whose immigrant parents or grandparents' strivings in America had allowed them to become educated and fluent in the language needed to tell their stories. Writers such as Jen and Cisneros, who move more easily from ethnic to dominant culture, are known as multicultural or cross-cultural storytellers, but almost all of them acknowledge the conflicts faced by immigrants of each generation to find an identity in which the old and the new culture can co-exist to some degree.

Although these essays have shown us a huge variation in immigrant assimilatory patterns, paradigms have been created by scholars and critics by which to compare them. The first generation of immigrants is thought to be more likely to be essentialist in their outlook, keeping their ancestral culture's traditions and roles intact, especially if they have limited use of English and/or are not accepted by the dominant culture because of race or class differences. The second generation is likely to be more assimilationist, particularly in older literature, rebelling against the old world ways of their parents by often uncritically trying to fit into American life. The third generation (and recently educated immigrants) feels secure and upwardly mobile enough to reconnect with lost strands of their ethnic community and ancestral traditions. Many of these writers proudly foreground these rediscovered rituals, mythologies, and philosophical perspectives, sometimes critically comparing them with what they see as the vacuousness of American mass culture.

Another literary phenomenon that occurred because of these social and political changes and the resultant broadening of the canon by ethnic writers, cultural studies scholars, and women's studies programs is the rediscovery and rereading of older literary works, using the tools of postmodernism to interpret them, such as postcolonial and feminist criticism. Because of the rediscovery of, for example, Rolvaag and Yezierska by a new generation of readers steeped in the feminist gaze, we have been afforded the opportunity to take another look at books some of us read in high school in the 1950s as quintessential pioneer tales focusing on male adventure and sacrifice.

Raychel Reiff's gender-centered critique of *Giants in the Earth* is clearly postmodernist in its reading of a book that was previously studied to tout the American virtues of self-reliance and rugged individualism. Reiff's reading can add to the richness of past readings since she explores a neglected aspect of these novels: the effect of early immigrants' pioneering life on women and on the male-female relationship. To some readers such as myself, this focus is more appealing and resonant than earlier approaches to this novel that emphasized and glorified pioneers struggling to build a new land, exemplifying how the puritan work ethic could make giants out of mere mortals. Early critics and English teachers used this book to instill national values and pride in a history forged by the forebears of what was then the dominant culture: pre-twentieth-century European Protestant immigrants.

Although fictional and nonfictional immigrant stories such as *Giants* helped to establish the literary paradigm for this genre, this study provides another, female perspective of the role women played in early immigrant experiences, and how such transplantations affected their identity, even their sanity. Beret, the wife of Rolvaag's protagonist in *Giants of the Earth*, unlike later female immigrants, has few choices to make regarding assimilation to American life. The wilderness lacks, for the most part, both Norwegian and American culture. The lack of communal, old world life and companionship is definitely a force that drives her to a mental collapse despite her attempt to find solace in old world traditions provided by the church affiliated with her Norwegian homeland. Reiff concludes that the foresaking of the old ways destabilizes Beret's life to such an extent that her psyche disintegrates. Her husband suffers the loss of his best friend and helpmate, but as Reiff interprets the ending, his suffering and death are offset by eyes "set toward the west, where lies an untamed land of adventure and romance."

In rural nineteenth-century America, the choice was not between old and new cultures; the culture of America was yet to be defined. Acculturation meant, pure and simply, adaptation to an often harsh, cultureless environment. Neither patriarchy nor assimilation are issues on the frontier of 1870s Midwest in the same way as they are in the 1920s East Coast urban settings of Antin, Stern, and Yezierska.

The protagonists in the works explored by Zierler and Japtok do, however, struggle with these issues, some more than others. The three Jewish American writers come from old world Eastern European traditions that demand patriarchal obeisance and adherence to culturally prescribed gender roles, especially for daughters. Japtok has explained the dialectical struggle between communally prescribed behaviors and roles that bespeak ethnic solidarity and the American ideal of individual freedom. The ancient Jewish reverence for education, though traditionally the prerogative only of males, provides the justification for Yezierska's, as well as Antin's and Stern's, assimilationist tendencies and their at least temporary rejection of Jewish old world cultural mandates. Departing from Jewish mores allowed them as females to seek an education and a profession, a way of supporting themselves and their families, allowing them to leave rundown ghetto neighborhoods they occupied as poor newcomers, and to assume an American identity.

The lives of these three writers were made difficult not just by their defiance of ethnic cultural values and gender roles, but also by negative attitudes toward immigrants during this period, discussed earlier. Orthodox *shtetl* Jews from Eastern Europe, who kept themselves cloistered and apart from the mainstream, had scant chance of finding vocations as writers, especially if they were females. But if they did, they had another burden as writers courting a readership. To be a success according to American values, they needed to portray themselves as becoming adapted to the mainstream lifestyle and as leaving behind the vestiges of old world, immigrant culture.

Martin Japtok's analysis of Anzia Yezierska shows how the author's personal experiences and awareness of what it took to be successful influenced the way she painted her protagonist, Sara Smolinsky: she is an appealing figure in terms of the mainstream ideology and a literary model for subsequent life stories in that she rejects the communalism of her Jewish heritage in favor of American enterprise and dynamism. "She establishes her personhood by accomplishing adult feats, [she] shows initiative. . . . Only she will break the pattern of poverty." Even as a youngster, she showed signs of becoming a Horatio Alger, valuing freedom, individuality, and especially success. She has the know-how and will to make money, whereas her father hides behind the cloak of an old world scholar to justify his unwillingness or inability to support his family in the new world ways. Taking on a male role and disobeying her father's dictates, Sara becomes the epitome of an assimilationist. However, as Japtok shows, although accomplishing her escape from the demands of her own culture's imperatives (at the price of feeling guilt about her sisters' lives and being disowned by her father), she leaves herself open to the criticisms and demands of both her ethnic family and the mainstream group she has so fervently fought to join and to write for.

Japtok rhetorically asks if the novel is therefore assimilationist, and by the end of his discourse, it becomes clear that such labels are at best problematic. Does assimilationist mean giving up culturally prescribed gender roles? If so, what are the female gender roles dictated by mainstream American society in the 1920s and 1930s? Most women were expected to marry and be a wife and mother. Although Sara marries an Americanized Jew who all but orders her to take in her ailing but still demanding father, she has rejected the lifestyle, proscribed gender roles, and religion of her family.

But neither Sara nor Yezierska would ever be considered 100 percent American because of their intrusion as Jews and females into a WASP male-dominated society and literary genre. Sara/Anzia would go on, however, to carve out new patterns for females from patriarchal families and to reconcile her family's harsh indictment of her straying from the fold with her need to have a life outside of its narrow strictures. As Japtok describes her new identity, "she experiences her ethnicity as a weight and shadow; its oppressive aspects help her justify the pioneering course she steers away from the constricting aspects of her father's generation in defining herself, but she will search for a way to be a Jew and a member of the family in her own new world way."

Are Mary Antin and Elizabeth Stern more or less assimilationist in their autobiographical narratives than is Yezierska? And, are their depictions of the immigrant's conflict between old and new world mores any easier to label? Probably not—it appears that even the smoothest transitions from immigrant to assimilated American do not come without pain and loss. Wendy Zierler describes both writers as undergoing turmoil in the process of becoming Americans and successful writers. Some critics faulted Antin and Stern for presenting a "too shiningly positive" view of American life, a too naively unrealistic portrayal of the difficulties of immigration and acculturation. Others asked whether this tone wasn't a blatant marketing device on the part of the writers to overcome gentile prejudices and to ingratiate themselves into mainstream American life and letters.

Zierler, like many recent critics who have rediscovered and reinterpreted these early twentieth-century novelists, sees the need to take a closer look at what seems at first reading, a much less turbulent transition than Yezierska's, from old world females to American mainstream writers. She shows that the anxieties discovered in the subtext are no less pervasive in the lives of both writers than those Japtok described in the plots of Yezierska's fictional creations. She also argues that through successive novels and autobiographies, both Antin and Stern employ literary strategies to reconcile the rejections of ethnic heritage and gender roles in initial writings; that these changes were necessary to appeal to mainstream readers whose expectations were that the protagonist of a *Bildungsroman* would develop in the direction of maturity and harmony rather than guilt and misgivings.

Antin is especially noted for separating herself from traditional gender roles and thus from her siblings. But, unlike Yezierska, she appears not to have had a difficulty with her family because of her deviations from their cultural norms. She seems to fit Gusdorf's qualification for writers of autobiography who individuate only to discover that their true essence or identities are perfectly consistent with their recovered childhoods, like Proust, whose recovery of the past reveals it as being part of a continuum with his current life. Like traditional male writers of autobiography or coming-of-age fiction from St. Augustine until the twentieth century, Antin speaks through a narrator who is self-possessed and confident in her pride and enthusiasm for the life she has won in the most wonderful of countries—America.

Zierler shows how Stern was less autonomous than Antin, needing the authorial convictions of her mother by her side as she "develops her authorial and autobiographical 'self,'" so she does not at first fit the model of rebelliousness from parents and ethnic communality of Yezierska nor of Antin's seamless independence from family. However, as Zierler notes, she goes on to write novels portraying increasing estrangement from the past and subsequently, heroines who become more and more conflicted and anxious about the choices made in the name of acceptance. Zierler's rereading of Stern's narratives reveal "an abiding concern for the past and a desire to maintain an interdependent version of self." Magdalena Zaborowska's *How We Found America* reveals that as an adult, Stern's personal life mirrored her fiction, but was without anxiety or conflict. Despite her upper-class lifestyle, she manifested an abiding concern with immigrants' plight in general, and the cause of her people in particular. She was very involved in promoting the cause of immigrants, but she also promoted the rights of women and fought against their oppression in Jewish family life.

Perhaps we as modern readers can only guess at the sacrifices to identity as women, Jews, and immigrants that Stern and others suffered in order to attract a mainstream readership curious about the making of an American, but not yet ready for one who spoke so easily of herself as an insider/American, and, to boot, one who intended to locate her fictional center in an ethnic neighborhood as though it were a typically American locale. According to Zierler, Stern was able to hide in her fiction the insider, upper-class status of her adult life as well as the breadth of the ethnic roots connecting her and her characters to their traditions and culture.

NEWER WRITERS

Turning now to essays that discussed the lives and works of recent writers of immigrant experiences, we find that although the settings of both earlier and recent narratives begin in the urban, lower-class environments, increasingly, the newer fiction describes second and third generations who are middle-class. Early and late twentieth-century writers also differ, however, in the apparent visibility of their "otherness," that is to say, in the color of their skin and the physical differences by which we define race.

Other differences between older and newer writers are evident. Some immigrants now come to this country highly educated and having professional credentials as did Mukherjee. Others, such as Marshall and Kogawa, are born into families of immigrants or are, like Jen, descended from immigrants. Because of the opportunities for education and social mobility, this last group of people have been able to integrate themselves into the mainstream more easily. Still others are like Ortiz Cofer, who as a Puerto Rican, is an American national but migrant to the mainland; or like Cisneros, whose childhood family was transnational, moving back and forth between homeland and adopted land. However talented and fluent in English these recent ethnic writers are, they are visibly not of European stock, though many share the heritage of several races and were educated by European colonials. Why is this worth noting? Because the authors discussed in later chapters of this collection have undergone even more overt and covert discrimination in their acculturation than have the Jews, Italians, and Irish in the first half of this century.

These immigrants are more "exotic" to mainstream Americans than earlier European immigrants not only because of their racial mix, but also because of the "strange" non-Judeo-Christian religions, cults, languages, foods, and attitudes of entitlement they bring with them. This second half of the century has seen a repeat of the first half's fights over immigration. However, this recent one has been more fierce because the perceived threat to the "American way of life" is seen as total by some. The civil rights laws of the 1960s allowed an American minority middle class to become politicized and to influence other immigrant minorities to storm the barricades to insist on respect for their cultures' right to co-exist. The political affected the social, which is reflected in the artistic.

No longer are writers willing to give up or hide their ethnic connectedness behind the mantle of assimilation and acculturation as were earlier writers. At best, recent writers show a willingness or comfort level with the idea of hybridity born of their double consciousness of two disparate cultures. Not all of these writers, however, would see themselves as embracing hybridity. Frank Chin and others mentioned by Qun Wang in his essay are seen as more essentialist in their stance, reflecting the attitude of some immigrants or descendants of immigrants that their communal mores must remain inviolate, or they will not be able to maintain their culture in the face of America's cultural colonization of the world.

And the 1980s revealed that the impact of those with an essentialist position is considerable; the backlash against the efforts of some ethnic groups to not only retain their traditions and language, but also to demand mainstream recognition, has brought about a new wave of intolerance. California's legislative measures to restrict services available to illegal aliens, and the academic "culture wars" have caused intellectuals, politicians, and readers to rethink their definitions of what it means to be an American, and which literature reflects mainstream ideologies. All of the known sociological and canonical markers for race, class, gender and genre have become so blurred and problematized by recent national life and literature, that finding one's identity is not just a psychological or genealogical matter.

Mukherjee's novel *Jasmine* is a fitting symbol for this state of affairs. Her protagonist undergoes many transformations in her assimilative process, each one representing an aspect of the current confusion over her ethnic, regional, or national identity. These confusions are associated by Mukherjee with the violence inherent in both the old and the new cultures, especially in their treatment of females. Citing other critics, Pultar suggests that this portrayal of misogyny could be an attempt by Mukherjee to appeal to American readers who view nations such as

India as primitive and congratulate themselves on their greater civility and equality for females. Jasmine's assimilative incarnations in America, according to Pultar, fail to bring her the hoped-for equality and security she had dreamed of when she escaped from India. In fact, Mukherjee portrays through her heroine's picaresque adventures a landscape of decay and corruption in the United States, which she juxtaposes with the mythical ideal conceptualized by Third World immigrants: the land of golden opportunity. Pultar and other critics who agree with her interpretation read Mukherjee's portrait of the United States as extremely dystopic, not unlike that of another portrait painted by immigrant novelist Nabokov in *Lolita*. Most American critics, however, read the ending of *Jasmine* quite positively, showing the protagonist's belief in the assimilative stance: despite its faults, she is greedy for the freedoms and opportunities living in the United States promises immigrants, particularly women.

The condemnation of America as a materialistic culture lacking in the communalism and commitment to values of other, perhaps poorer cultures is a theme in many recent immigrant novels. Although extremely condemning of America's moral climate, these immigrant writers and critics are equally alienated by the treatment of women in the more patriarchal cultures of their heritage. Pultar's perspective of *Jasmine* as a moral indictment of new world culture, found wanting even when compared with the patriarchy of India, poses the question of what old world traditions are useful for immigrants to retain in a new world setting, and which, especially for females, are useful only as artistic tools to explain the old culture to the new. This question leads us to the conflicts cited by Qun Wang in his assessment of Asian American literary critics such as Frank Chin. The conflict between his call for authenticity on the part of Chinese American writers clashes head-on with feminist writers such as Maxine Hong Kingston. Those who oppose essentialist ideas feel that Chin's call for historical verisimilitude and loyalty to Asian ethnic traditions prevents discussion of the suffering and discrimination faced by women in certain old world cultures. Although both Mukherjee and Kingston respect and acknowledge the part their ancestral traditions play in their identity, they feel equally justified in imaginatively transforming tradition and myth to portray the pitfalls of both old and new world cultures. They would eschew the essentialism of Chin also because both artistically and personally they feel restricted by it. However, some say the writings of those who use traditional culture as the raw materials for social and gender criticism have led to the "abandonment" of commitment and values seen by Pultar in Mukherjee's novel. Other observers of the literary scene have seen essentialist criticism as "sour grapes" on the part of some male critics reacting to the popularity of newly powerful and prolific female multicultural writers compared with their less-lionized ethnic brothers.

Another writer like Mukherjee, who juxtaposes the pitfalls of life in the United States with those of her colonial homeland, is Jamaica Kincaid. Jacqueline Doyle's essay on the novel *Lucy* focuses on the parallel depiction of development of emotional and artistic identities by its Afro-Caribbean protagonist. Lucy's coming-of-age as an immigrant *au pair* in New York City is chronicled by her photographs of the process. "Reading" beneath the surface of these snapshots of her all-American employers, their friends and family, Lucy's narrator finds the same hypocrisies, racism, and arrogance that she saw in the dominant white culture of colonial Antigua and among those who have been colonial subjects like her mother. However, as Doyle points out, it is only as an immigrant that she is able to make such comparisons. The freedom she has away from colonial life (with her mother) has given her new insights into both cultures' power to erase identity by interposing that of the dominant culture.

Toward the end of the novel, Lucy's view of the place, New York, becomes clearer, and she hopes for a time in the future when she will see it as more beautiful. But framed in the metaphors of Lucy's photographic insights, are, according to Doyle, Kincaid's accusations about the void in American middle-class life. Unlike Mukherjee's Jasmine, who is seen as still eager to find herself in the unexplored wastelands of America, Kincaid does not write her hero into an assimilative resolution. Instead, Doyle finds that Lucy's "assertion of self seems oddly blurred and incomplete" for the ending of a novel of development of both artistic and personal identity. She connects this state of "in-betweenness" of Lucy with what Homi Bhaba says is typical of migrants, exiles, and the colonized. Kincaid, Doyle notes, claims the right to use this state of ambiguity, along with the disillusioning clarities Lucy (read: Kincaid) has found in her adopted land, as the conflicted state necessary for artistic expression.

Cultural conflict is a necessary but not invariable component of immigrant literature, so it is not surprising that Kincaid and another black female writer discussed in this book differ in their depiction of antagonists, of who or what provides the obstacles to wholeness and happiness for the immigrant in First World nations. The American-born daughter of Barbadian immigrants, Paule Marshall creates female protagonists in Selina and Ursa who are conflicted by their love and loyalty to their culturally disparate parents. Unlike Lucy, who desires total erasure of her mother from her life, Selina and Ursa must decide whether to follow the assimilative model of one parent or the anti-materialistic/idealistic leanings of the other: immigrant Silla's desire to buy a Brooklyn brownstone, or Deighton's desire to leave the rat race of America for his idealized Caribbean homeland; the self-aggrandizing politics of Primus in the postcolonial Caribbean, who chooses status and greed over racial identity and solidarity, or Estelle's political activism on behalf of the poor. Eventually, the female protagonists, whether parent or daughter, seek a healing and reconciliation with their ancestral cultures after they have carved out their psychic and individual spaces in the dominant culture.

Again, in the Afro-Caribbean culture of Paule Marshall's Brooklyn, as well as in most Third World immigrant and American minority cultures, there is a tension between the American offer of freedom, social mobility, and individualism, and the racial and ethnic solidarity offered by communities and homelands; the choice is more problematic to females of patriarchal cultures. Solidarity is necessary, according to Chin and others, to combat racist stereotypes perpetrated by the white dominant culture on minority and immigrant groups, especially males. Writers such as Marshall, however, go beyond the issues of ethnic and racial solidarity to portray female characters who, having transcended identity crises based on race, class and gender, bump up against neocolonialist impulses among their own leaders both in the United States and in the formerly colonized islands. The key to maintaining their balance and healing fractures in their identities, is having a cultural and spiritual connection to their traditions but being equally willing to shoulder individual responsibility for the welfare of others, even if it means internecine conflict.

Marshall, according to my estimation of her evolution as a novelist, is critical of the dominant culture's racist treatment of diasporan blacks and of the American consumer society, which encourages upwardly mobile black people to trade affiliation with their community for mainstream acceptance and material comfort. However, unlike Kincaid, Marshall portrays in her fiction the notion that individuals, females especially, must take responsibility for the world they inherit and change it. Having a strong hybrid identity grounded in the past will help women overcome the present-day obstacles posed by those in the dominant culture or in their own ethnic group, so that they can help their people, whether in diasporan communities or in their homelands, improve their lives and carry on ancestral traditions. I see the pattern in Marshall's novels as pointing to a global interdependence of races and communities, as the integration of black diasporan identities becomes a reality and as females are able to secure their roles as healers and conveyers of tradition to the next generation. In this sense, Marshall's later fiction belongs philosophically to the group that will be identified in this essay as "Third Wave Hybridists," though Marshall is a generation older than they are.

This issue touches on a theme encountered in *Bread Givers* and discussed in relation to the controversy between Chin and Kingston: women often separate themselves from their ancestral traditions because they include repressive roles for females. The relative emancipation of women's roles in American society since Yezierska's Sara walked away from her patriarchal family have evolved into the most recent of Marshall's female characters who oppose restrictions from anyone—male or female, tradition bearers or emancipated people. They do, however, seek a reconciliation and healing with their culture once they have carved out their psychic spaces in the dominant and ethnic societies.

Another aspect of the essentialist/assimilationist/hybridist conflict centers on the issue of language. In both *Native Speaker* by Chang-rae Lee and *Obasan* by Joy Kogawa, the protagonists hide their discomfort with the process of acculturation by repressing their own voices, literally and figuratively. For Kogawa's fictional alter ego Naomi, the lost words and language result from a political and a personal trauma—the political trauma being the internment of Japanese Canadians during World War II and their dispossession and dispersal after the war, and the personal trauma being the effect of that internment on one Japanese Canadian family.

Because he is not a "native speaker" (although he speaks excellent English) and does not feel American, Lee's protagonist Henry uses a "voice" characterized by coolness and repression of emotions. This helps him in his job as a spy, which June Dwyer sees him "uniquely fitted for . . . by dint of his second-generation American status and his Asian cultural heritage of reticence and self-control." The metaphorical use of spying to describe the perspective of marginalized immigrants is apt, according to Dwyer: "Specifically, they find out things about ourselves that we would rather not have known." But Henry finds out as much about the limitations of this guarded emotional stance as he does about the shortcomings of American capitalism's exploitation of immigrant labor and about their treatment of minority politicians who quest for social acceptance. Henry is finally able to go beyond his assumed, shifting voices and identities and through therapy to discover a newfound American volubility and openness that is acceptable to everyone including himself. Equally Henry is able to forge a new relationship with his Caucasian wife and with his Korean heritage, signifying an assimilative stance by Chang-rae Lee but not one that involves loss of one's native language.

It is only when both Kogawa's and Lee's characters come to terms with their pasts that they are able to find identities and voices that allow them to feel at home in a society of, in Matthew Beedham's words, "false dichotomies of 'indigenous' and 'immigrant.'" According to him, realizing the hypocrisy of these terms used to describe hybrid societies such as the United States and Canada "allows us to develop a new perspective of who we are and who we will become." Beedham sees the hypocrisy as the existence of an identity fixed by the dominant culture to include only characteristics typical of Canadians and Americans of European descent. He calls for an openness of identity in which ethnic groups could define themselves as North Americans rather than having their identity defined for them. Further, he hopes for a new attitude by the dominant culture of the future in which ethnic cultures will not merely be tolerated or accepted, but one in which they can add their voices to the richness of existing North American voices.

THIRD WAVE HYBRIDISTS

Finally, it may be useful to note a distinction made in these essays either implicitly or explicitly about very recent writers such as Gish Jen and to a lesser extent Ortiz Cofer and Cisneros. These second- and third-generation writers of immigrant descent who were born in or have lived all or most of their lives in America offer a true hybridity as the obvious resolution to binary ways of identifying oneself or one's group. These "new wave" hybridists consider a dual identity not to be the problem that previous generations made it, as long as the dominant culture accepts their unwillingness to be labeled by cultural affiliations or hyphenated identities. They claim the right to move back and forth across identities and to become citizens of the world as well as Americans.

Jen, especially, considers herself beyond the point of needing to strive for identity through her fictional alter egos. As Zhou Xiaojing notes in her essay, the novelist is no longer interested in dismantling stereotypes or fighting prejudices. She feels free to concentrate on the aesthetics of her characters' inner dialogues with themselves. Jen does, to a certain extent, portray the negative preoccupation with money of some middle-class Chinese Americans, but she considers that flaw a function of an immigrant character being pulled into the consumer culture of America rather than as a negative quality of Chinese immigrants or as a necessary part of acculturation. For Jen and other writers, America provides so much freedom that it is difficult to find one's moral center since boundaries and borders are lacking:

Like Jen's consumer-dreamers, we hunger for the same convertibles and ownership of property; we come armed with professional degrees and a spirited belief in our invincibility. Once here, we seek for ways to constantly renew ourselves, moving braille-fingered over our everyday experiences, hoping a coherent language will surface . . . men and women, experimenting with connections across cultures and looking like children among toys for the redeeming grace of love. As America becomes more and more real to us, we fear becoming more and more insubstantial, not knowing what myths sustain us or what flags call us home. (Samarth 100)

Cofer, too, represents a variation on the hybridist perspective in her portrayal of how both the Puerto Rican American daughter's assimilationist tendencies and her mother's essentialist refusal to integrate herself into her adopted homeland spell loss of self or isolation. By inference, she shows, according to Faymonville's estimation, a weakness with both of these approaches, thereby implicitly moving toward hybridity as a useful stance. Faymonville describes Cofer's use of hybridity as the consciousness of national identity assuming an international context and that nations "must be imagined as a nation among other nations." Assuming identities are becoming increasingly transnational as well as transcultural helps to alleviate the limitations immigrants have put on themselves or had put on them, without sacrificing their ability to bring their culture into the mix.

Cisneros's search for a "Chicana" identity as detailed in Payant's essay points to yet another positioning of identity that could be seen as hybrid. The problem of being female and Hispanic (Mexican-American) in America's culture results in an inability to have a comfortable border crossing, since her natal culture values machismo and contemporary America strives for gender equality, but Cisneros, especially, points to a fluidity in the idea of national identity as the obvious solution to the kind of pigeonholing of identity that leads to insiders and outsiders, powerful and powerless. To accomplish this fluidity, Cisneros reinvents legendary ancestors for women to emulate by combining the best of historical models, such as, the compassion of the Virgin of Guadeloupe with a powerful Aztec goddess. Like Kingston and others, she finds lyricism and political utility in the artistic transformation of her cultural heritage. To this generation of writers, a predetermined identity, whether postulated by inherited traditions, writers, or critics with essentialist agendas, is as harmful as the stereotyping of immigrant groups such agendas were intended to eradicate.

CONCLUSION

The issues covered in this collection have spanned the whole range of disciplines: religion, education, psychology, sociology, and gender studies. Each aspect of immigrant life as presented in these critical studies of fiction have pointed to patterns of human behavior that are specific to an ethnic group and yet generalizable to the cultural conflicts we all face as members of a multifarious political and geographical entity. The ideologies of the United States and Canada offer opportunity for cultural difference and individualism while at the same time opposing these freedoms with the democratic tenet that we speak and act as the dominant majority. Each cultural group's acculturation process during the first few generations has been conflicted at the prospect of the loss of its unifying traditions to the mass culture of an increasingly homogeneous America. The fictional renderings of these conflicts are enlightening and instructive for all Americans as we try to secure our personal and affiliative niches.

What of the future? Is there an immigrant literature of the twenty-first century that will shed a different light on the experience of immigrants? Perhaps a headline in a recent series in the *New York Times* foreshadows the new immigrant experience yet to be written: "The New Immigrant Tide: A Shuttle Between Worlds" (Sontag and Dugger). This article extends a recent trend in immigrant or multicultural literature wherein both cultures are easily bridged not merely by hybrid lifestyles, but by the ability to live and work in more than one culture with equal ease. New immigrants are often people who understand the opportunities an economy like the United States can offer, but who also know what their culture offers in terms of a smaller, more intact community and a less hectic lifestyle.

The writers explain this willingness to travel back and forth, to inhabit two cultures by noting:

> For modern immigrants . . . the homeland is no longer something to be forsaken, released into a mist of memory or nostalgia. As the world has grown smaller, the immigrant experience has inevitably changed. Unlike the Europeans who fled persecution and war in the first half of the century, few modern immigrants abandon their motherland forever. . . . Instead they straddle two worlds, in varying degrees, depending on where they came from and what they can afford." (1:1)

A similar perspective offered by a literary critic traces this trend in terms of its effect on writers: "Earliest white Europeans sought dominance in the new land. Earlier writers wanted cultural opportunities not offered them in their birth nations or cultures; now minority voices seek a space within the society at large while insisting on their own cultural validity" (Miller 31).

Does the apparent ease of straddling two cultures spell the end of a genre based on conflicting identities and cultural imperatives? Probably not, since we as postmodern readers want to relive all of the immigrant experiences, those different from our ancestors' own and those that directly tell our familial stories, as they all help us construct and deconstruct the mythos that belongs to all of us—the American dreamscape.

WORKS CITED

Miller, Wayne. "Cultural Consciousness in a Multi-Cultural Society: The Uses of Literature." *MELUS* 8.3 (Fall, 1981), 29–41.

Samarth, Manini. "Affirmations: Speaking the Self into Being," *Parnassus: Poetry in Review* 17:1, 88–101, 1992.

Sontag, Deborah, and Celia W. Dugger. "The Immigrant Tide: A Shuttle Between Worlds."
("Here and There: Holding On to the Homeland"). *New York Times* 19 July 1998, sec.
1:1+.

Zaborowska, Magdalena. *How We Found America: Reading Gender through East European Immigrant Narratives.* Chapel Hill: U of North Carolina P, 1995.

Selected Bibliography

GENERAL WORKS ON IMMIGRATION AND CULTURE

Antin, Mary. *They Who Knock at Our Gates: A Complete Gospel of Immigration*. Boston: Houghton, 1914.

Barhai, Avraham. *Branching Out. German-Jewish Immigration to the United States: 1820–1914*. New York: Holmes and Meier, 1994.

Boelhower, William Q. "The Immigrant Novel as Genre." *MELUS* 8 (Spring 1981): 3–13.

Brimelow, Peter. *Alien Nation: Common Sense about America's Immigration Disaster*. New York: Random, 1995.

Choy, Bong-youn. *Koreans in America*. Chicago: Nelson, 1979.

Coolidge, Mary Roberts. *Chinese Immigration*. New York: Holt, 1909.

Daniels, Roger. *Not Like Us: Immigrants and Minorities in America: 1890–1924*. Chicago: Ivan R. Dee, 1997.

Ehrlich, Paul R. Loy Bilderbach and Anne H. Ehrlich. *The Golden Door: International Migration, Mexico and the United States*. New York: Ballantine, 1979.

Fitzgerald, Keith. *The Face of the Nation: Immigration, the State and the National Identity*. Stanford: Stanford U P, 1996.

Garcia, Maria Christina. *Havana USA: Cuban Exiles and Cuban Americans in South Florida 1959–1994*. Berkeley: U of California P, 1996.

Glazer, Nathan, ed. *Clamor at the Gates: The New American Immigration*. San Francisco: ICS, 1985.

Gutierrez, David G. *Walls and Mirrors: Mexican Americans, Mexican Immigrants and the Politics of Ethnicity*. Berkeley: U of California P, 1995.

Handlin, Oscar, ed. *Children of the Uprooted*. New York: Braziller, 1966.

———. *Immigration As a Factor in American History*. Englewood Cliffs: Prentice Hall, 1959.

Hing, Bill Ong. *To Be an American: Cultural Pluralism and the Rhetoric of Assimilation*. New York: New York UP, 1997.

Jensen, Joan. *Passage from India*. New Haven: Yale UP, 1990.

Jones, Maldwyn Allen. *American Immigration*. Chicago: U of Chicago P, 1992.

Lee, Joann Faung Jean, ed. *Asian American Experiences in the United States: Oral Histories of First to Fourth Generation Americans from China, the Philippines, Japan, India, the Pacific Islands, Vietnam, and Cambodia.* Jefferson: McFarland, 1991.

Maharidge, Dale. *The Coming White Minority: California's Eruptions and America's Future.* New York: Random, 1996.

O'Brien, David J. *The Japanese American Experience.* Bloomington: Indiana UP, 1991.

Perea, Juan A., ed. *Immigrants Out!: The New Nativism and the Anti-Immigrant Impulse in the United States.* New York: New York UP, 1997.

Pozsetta, George F., ed. *Assimilation, Acculturation and Race in the United States: The Twentieth and Twenty-first Centuries.* Boston: UP of America, 1992.

———. *Contemporary Immigration and American Society.* New York: Garland, 1991.

———. *Ethnicity and Gender: The Immigrant Woman.* New York: Garland, 1991.

Salins, Peter. *Assimilation: American Style.* New York: Basic Books, 1997.

Sanchez Korrol, Virginia. *From Colony to Community: The History of Puerto Ricans in New York.* Westport: Greenwood, 1995.

Scally, Robert James. *The End of Hidden Ireland: Rebellion, Famine, and Emigration.* New York: Oxford UP, 1995.

Suro, Roberto. *Strangers Among Us: How Latino Immigration is Transforming America.* New York: Knopf, 1998.

Takaki, Ronald. *Strangers from a Different Shore: A History of Asian Americans.* New York: Penguin, 1989.

Ueda, Reed. *Postwar Immigrant America: A Social History.* Boston: St. Martin's, 1994.

Weinberg, Sydney Stahl. *The World of Our Mothers: The Lives of Jewish Immigrant Women.* Chapel Hill: U of North Carolina P, 1988.

West, John Isbester. *Immigration Debate: Remaking America.* West Hartford: Kumarian P, 1996.

Williamson, Chilton. *The Immigration Mystique: America's False Conscience*: New York: Basic Books, 1996.

WORKS ON IMMIGRATION AND LITERATURE

Acosta-Belen, Edna. "Beyond Island Boundaries: Ethnicity, Gender, and Cultural Revitalization in Nuyorican Literature." *Callaloo* 15.4 (1992): 979–998.

Brannon, Lil, and Brenda M. Greene, eds. *Rethinking American Literature.* Urbana: National Council of Teachers of English. 1997.

Cheung, King-Kok, ed. *An Interethnic Companion to Asian American Literature.* New York: Cambridge UP 1997.

Cudjoe, Selwyn R., ed. *Caribbean Women Writers: Essays from the First International Conference.* Wellesley: Caloux, 1990.

Edmondson, Belinda. "Race, Tradition, and the Construction of the Caribbean Aesthetic." *New Literary History* 25.1 (1994): 109–120.

Fitz, Earl. *Rediscovering the New World: Inter-American Literature in a Comparative Context.* Iowa City: U of Iowa P, 1991.

Hicks, D. Emily. *Border Writing: The Multidimensional Text.* Minneapolis: U of Minneapolis P, 1991.

Knippling, Alpana Sharma, ed. *New Immigrant Literatures in the United States: A Sourcebook to Our Multicultural Literary Heritage.* Westport: Greenwood, 1996.

McKenna, Teresa. *Migrant Song: Politics and Process in Contemporary Chicano Litera-*

ture. Austin: U of Texas P, 1997.

Moraga, Cherrie, and Gloria Anzaldua, eds. *This Bridge Called My Back: Writings By Radical Women of Color*. Watertown, MA: Persephone P, 1981.

Oyama, Richard. "Ayumi: 'To Sing Our Connections.'" *A Gift of Tongues: Critical Challenges in Contemporary American Poetry*. Ed. Marie Harris and Kathleen Aguero. Athens: U of Georgia P, 1987. 249–256.

Peck, David R. *American Ethnic Literature*. Pasadena, CA: Salem P, 1992.

Rahming, Melvin R. *The Evolution of the West Indian's Image in the Afro-American Novel*. Millwood, NY: Associated Faculty, 1986.

Simone, Roberta. *The Immigrant Experience in American Fiction: An Annotated Bibliography*. Lanham: Scarecrow, 1995.

Vaid, Jyotsna. "Seeking a Voice: South Asian Women's Groups in North America." *Making Waves: An Anthology of Writings by and about Asian American Women*. Ed. Asian Women United of California. Boston: Beacon, 1989. 185–194.

Wong, Sau-ling Cynthia. *Reading Asian American Literature: From Necessity to Extravagance*. Princeton: Princeton UP, 1993.

Index

About the Contributors

MATTHEW BEEDHAM is Visiting Professor at Chonnam National University, in Kwanju, Republic of Korea. His research interests are in cultural theory, especially minority discourse. He has previously won the Rabbi Isserman Award for work on international and interracial relations, and published articles on the translation of Chinese logographs and Chinese Canadian literature. He is presently preparing the entry for Jacques Derrida in the *Dictionary of Literary Biography*.

JACQUELINE DOYLE is Associate Professor of English at California State University, Hayward. She has published journal articles on women writers from multicultural backgrounds.

JUNE DWYER is Professor of English and Chair of the department at Manhattan College in New York City. She has written two books, *Jane Austen* and *John Masefield*, articles on women and patriotism for *Studies in Short Fiction*, *Modern Language Studies* and *The Faulkner Journal*, and articles on immigration for *Proteus* and *MELUS*. She is working on a book called *Greenhorns, Greenbacks, and the Green Land: Immigrants and the Literature of the American Dream*.

CARMEN FAYMONVILLE is Assistant Professor of Comparative Literature and Composition at the University of Wisconsin at Platteville. She has published in the areas of World Literature, Emigrant and Immigrant Literature, Postcolonial Studies, and Writing Pedagogy.

MARTIN JAPTOK received his Ph.D. from the University of California at Davis, where his dissertation concerned African American and Jewish American coming-of-age stories and ethnic nationalism. He has published articles in *African American Review*, *The Southern Literary Journal* and in several anthologies. An article is forthcoming in *MELUS*. Professor Japtok teaches at West Virginia State College and is working on an essay collection entitled *Postcolonial Perspectives on Women Writers from the U.S., the Caribbean, and Africa*.

KATHERINE PAYANT is Professor of English, Director of the Gender Studies Program, the Liberal Studies Program, and Distinguished Faculty Award winner at Northern Michigan University. Her teaching interests center on women's studies. She has published articles on contemporary women's literature and related subjects. Her book *Becoming and Bonding: Contemporary Feminism and Popular Fiction by American Women Writers* was released by Greenwood Press in 1993.

GÖNÜL PULTAR is the Director of the Center for Literary Studies and a member of the Department of English at Bilkent University in Ankara, Turkey. During 1998 she was a fellow at Harvard University. She is the founding editor of the *Journal of American Studies in Turkey* and the author of *Technique and Tradition in Samuel Beckett's Trilogy of Novels* (1996) and two novels. Presently, she is finishing a study with the working title "Negotiating between Cultural Resistance and Resignation: A Turkish-language Narrative of the Turkish-American Immigrant Experience."

RAYCHEL HAUGRUD REIFF is Associate Professor at the University of Wisconsin at Superior, where she teaches a wide variety of American and British literature courses as well as composition. She has published two articles on O. E. Rolvaag and a book, *Ole Rolvaag: Artist and Cultural Leader*, edited by Gerald Thorson. She has also published articles in *American Literature* and *Journal of the Colorado Language Arts Society of the NCTE*.

TOBY ROSE is Professor of English at Northern Michigan University. She has degrees in English pedagogy and in Teaching English to Speakers of Other Languages. She has taught in many cultures including France, Japan, Venezuela, and Belize, where she was a Fulbright Scholar. She currently teaches Caribbean Literature and Postcolonial Theory and Literature.

QUN WANG is Associate Professor of the Humanities at California State University, Monterey Bay; he has authored two books and numerous articles on American drama and American ethnic literature and cultures. His research interests include the study of American literature and ethnography.

ZHOU XIAOJING is Visiting Assistant Professor at the State University of New York at Buffalo, where she teaches Asian American literature and Asian American Studies. Her areas of concentration include contemporary Asian American fiction and twentieth-century American poetry, especially Asian American poetry. She has published in journals and anthologies on her areas of interest, and is co-editing a critical anthology on Asian American literature.

WENDY ZIERLER received her Ph.D. in Comparative Literature from Princeton University. She is currently a Research Fellow in the English Department of the University of Hong Kong. She is completing a book entitled *Border Crossings: The Emergence of Jewish Women's Writing in Israel and the USA and the Immigrant Experience*. Her new project is "Literary (Un)Orthodoxies: Feminism, Religion and the Woman Writer."

ISBN 0-313-30891-8

90000>

HARDCOVER BAR CODE